BEYOND THE LENS

Published by The Association of Photographers Limited
Studio 9
Holborn Studios
49/50 Eagle Wharf Road
London N1 7ED

00 44 (0) 7739 6669
info@aophoto.co.uk
www.the-aop.org

4th Edition 2014

Edited by Gwen Thomas and Ella Leonard
Typesetting & Design by Bettina Brux
Printed by Spinnaker Print

Disclaimer
This book is intended as a guide for those people involved in photography and it is not intended to take the place of legal advice. The authors, publisher and consultants can take no responsibility for the consequence of any reliance placed on its contents. The editorial content of Part 3 'Making a Living' (except Chapter 8 Standards and Codes for Assisting Photographers & Chapter 9 Negotiating Licences and Usage) does not necessarily reflect the attitude of the AOP Board or the membership.

ISBN 978-0-9573891-2-0

INTRODUCTION

TERRY O'NEILL

Nearly 50 years ago, Ava Gardner gave me a letter of introduction to her ex-husband Frank Sinatra. He was my hero. He was the biggest star in the world. So I flew to Miami where he was filming, walked up the beach to his hotel and bumped into him on his way to the film set. I handed him the letter, he ripped it open and turned to his minders." This kid's with me".

That's all he said. For the next three weeks I was his shadow. Nothing needed to be signed, no clearances, no contracts, no restrictions. No managers, no publicity agents, no busy bodies putting their hands over my lens. I got Frank up close, in private, backstage, on stage, immersed in concentration or casually chilling out.

They were my pictures, my negs, my copyright, like everything and anyone else I photographed, there never was an issue of ownership. Either we originated our own work and offered it to art editors, or they called me and my contemporaries and assigned us. Often the magazines could only get to their famous subjects if they were using reputed photographers such as myself, or Bailey or Avedon.

There was a simple deal – because most frankly couldn't afford our day rate. Duffy, me and others – we took the pictures, allowed them first publication rights and syndication on a 50/50 split for three months. After that, the negatives and prints were returned to us.

Except in many cases they weren't. In those days photographers concentrated on the next job, and it was easy to forget who you'd sent images to or when. Likewise our agencies would duplicate the negs and prints for syndication overseas. The better magazines insisted on original negs. Then, if we switched agencies, often those agencies we were leaving would not return all of our work.

The net result was newspaper, magazine and agency libraries all over the world could accumulate a sizeable chunk of your life's work by default.

And then the digital age hit us. Initially those libraries became white elephants taking up expensive storage space and companies sought to cut costs. Entire files of contact sheets, original prints and negs disappeared into landfill – or its economic equivalent – amalgamation and buyout by those who saw the future in digitized libraries.

Suddenly ownership and copyright became a legal tug of war. Was a piece of paper signed giving away copyright? Copyright law is a quagmire with competing definitions – in Britain for instance I can put one of my photographs on a T shirt if I choose, after all it's my work, my photograph, my art, but in America I need permission from the "face".

For the past three years I have been cataloguing my archive –there must be millions of negatives accumulated over 50 years – and I realized how much was missing. So began the long haul – not only of identifying where they might be but also reclaiming them. I discovered that in this new digital age possession was nine tenths of the law as far as some carpet baggers were concerned.

One library had dozens of my shoots, original negs and prints from the 60s through to the 80s. First they spuriously claimed they owned them until I produced affidavits – from their own picture editors and art directors. Then they stonewalled, claiming they couldn't find any, then (when we proved they existed) that they owned a share in them because they'd stored them for so long.

Eventually we blew that claim out of the water – after two years and thousands in legal fees they finally folded. When we got into that deserted, unused storage facility, to reclaim a fat box full of negatives we were flabbergasted how much work from other famous name photographers was gathering dust there.

Another obstructed us at every twist and turn, eventually only giving up original work we'd consigned decades earlier, when we paid them to search for it and return it. Yet they still refused to give us copies of my images they had scanned from original negs or prints that they couldn't find. Why? They couldn't use them anymore, they were just being spiteful. They ludicrously offered us the scans which were pretty poor and low-res, at an exorbitant rate – and the agency actually said they'd rather destroy them than let me have them back.

Then we found that some of my original negatives, dupes and prints from that same library were being openly sold to collectors on the Internet and at auction. A guy in Holland has scores of my transparencies. How?

And who owns a dupe or a copy print? One agency that printed my work and sent out hard copies for repro in the pre-digital age claim ownership of the prints. Well they paid for the paper and printing, but they benefitted from that from their share of repro fees for years. Who owns the image that gives that paper its face value? Their copy prints have been plucked out of skips as newspaper libraries have discarded hard copies and now they are being openly sold on e-bay.

Now that libraries are consigned to storage facilities like time capsules buried for their asset value, old librarians who knew where everything was, have been pensioned off and photographers trying to identify or reclaim work are baulked and obstructed and forced to employ lawyers.

One executive of a large media company with millions of negatives in store, told a mutual friend, "we'll just hang on to it and wait for all the old photographers to die – then there'll be no-one to contest ownership."

Some agencies are honest and have been helpful and decent – I now have my archive with Getty Images, which is a partnership I can trust. Others are gambling on photographers being afraid to employ lawyers to fight for their rights – my guess is determined photographers like myself can call their bluff and force them to do the right thing because the agencies can't afford lawyers either.

The digital age has given photographers the facility to deliver their work speedily, to enhance it and retouch it and to archive it economically – and yet photographers, old and new, are increasingly finding ownership of their work hidden or hijacked.

Photographers are under attack from other directions too. In my day film companies, or rock n roll management, needed photographers like me to get them the publicity that would sell tickets and albums – they were just grateful for great shots and cover stories. Now many stars of today have management who insist on control of the work, they insist on choosing the photographer, what image is released, how it is retouched, what copy and headline is attached, even how it is cropped and many insist on a percentage of repro fees.

They want to control and monetise their "image rights". Many media companies will only commission a photographer if copyright is signed over to them. It's not the skill and art of the photographer but his or her compliance with the commissioners' commercial interests that matter. And it's understandable that many photographers acquiesce for the work.

It's reduced photography, just as Photoshop has killed its honesty. And perversely it's boosted the paparazzi – as good or bad as their shots are, at least generally you are seeing some reality, not the digitalized distortion of marketing departments or the complicit sycophancy of the media.

It's why I only photograph friends like Michael Caine or Eric Clapton now as a favour if they need an album or a book cover. I'd rather concentrate on cataloguing and reclaiming my archive and organizing exhibitions.

My advice to any young photographer is to hold onto their copyright and use the power of the Internet to archive, market and sell their work.

Photographers need a strong professional body to back them up more than ever – to represent them, lobby for them and fight for their rights. Perhaps a concerted action by a strong alliance of photographers will force those companies hoarding their original work to return it to the rightful owners. It would be a start. And eventually I can see the return of a Magnum style international coalition that exists to protect and serve photographers, professionally and commercially.

Terry O'Neil

ABOUT THE PUBLISHER

The AOP was formed in 1968 by a small group of photographers. United by a common aim to challenge the then unreasonable demands of model agencies, it brought together professional photographers, to protect their rights and promote photography.

Constituted as a non-profit distributing trade association, today its membership exceeds 1,000 photographers and photographic assistants covering advertising, fashion, editorial, architectural and design sectors and is supported by photographers' agents, manufacturers and suppliers of photographic equipment and services. The AOP also has a number of affiliated college and university courses and plays a significant role in promoting, maintaining and developing relationships between all levels of higher and further education and the professional industry. A board of directors comprising 7 photographer members, three non-member directors and an assisting photographer member governs the AOP.

The AOP's principal aims have remained the same over the past 46 years and, through its campaigning and education work, has improved rights for all photographers creating a unique community of professionals. We are proud of our history, and rightly so: we negotiated reforms which led to the Copyright, Design and Patents Act 1988; we developed the widely accepted Standards of Practice, which afford photographers greater protection and ownership of their work; produce 'Beyond the Lens'; created the OPEN awards and the AOP Awards, the most prestigious accolade in the photographic industry, running for over thirty years at the time of press.

Recognising the many pressures photographers face, the AOP Legal, Education and information service aims to provide members with practical help to reduce the administrative burden of running a business; it includes workshops, guidance on how to resolve business and rights matters, and a database of worldwide services. We also act as a forum for discussion and exchange of information about changes in the industry and the impact of new technologies.

Membership details and further information about the AOP's activities can be found on our website: www.the-aop.org.

CONTENTS

CONTENTS

CONTENTS

PART 2: THE BUSINESS END

CONTENTS

CONTENTS

PART 3: MAKING A LIVING

CONTENTS

Appendix

AUTHOR BIOGS

Stephen Barnett
Stephen started his business in 1985 after taking a BA in photography at Harrow. An AOP member, he works on report & accounts and corporate identity, often overseas and usually in difficult environments, for design groups and client direct. Stephen is never happier than during the nervous anticipation of a good trip!

Norman Childs
Norman Childs has had a very successful award-winning career, in running his own business in industrial and architectural photography for the past 30 years. He has been commissioned by many well known clients on assignments in over seventy of the world's countries. Together with his wife Pat he has operated in some of the most remote and hostile terrains imaginable. Norman has a very dynamic approach to marketing that has led to creating niche markets in making his business truly global, with most of his clients headquartered in the US and Europe. He is a Fellow of the Chartered Society of Designers.

Contact: norman@greenshoots.co.uk Website: www.greenshoots.co.uk

John Cole
John is a photographer and Life Coach. A free lance photographer for over 35 years, John specialises in reportage and documentary photography and has shot features for a number of international publications, including the Sunday Times, the Independent and the Observer magazines, as well as annual report and corporate brochure work for leading design firms and ad agencies in the UK and abroad. A member of the AOP for 25 years John is especially interested in coaching in the creative industries, and brings to his coaching work years of experience as a professional photographer.

Contact: ClarityWorks@johncole.co.uk Website: www.clarity-works.co.uk

Peter Dazeley
Dazeley is an award-winning advertising, fine-art photographer and writer, born and brought up in London. His personal work is an on-going journey of discovery, looking for and photographing people and things he finds visually stimulating. "Making the ordinary look extraordinary is Dazeley's gift," says Sarah Ryder Richardson, who represents Dazeley in the UK.

Nick Dunmur
Nick Dunmur is a professional photographer and a member of the Association of Photographers. He works mainly in the advertising and commercial sectors of the industry and has used various platforms since adopting digital in 1999.

90% of the work he produces is digitally originated but he still uses film and believes in its continued existence as a means of recording and making pictures.

Michael Harding
Michael Harding is a former Chairman of the AOP. He is based in London, from where he travels around the world shooting for blue chip companies and ad agencies.

Philip Haynes
Philip is a freelance assisting photographer based in London. He graduated from Norwich School of Art & Design in 2009. As a student his work was recognised by both the AOP and D&AD at their annual student awards. Philip has been assisting since graduating and has worked for many high profile international photographers. When he isn't assisting he is supporting his beloved Norwich City FC or out shooting sports.

Niall Horton Stephens

Niall has been representing photographers for over 25 years, mostly in the commercial field but has also had the pleasure of representing such luminaries as Bob Carlos Clarke, Patrick Lichfield and Gered Mankowitz. His agency was probably the first to represent new talent as a distinct section within an agency, the first to represent CGI and a very early adopter of web based promotion of photographers. He's had the pleasure of working with the AOP on numerous lectures, folio critiques and judging the AOP Awards. He has guest lectured at Blackpool College and the LCC amongst others. He was a founder of the trade body PhotoAgentsLondon which seeks to establish industry best practice.

Janet Ibbotson

Chief Executive Officer of the British Copyright Council since 1998, Janet is also copyright consultant to the Broadcast Entertainment Cinematograph and Theatre Union (BECTU) and a freelance consultant. Whilst working for the Association of Photographers (AOP) in the 1980's, Janet realised that a lack of copyright awareness lay at the heart of many of its members' problems. She was AOP staff member responsible for the Magazine Action Group in the mid 1980's, was instrumental in developing and negotiating the Base Usage Rate system with advertising agencies and prioritised the development of legal and professional practice services for members and, through the then Committee on Photographic Copyright, she also campaigned successfully for changes in UK copyright law. Janet has twice been Managing Director of the Association of Photographers (1984-1992 and 2005-2007). Between 1992 and 1998 she was Deputy Chief Executive of the Design & Artists Copyright Society and was responsible for developing it as the UK collecting society for all visual artists including photographers. She also worked on developing a first policy for DACS on licensing what were then the 'new technologies'. During her time at DACS, Janet chaired, or was a member of, a number of European and international committees within IFRRO and CISAC. She has also been a Vice Chairman of the Educational Recording Agency (ERA). Janet has also worked on a number of research projects within the Creative Industries, her most recent in 2012 being a Feasibility Study for the ARROW Project on the incorporation of diligent search of artists and works which have been included in books, a project with implications for orphan works and the digitisation of collections. Her work for the British Copyright Council keeps her at the centre of legislative developments and well informed on industry views.

Simon Leach

Simon has spent 25 years in the photographic industry working in a variety of disciplines and studying through colleges in Gloucester and Blackpool. He has always understood the significance and importance of maintaining rights for the individual creator, which led to a greater involvement with the Association from 2007. His own photographic work is built on craft and can be seen at http://www.simonrleach.co.uk

Philip Lee Harvey

Born in Canterbury, England in 1969, Philip completed a Graphic Design degree at the Norwich School of Art and Design, before going on to assist some of the UK's leading advertising photographers. Eager to develop his photographic career, he soon started taking on editorial and advertising commissions of his own. Since then, he has worked in over 100 countries, in environments ranging from Antarctica to the Sahara desert. His journeys have taken him to some of the worlds most inhospitable and demanding destinations.

Philip has won numerous awards including ones given by the Association of Photographers, Creative Circle, Royal Photographic Society, John Kobal, Travel Photographer of the Year, the International Colour Awards and Campaign magazine.

Website: http://www.philipleeharvey.com

Ella Leonard

Having worked for the Association of Photographers for eight years Ella is now freelancing as a Project Co-Ordinator. Whilst at the AOP Ella worked on Education, Events and Awards.

Contact: ellaleonard@me.com

Conor Masterson

After studying photography and graduating in 1991 Conor began working in the UK as a photographer in the Midlands in 1994. In 1997 he moved to London and began working as a full time and then freelance assistant to a variety of photographers working for advertising, design and fashion clients.

Since making the transition from assistant to full time photographer he has shot location and portrait work for advertising. He has revised his original contribution to Beyond the Lens, written at the end of his assisting career, and brought it up to date in 2012.

Website: www.conormasterson.com

Richard Maxted
After graduating with a degree in photography from Blackpool College in 1995, Richard opened his east London studio in 2000. Quickly establishing himself within the industry his eye for detail and obsession with 'getting it right' earned him respect and admiration in equal measures from his peers. Considered and meticulous Richard's work is perfection in the world of still life advertising photography. His award winning images are both challenging and fascinating and his controlled use of studio lighting is an art form in itself. With a list of high profile clients Richard's passion for photography is almost tangible.

Website: www.maxted.com

Ian McKinnell
Ian graduated in Fine Art from Brighton in 1976 and has been a freelance illustrator and photographer since 1981. In 1984 he was one of the first people in Britain to own an Apple Macintosh. He has used Photoshop & 3d programs from their very inception and closely followed their development. Ian and the Macintosh have grown together.

He specializes in 3D & cgi photo-realism and works for a wide variety of design, advertising & editorial clients. His library images are represented by Getty.

Website: www.ianmckinnell.com

Paul McMullin
Paul started his career in photography with a small general practise studio in 1977 in Liverpool. After being an assistant with this company and then as a staff photographer with a multi-national industrial business, Paul moved into the wide world of the self- employed in 1987. Since then he has specialised in both corporate and architectural location photography. Architecture and the built environment are now his passion and he works with a select group of construction and architectural clients for assignments around the world. As a 'Liverpudlian' he has a keen interest in the resurgence of the City and is regularly commissioned as photographer for books and articles as well as providing images from his own collection of Liverpool which he shoots for his own pleasure for use in advertising / marketing but also as an historical record.

Contact: paul@paulmcmullin.com Website: www.paulmcmullin.com

Paul Rochman
After qualifying as a Chartered Accountant, Paul worked on the financial side of commerce for a number of years, mostly in creative fields – in industries including fashion, journalism, and music. He then moved into practice and worked with Vic Goodman, an accountant specialising in the world of commercial photography and related fields. Following Vic's untimely death nearly 20 years ago, Paul took on Goodmans' clients and developed the practice, now called Rochman Goodmans, continuing to specialise and expand as accountants for photographers and others working in creative fields. His clientele includes sole traders, partnerships and limited companies. As well as photographers, Paul's practice acts for studios, agents, make-up artists, designers, location finders and other related professionals.

Contact: paul@rochgood.co.uk

Sentinel Independent Financial Advisers:
Financial Planning can be daunting. There are an enormous range of Protection Insurance, Investment and Pension options to consider. Sentinel is a leading firm of Independent Financial Advisers with considerable experience in meeting the needs of individuals and businesses within the photographic industry. Whatever your requirements – from Life Assurance, Critical Illness Cover or Income Protection policies to investment and pension planning – we have access to the entire market and are committed to sourcing tailored, competitive solutions that offer peace of mind for all circumstances and budgets.

Contact: info@sentinelifa.co.uk Tel: 0207 959 2430 Website: www.sentinelifa.co.uk

Grant Smith

Grant is an Australian born photographer, who has lived and worked in London for the last 30 years. During that time he has captured the changing face of the city and developed an extensive knowledge of London's architecture. It was on one of his architectural assignments in the City that he first encountered the unwelcome effect of the Terrorism Act 2000 on working photographers. As one of the organizers of 'I'm a Photographer, not a Terrorist', he has become a leading spokesperson for photographers' rights while working in public. Smith also lectures on photography at City Lit and runs photo tours of the City.

Website: http://www.grant-smith.com

Swan Turton

Charles Swan has been the AOP's solicitor since 1990 and was its first non-photographer director. He heads the Photography group at media law firm Swan Turton and advises photographers on copyright and other legal issues.

Anne Mannion is a solicitor in Swan Turton's Photography group who specialises in copyright enforcement and other dispute resolution matters.

Website: http://www.swanturton.com

Gwen Thomas

Gwen began working at the AOP in 1987. Currently the Director of Business and Legal Affairs and Company Secretary of the AOP, Gwen has been advising members on copyright, contract and ethical problems; negotiating on behalf of members; lobbying for photographers rights; responding to Government papers on proposed legislation affecting photographers; and lecturing on copyright and ethics since 1992. She is a Director of the British Copyright Council, representing the visual arts, and as General Manager of Pyramide Europe Ltd. Gwen is involved with ensuring the European Commission are aware of the needs of visual artists when legislation is discussed and prior to directives being issued. She represented visual arts on the Copyright Licensing & Steering Group, formed in 2012, and tasked with overseeing the implementation of the primary recommendations of the report to Government 'Copyright Works: Streamlining copyright licensing for the digital age' and ensuring continued cross-sector collaboration focused on further streamlining of copyright licensing. http://www.clsg.info

Gwen co-wrote *Whose Rights?* a book examining restrictive contracts throughout the EU, published by Pyramide Europe; was a contributing author to the first three editions of Beyond the Lens; and is an author and editor of this edition. mailto:gwen@aophoto.co.uk

Andrew Wiard

Andrew began a career in photojournalism working with Simon Guttman of Report, London, in 1975, and was the main photographer there during the 1980s. He represented the National Union of Journalists on the British Copyright Council during the campaign for copyright reform resulting in the Copyright Designs and Patents Act 1988. He is a founder member of EPUK (www.epuk.org) and Stop43 (www.stop43.org.uk), is on the board of the British Press Photographers' Association, and on the NUJ's Photographers' Council. Website,

Contact: mailto:andrew@reportphotos.com Website: www.reportphotos.com

Nick Wilcox Brown

Nick is an editorial and advertising Photographer turned Filmmaker, now producing and shooting films for commercial and broadcast clients.

Website: http://www.nickwb.co.uk

Williamson Carson & Co. Ltd.

Williamson Carson & Co. Ltd. Was formed in 1986 by John Williamson and Tom Carson who between them had 40 years experience working in the city with Lloyds Brokers. The Company was primarily involved in the entertainment industry, insuring filmmakers, advertising agencies, and professional photographers. It still specialises in these activities but has now expanded to include all forms of general and personal lines Insurances, including property; marine (hull & cargo); liabilities; professional indemnity; directors and officers, business interruption; travel; motor and household. Williamson Carson are the appointed insurance brokers to the AOP.

Website: http://www.williamsoncarson.co.uk

PART 1: THE LAW AND THE PHOTOGRAPHER

CHAPTER 1: COPYRIGHT & MORAL RIGHTS

JANET IBBOTSON

COPYRIGHT

Copyright is a complex area of law and its successful interpretation is dependent on case law, much of which is not photography specific. Contributing to the complexity are overlaps and interplays between copyright and other areas of law such as contract, passing off, competition, insolvency and human rights. Added to this is the difficulty of describing, with any certainty, the market in creative content and the role that photographers' rights have in that market.

In the 10 years since BTL was last published, the market for photography and indeed for all creative content has changed beyond recognition. Traditional divisions between creators and exploiters marking adversary, ally or friend have gone. We are all content creators now. Digital and online services and products drive the content market and have produced a very different kind of consumer demand. Some of those services and products are already dominating the market and, while taking a rigorous approach to protection of their own rights, they lobby actively to weaken the rights of others not just through acquisition but also by encouraging consumers to expect free access to creative content. In turn, this has led to a change of approach among policymakers and legislators. The tone of this quote from a political debate on a new piece of UK copyright law is typical of how this feeds through: -

> *"...we should look at copyright as a means of increasing national wealth, not just of producing a nice little rose garden to enable creative people to live comfortably and have everything exactly the way that they want it. It is a bargain between two sides. It is an agreement to use something that is essentially an evil – a monopoly – in order to enable something good to happen."*(1)

This chapter of BTL cannot attempt to cover all this detail, particularly if it is to stick to its original aim of providing photographers with a straightforward and simple entry point into copyright and a basic understanding of their rights. While reading BTL, its readers should be aware that the law itself may no longer be enough in an increasingly complex and hostile environment for rights holders and that photographers themselves no longer seem to have a solid view on what is best for them.

At a time of such change and in this brave new world, a re-write of these chapters of BTL for the 4th edition is a difficult task, though a much needed one.

What is copyright?

- the exclusive right of the copyright owner to authorise or prohibit certain "restricted acts"
- a collection of rights
- includes certain acts over which the copyright owner has little or no control, known as the "permitted acts" or exceptions and limitations to copyright
- a monopolistic right
- a balance between public interest and freedom of access
- an author's right, a property right and an incentive to creativity
- a human right
- a form of intellectual property

Protection, payment and permission

Copyright gives the photographer alone the right to control the use of their photograph, through the "restricted acts". That is, it allows them to make that photograph available for a payment, with their permission and subject to certain conditions, including "exclusivity", and to protect their photographs by giving them the ability to pursue those who have made unauthorised and infringing copies.

The law also sets limits on those rights through "permitted acts" which permit certain uses of benefit to society, or certain sections of society, without the need for permission or payment to the photographer. These are all set out in the law, but at the boundaries between the restricted and permitted acts tensions arise and the courts take over and this is why case law is so important in copyright.

(1) Lord Lucas, Hansard, 16 Jan 2013: Column GC302, Grand Committee, Enterprise & Regulatory Reform Bill

Exclusivity and a Monopoly Right

Copyright is a property right and exclusive to the owner, meaning no one can copy or use the creations of an author without their permission. For photographers this has three main implications: -

As the owner of an "exclusive right" the photographer can prevent others from copying the photograph and, if they do so without permission, the photographer can pursue them for infringement.

The second is an essential part of every photographer's business: they can grant rights to a client on an "exclusive" basis. For example, where exclusive rights to a photograph will protect a client's interest in that image as well as its association with their product or name. From the photographer's point of view granting that exclusivity comes at a higher premium and should result in more income for the photographer.

There is, however, an additional responsibility that comes with exclusive control over a piece of property, and copyright is legally a form of property (see Intellectual Property Rights below). As the photographer holds the exclusive right they also have a monopoly. Built into copyright law are rules intended to balance the interests of the creators of works protected by copyright with those of the users of such works. There are a range of checks and balances built into the law but these are most clearly seen in the "permitted acts", perhaps better known as exceptions and limitations to copyright. Their purpose is to ensure that the public interest is protected and that certain types of users of protected works have the access they need with the fewest possible restrictions. Within those limits, users do not need permission for use, or to make payment for use to the copyright owner.

This is one of the areas where the digital and online market for creative content has had the greatest impact and where lobbying is resulting in the greatest number of changes. There is considerable pressure at international, European and UK level to widen existing exceptions and limitations to copyright in ways which are likely to result, not in freedom of access, but in free access to creative content including photographs.

A Human Right

Article 27 of the Universal Declaration of Human Rights states that:

"1) Everyone has the right to freely participate in the culture of the community, to enjoy the arts and to share in scientific advancement and its benefits.

2) Everyone has the right to the protection of the moral and material interests resulting from any scientific, literary or artistic production of which he is the author."

The freedom of access debate based on fundamental human rights is a hot topic but it gets tangled up in arguments in favour of promoting free access to information/content. Those who argue in favour of free access should remember that human rights also support and promote the interests of the creator by guaranteeing respect for their economic and moral rights and copyright law is the means by which this is achieved.

The Common Law tradition or Droit d'auteur

The Common Law tradition of the UK and the USA, and normal throughout countries which were once rule by Britain, places an emphasis firmly on the economic exploitation and dissemination of creative works, treating them as pieces of property. The droit d'auteur principle behind most, though not all, European legislation (also strong in South America, some parts of Asia and Africa) derives from civil law codes and is more of a human right, placing the personal or moral rights of the creator before commercial interest. In short, under the droit d'auteur tradition, the economic rights arise from the personal or moral rights, whilst in the Common Law tradition economic rights come first.

This is really only of importance for those working across borders. In the UK, the Common Law approach has encouraged policymakers to take a stronger interest in the economic value of rights e.g. those of the entrepreneur, rather than in the needs or wishes of the creator or photographer. This difference in approach between the UK and the rest of Europe has an impact on the way in which the UK responds to and adopts European legislative initiatives (see Which Copyright? below).

Intellectual Property Rights (IPR's)

Copyright is one of a wider group of rights called intellectual property rights. "Intellectual" because they are products of the human mind and "property" because they are owned like a house or other form of property. Copyright legislation in the UK also includes Moral Rights.

Intellectual property in the UK includes patents, trade marks, design rights and database rights and protects performances as well as works protected by copyright.

Performances are protected in a slightly different way and by a parallel set of rights known as "related rights". It is a performance and not a work which is protected. The interests of performers e.g. actors, singers, musicians, etc are similar to those of other right holders, particularly creators and authors.

Before going further there are two frequently misunderstood points about copyright to be cleared up: -

Registering copyright in a photograph

There is no system for registering copyright in a photograph, or in any other work for that matter, in the UK. Copyright exists automatically from the moment the photograph is created.

American law is slightly different but even there photographs are still protected irrespective of whether they are registered or not. What is different is that the level of protection, particularly when it comes to enforcement of rights, for unregistered photographs, is not as high. Those photographers working regularly for American clients or whose works are distributed in the USA should consider registering their works http://www.copyright.gov/forms/

Protecting ideas through copyright

Ideas are not protected by copyright.

Though copyright attaches to "products of the human mind", the rights only come into existence once the work is "fixed" in the form of a painting, cast as a bronze, or "fixed" on film on paper or in digital form. It is only when the idea is expressed in material form, that is, the painting, manuscript, photograph or sculpture, that copyright exists.

Copyright law in the UK

Which Copyright law?

In the UK, copyright works are protected under the Copyright, Designs and Patents Act 1988 as amended (CDPA 1988), which became effective on the 1st August 1989, though in some instances provisions from the 1956 Act or 1911 Act apply to older works. Guidance on these are to be found in the 1988 Act.

The "as amended" is relevant because since the 1988 Act was introduced it has been changed a number of times. These changes are the result of overlaps with other areas of UK legislation (e.g. Acts covering Broadcasting, Communications, Enterprise or Growth) and in many cases implement European Directives intended to harmonise copyright law across the European Union. In the UK changes to the law which result from these Directives are normally implemented in the form of a Statutory Instrument, that is a form of secondary legislation. Some of these changes also make the UK, along with other Member States of the European Union, compliant with recent changes at international level.

A free online unofficial version of CDPA 1988, though consolidated only up until 2007, is available at http://www.ipo.gov.uk/cdpact1988.pdf

Whose Copyright Law?

CDPA 1988 was probably the last truly British copyright Act. In matters of copyright law and other areas of intellectual property, the UK has since followed the lead of the European Union. This has presented some challenges because of the fundamentally different approach to copyright taken by the UK to that of other European countries (see Common Law tradition v. Droit d'auteur above). On the whole, representatives of photographers and other authors have found the European approach more sympathetic to the needs and interests of creators, though some are now expressing concern about the possibility of introducing some less popular "European" concepts into future legislation (see Extended Collective Licensing).

Whose Contract Law?
Remember that these laws are all about copyright, they do not affect what photographers agree with clients in their contracts.

Any UK photographer who wants to do business with an overseas client should try to ensure the contract is made under UK Law (i.e. English and Welsh law, Northern Irish or Scottish law), not because UK law is best, but because familiarity with UK law makes it easier for the photographer and their adviser to negotiate terms and enforce the law if necessary. See Chapter 2 for more information on contracts.

For those photographers who are interested, a context for current legislative developments can be found at the very end of Chapter 1.

Copyright, Designs and Patents Act 1988 – key points

This first section looks at the works protected by copyright, authorship and ownership, duration of copyright in a photograph, restricted acts i.e. the exclusive rights which the photographer can control and permitted acts/exceptions and limitations i.e. those which the photographer cannot control or over which they only have limited control. The following section looks at how photographers deal with their exclusive rights i.e. licences and assignments and at the protection and enforcement of rights. Moral Rights are also covered later in the Chapter.

Types of Work protected by Copyright
Protection under the 1988 Act is afforded to creators of original literary, dramatic, musical and artistic works and certain others categories of works including films.

Included in the category of protected artistic works are paintings, graphic designs, sculptures, illustrations, works of artistic craftsmanship and, of course, photographs.

Definition of a Photograph
The law protects photographs as artistic works, so the next important question is what is meant by a 'photograph'? The definition in the 1988 Act reads as follows:

> *"'photograph' means a recording of light or other radiation on any medium on which an image is produced or from which an image may by any means be produced, and which is not part of a film".*

It is clear that this definition covers photographs in all their forms, including those which are digitally produced. It does not include a still taken from a 'film', that is from a movie or video. The rules which apply to films are quite separate.

Stills from Films
A still taken from a film, including a screen grab, is not protected by copyright law as a photograph. It is protected as part of a film and the director and the producer are its authors and the first owners of copyright in the still.

Computer Generated Works
The term "computer generated work" has a special meaning in UK copyright law. It is a work generated by a computer with no human author. The first owner of copyright in such a work is the "person by whom the arrangements necessary for the creation of the work are undertaken" and copyright in such an image lasts only for 50 years from the end of the year in which it is made.

Photographers should not refer to photographs created digitally or digitally manipulated photographs as "computer generated". It could be confusing.

Originality, photographs and copyright
The 1988 Act protects original photographs as artistic works irrespective of artistic quality. However, the main point for photographers is that in the UK the threshold for originality has traditionally been low. In effect that means that virtually every photograph is protected by copyright.

The term "original" is not defined in the Act or elsewhere, though here are some very old cases on photographs and originality. Issues raised in case law over the years are: whether the photograph is a 'slavish copy' that is, akin to a photocopy; what skill, labour and judgement were involved; composition and creative choices; was there a sufficient difference in the change of medium i.e. from painting to photograph.

As a result of the harmonisation of European copyright law, this approach is changing. Notable cases such as Infopaq and Painer demonstrate that the European concept, that is that only photographs which are the photographer's "own intellectual creation" are protected by copyright, should now be taken as the test for originality in the UK. Given that the UK threshold for originality has traditionally been lower than that elsewhere in Europe, that is, more photographs are protected by copyright in the UK, the decision in the Red Bus case might give greater guidance. In that case, the Judge's decision on whether the copied photograph was protectable was based on the angle of the shot, the field of view and computer manipulation post-processing with the aggregate result being a composition which can be a product of skill and labour/intellectual creation and is therefore original and protected.

If the approach demonstrated in the European cases is the correct approach for testing for originality and thus for copyright protection, then there is a question of how other photographs should be protected in the UK. It is worth noting that the European test for originality in photographs was itself introduced as part of the Directive on how long copyright should last (the Term Directive) and the Directive itself permits Member States to provide protection for other photographs. For example, in Germany photographs which are not treated as original are afforded protection under a different law which protects them for a much shorter length of time. These differing levels of protection for photography in EU Member States do not appear to have caused many problems so far but there is always potential, in which case perhaps the German approach could be mirrored in the UK.

Adaptations, Appropriation, Collage and copyright in photographs of other protected works

An adaptation right exists for most categories of work but not for artistic works including photographs. The adaptation right is in fact a right given to the copyright owner to license others to make an adaptation of their work, for example, by turning a book into a screenplay. Without the adaptation right, photographers (and other creators of artistic works) must use other rights under their control, such as the right of reproduction (that is, the right to authorise the making of copies): any adaptation must be based on the original work and thus the making of the adaptation must involve making a copy of the whole or part of the work.

Before the adaptation is made, permission should be obtained for the copying from the photographer or artist who created the original work. If there is then sufficient creative input into the second work, that is the adaptation, it will be treated as an original copyright protected work in its own right. However, that does not affect the copyright protection afforded to the underlying work, which in the case of a photograph will belong to the first photographer and which should be respected. Again, this is the same for other categories of works where, for example, a screenplay from a book is protected in its own right as well as being an adaptation of the original book.

Misunderstandings of this type frequently arise with photographs of other artistic works, whether these are flat artworks or three-dimensional objects such as works of sculpture. The resulting photograph probably carries copyright protection as an original work itself, subject to originality (see above), but this does not negate the copyright in the underlying artistic work included in that photograph.

In the case of a photograph of another artistic work, while the photographer may have been given permission to take the photograph, this does not mean they can permit others to make copies from that photograph unless the artist who owns the copyright in the underlying artwork has also given their permission. As some photographers make their living from this type of photograph they should always make these dual rights clear when making such photographs available for publication purposes. The onus is then on the publisher to clear the copyright with the owner of the copyright in the underlying work, normally the artist.

Example A photographer operating a picture library is asked by a well known ceramicist to take photographs of his latest collection of pots (works of artistic craftsmanship). Their agreement is that the ceramicist may use the photographs in his exhibition catalogue. The photographer is paid a fee for taking the photographs and expenses. In exchange for the photographer's time and expertise, she may include the resulting photographs in her online portfolio. In simple terms this is the contract including the licensing agreement between the two parties.

Subsequently the ceramicist is approached by a consumer magazine wanting to use the photographs in a feature. Permission from the photographer is needed because it falls outside the original agreement.

The photographer puts the photographs into her online portfolio but clients interested in purchasing rights to these photographs should be made aware, at the first point of contact with the photographer, that the permission of the ceramicist is needed before any reproductions may be made.

Appropriating the work of another photographer or artist without permission and using parts of it, or manipulating and adding to that work to create an entirely new one, is neither good practice nor legal.

There is some confusion over collages. However, such artworks created using hard copy e.g. from cuttings from magazines or newspapers do not in their creation involve copying. Copying only arises when the resulting artwork is scanned, or it's reproduced in a magazine, newspaper or on television. So merely displaying the original collage artwork is not a problem. However, a collage created digitally will be made up of images which, at the very least, will have been scanned and stored in a computer, that is, they will have been copied as part of the process. The resulting digital collage, once printed and displayed in a gallery will be made up of copyright infringements unless permission to use the images has been obtained in advance.

Currently there is no copyright exception in the UK which permits parody. Despite the lack of such a law, the UK has a very strong tradition of parody. However, it seems likely that the law will be amended to incorporate an exception for parody in the Spring of 2014. There is no indication what that exception will permit but it may change certain types of practice in this area.

Derivative Works and Copyright in the digital version of a photograph

No separate copyright exists in the digital version of a photograph. Such a concept is not recognised by either UK or other European legislation and its status in the USA remains doubtful. The digital version is merely a copy of the original photograph.

Photographers entering into contracts, mainly representation or acquisition agreements with stock agencies, which state that such a right in the copy exists (sometimes referred to as a Derivative Work) and that it belongs to the producer/client, should contact their professional organisation for advice.

Authorship and Ownership

Who is the Author of a Photograph?

The creator of a protected work is its "author". An "author" is not just a writer, it is a term that applies to every creator of a protected work and has a legal meaning of its own. In the case of a photograph, the author is "the person who creates it" and that, normally, is the photographer, nor the art director who came up with the initial concept, or the stylist. It means the photographer. In the case of Creation Records v. News Group the Judge picked up on this point: -

> *"It seems to me that ordinarily the creator of a photograph is the person who takes it. There may be cases where one person sets up the scene to be photographed (the position and angle of the camera and all the necessary settings) and directs a second person to press the shutter release button at a moment chosen by the first, in which case it would be the first, not the second, who creates the photograph."*

Photographers have not always been recognised as the authors of their photographs and these old rules continue to cause some confusion. Under the 1911 and 1956 Copyright Acts, the commissioner (whether a person or a company) owned the copyright in the photograph they had commissioned. To make matters worse, "the author" was the person who owned the film at the time the photograph was taken. Thankfully this no longer applies; photographers are, however, frequently approached by clients who think some part of the old rules is still valid.

Clients have been known to argue that having paid the photographer to take the photograph, they own both the photograph and the copyright in it. The photographer's response should be: -

> *"You are paying me for my skill and creativity; you are paying for my time and the expenses of the photographic shoot; you are paying for the right to use the photograph in your advertisement or editorial; but you do not own the copyright and ultimately you cannot own the photographic image. The photograph is my copyright and I am the person best placed to preserve and protect my work."*

How authorship is linked to ownership of copyright

The law states that the author of a work is the first owner of any copyright in that work. As the author of a photograph is almost always the photographer, it follows that the photographer is the first owner of copyright in every photographic work they create.

Is there a difference between ownership of Materials and ownership of Copyright?
The ownership of copyright in any artistic work, including photographs, is quite separate from the ownership of the actual physical work.

For example, if a painter sells a painting for a sum of money, to be hung on a collector's wall, the collector does not acquire the copyright with the right to hang it on the wall. The copyright remains with the painter and it is their choice whether or not they exploit their copyright. The same applies to photographs.

Although the material object and the copyright are quite separate, most photographers, illustrators and graphic designers will find it easier if they make it clear to the client in advance who owns any physical material, should it still be needed. Similarly with images provided to the client in digital form the client should be made aware that they only have access to the digital image for the purpose for which it was commissioned or the use for which it was licensed and it should be destroyed or at the very least recorded as not licensed for further use without the photographer's permission in the client's archives. The photographer's terms and conditions of business (see Annexe) should also incorporate words to this effect.

For photographers, particularly where a shoot results in a great many digital images, controlling access can be vital though arguing for the return of photographic images may sound a little out of date to clients who are sent digital files every day. Perhaps the best form of long term protection for the photographer is to ensure that metadata containing their name, contact details and other information about the creation and ownership of the image is embedded somewhere in the digital file and again, that terms of business oblige clients to preserve rather than remove that metadata.

Can a photograph have more than one author?
It is possible for a single photograph to have two or more authors and thus two or more copyright owners; however, it is not an ideal situation because of the obvious complications over who controls the work. Joint authors should not just rely on the future goodwill of their creative partner but should have an agreement about copyright (and moral rights) in writing from the very beginning, perhaps forming part of a wider partnership agreement covering all aspects of the business relationship. Leaving joint copyright matters to fate and the vagaries of friendship is unwise and could ultimately be very expensive.

Are there any complications to working under a pseudonym?
Some photographers do use a pseudonym or a nom de plume, although quite why a photographer would want to make it more difficult to be identified and located than it already is, is unclear. Any photographer using a pseudonym should ensure that their professional body has the pseudonym listed as well as and alongside their real name.

As far as copyright is concerned, it is only important if the real identity of the photographer cannot be traced. At present such a work would be treated as a work of unknown authorship and protection under copyright will only last for 70 years from the year in which the photograph was taken, or if during that period the work is made available to the public, 70 years from the year when that happens. Though it would revert to life plus 70 years if the photographer's real identity became known during that time.

With forthcoming legislation on orphan works (those where the author cannot be identified or located following diligent search), such works run a much greater risk of being treated as orphaned under Government authorised schemes which will permit licensing of those works.

What is the position for employed photographers?
Employed photographers do not hold the copyright in any work produced 'in the course of their employment'; instead, unless otherwise agreed, copyright is owned by the Employer.

In UK law, generally there is very little clear guidance as to what constitutes an employed person; however, it is generally taken to be someone who works under a contract of employment (or contract of service), whose tax and National Insurance contributions are deducted before receipt, and whose employee contributions are paid by their employer. Where possible, employed photographers should ask their employers to insert a clause into their employment contract which states that it is the photographer who owns the copyright and not their employer, though recognising that it is very difficult for those seeking employment or accepting a position to insist on, or even ask for, such a clause to be included in their employment contract.

A freelance photographer who accepts a commission from a client which lasts for a short period of time, e.g. a photographic residency, should ensure that they are issued with a contract for services and not an employment contract or contract of service. Even better, as a responsible freelancer, the photographer should issue their own contract. In both cases, the contract should make specific reference to ownership of copyright.

Employed photographers should be careful about how and when they take photographs outside their hours of employment. For example, if an employed photographer uses their employer's equipment, film, darkroom and business contacts, or takes their own pictures at the end of a shoot for their employer, then based on these factors a court could decide that copyright lay with the employer.

Photographers who own a limited company are normally employees of that company and so the copyright belongs to the company and not to the photographer and will be treated as an asset of that company and, should the company be wound up or liquidated, the copyright will be lost and sold on as part of the company's assets. The solution is a short legal document between the photographer and his limited company, transferring copyright and other rights in the work back to you.

How long does copyright in a photograph last?

Most photographers will only ever need to know that **copyright in a photograph lasts for the life of the photographer plus 70 years**. The countdown starts at the end of the year in which the photographer dies. This is, however, one of those technically complex areas of copyright law and if you are anything other than a photographer with photographs taken since the 1st August 1989, it may be worth getting an expert opinion.

Initially under the 1988 Act (which came into effect on 1st August 1989), it was not the case that copyright in a photograph lasted for life + 70, but on 1st January 1996, Regulations amending the 1988 Act were introduced which increased the duration of copyright in the UK in line with a European Union Directive.

A second set or Regulations on duration came into force at the end of 1996.

The first set of regulations (SI3297 and available at http://www.legislation.gov.uk/uksi/1995/3297/contents/made) relate to:

- new works created on or after 1st January 1996;
- existing works.

To understand the regulations, it is important to know the meaning of two key terms. These are "extended copyright" and "revived copyright".

"Extended copyright" applies to works protected by copyright under the 1988 Act immediately before January 1996. These are works which were still in copyright at the end of 1995 under the life plus 50 years rule.

"Revived copyright" applies where the term of protection had previously expired in the UK before 31st December 1995, but where the works were protected by copyright in any EEA State on 1st July 1995.

Separate provisions apply to each.

General points worth noting are that the regulations legislate on ownership of both revived and extended copyright. They cover existing licences, agreements and waivers or assertions of moral rights, and use of revived works, introducing a compulsory licence for the use of these works. This compulsory licence means that, with certain exceptions, the work may be used without the permission of the copyright owner if the owner is given sufficient notice and a reasonable fee is paid. Nothing in the regulations affects pre-existing moral rights.

The regulations are intended to apply to photographs in exactly the same way as they do to other artistic works, that is, for the life of the author plus 70 years (except where the term of protection is longer under the 1988 Act), thus increasing the term of protection by 20 years.

Rather than reproducing all the details here, it is recommended that those interested should read the more detailed factsheet available on the DACS website at http://www.dacs.org.uk/knowledge-base/factsheets/copyright-in-photographs – duration

Within the photographer's control

Restricted Acts

The restricted acts are those over which the copyright owner has exclusive rights and for which they can grant or refuse permission. They are the basis on which the photographer protects their work and earns a living.

The restricted acts for photographs and other artistic works are:

Copying;

Communicating the work to the public;

Issuing copies to the public;

Renting/lending the work to the public.

All copyright owners have these rights, though there are differences and different types of copyright owners find some rights more valuable or relevant than others.

The rental and lending rights are not particularly relevant to photographers.

Photographers rely more on the right to control the making of copies and of increasing importance is the right to communicate the work to the public.

Copying

Also known as the reproduction right. Copyright gives photographers the right to authorise the reproduction or copying of their work and to prevent others from reproducing or copying that work. For most artists and photographers it is the most important right and most often used in cases of copyright infringement.

The law states that the reproduction or copying must be in a material form. "Material form" includes storing the work on any medium by electronic i.e. digital means.

So, irrespective of whether the copy is made by a photocopier, or scanner, or is broadcast or distributed via the Internet, or is published in a newspaper magazine or book, or is on paper, computer screen or on CD, it is still a copy and the photographer has the right to control the making of those copies.

Communication to the Public

This right is only now starting to come into its own. This is because it incorporates the "making available" right and that gives photographers an additional tool against online infringement.

Outside the Photographer's Control?

Copyright law isn't all about protection and exploitation, it is also intended to provide a balance between the interests of copyright owners and those who want to access and use copyright works. For this reason UK law includes a long list of exceptions and limitations. These are called the "Permitted Acts".

While an understanding of some has long been essential in the photographic business, others are only now becoming important. The list below deals with the essentials first and then includes a quick analysis of the rest.

When an infringing user claims that their use is covered by one of the exceptions to copyright the courts use pre-existing case law and the "Three-Step test" to help them to reach a decision.

Berne Three-Step Test

The "Three-Step Test" underlies all the permitted acts, that is, exceptions can only be applied:

1. In certain special cases;
2. Which do not conflict with a normal exploitation of the work; and
3. Do not unreasonably prejudice the legitimate interests of the author.

The Berne Three Step Test comes from an international copyright convention known as the Berne Convention http://www.wipo.int/wipolex/en/wipo_treaties/text.jsp?file_id=283693. It is not explicitly repeated in UK law, though it is incorporated into the relevant European Directive. It would be helpful for photographers and users alike, if it were included. It is, however, considered to be implicit in the legislation and it is certainly referred to time and again in case law.

Fair Dealing
Certain exceptions are known as "fair dealing" exceptions. "Fair dealing" is a difficult term to explain as again, there is no definition in the law and it relies on principles established in case law. Much depends on what is considered "fair" in the circumstances and again the "Three-Step Test" applies.

Criticism, Review and Reporting current events
This fair dealing exception covers use for criticism and review and for reporting events which includes news reporting.

Those taking advantage of the exception must ensure that the original photographer receives sufficient acknowledgement i.e. a proper credit. The original work must also already have been made available to the public (that is, published or displayed in some form).

Criticism & Review
A photograph may be used for the purpose of criticism or review of the photograph or of another copyright work, provided the photographer is credited.

So, for example, if a photographer finds that one of her photographs has appeared in a television programme without her permission, and the production company or broadcaster argues that it used the image under the exception for criticism and review, the photographer may argue that it was not for the purpose of criticism and review and/or that it was not fair dealing. Her case would be supported by existing case law. She might also want to support her case with evidence that the acknowledgement given to her was insufficient.

Reporting Current Events (includes News Reporting)
Although other artistic works may be "dealt" with for the purposes of news reporting and reporting current events, photographs may not.

In the course of reporting current events, such as the theft of a famous painting, it may be desirable to show an image of that painting or of other paintings stolen along with it, but to permit the free use of photographs of a sports event or a news scoop would mean that sport and news photographers would rarely be paid for their work and could not preserve 'exclusive' agreements with their clients and other publications would be free to lift the images. Photographs are therefore excluded from this exception.

Incidental Inclusion
If a photograph has been included in another work without the permission of the photographer then the photographer must decide whether that use is incidental.

To make that decision, a number of points are considered:

- is the whole or part of the photograph used;
- is it a significant part or a minor part of the photograph (e.g. a key element);
- does the use of the photograph enhance the work in which it appears;
- does the use of the photograph endorse a product;
- is the photograph there purely by chance.

If the use is not incidental then there is an infringement of the photographer's copyright.

It is perhaps easier to look at incidental inclusion by taking three examples from the point of view of a photographer who is incorporating someone else's work into their own:

- If a portrait photographer is working in someone's home and in the background a portion of painting can be seen, it is likely that this would be treated as incidental use. However, if it can be argued that the photographer has deliberately positioned the subject in front of the painting to make the photograph more attractive, then it is unlikely to be seen as incidental.
- A stylist selects a painting and then dresses a scene around that painting, selecting colours and shapes to reflect the painting. This is unlikely to be incidental use.
- A client from a furniture company wants his product associated with quality and the photographer is asked to photograph a chair by Le Corbusier next to a sofa made by the client. The copyline reads 'Quality speaks for itself'. The Le Corbusier chair has been used to promote the client's product and to associate the qualities of the one with the other. This is not incidental use.

CHAPTER 1

Advertising the Sale of a Photographic Work

This exception permits a gallery or saleroom to include a photograph in its catalogue but only for the purpose of advertising the sale of the photograph. If, after the sale, the gallery continues to sell the catalogue to the public, this is not for the purpose of advertising the work for sale and the exception no longer applies.

Increasingly such catalogues are freely available online even though the exception does not currently apply to making catalogues available online. It is possible that the Government will extend the exception to cover online availability.

Certain Artistic Works on Public Display

This permits photographs to be taken of the following artistic works:

- a building
- sculptures, models for buildings and works of artistic craftsmanship permanently situated in a public place or in premises open to the public.

A work of architecture which is a building may be freely photographed (in the UK) and that photograph reproduced. However, the model for that work of architecture can only be photographed if it is permanently situated in a public place or in premises open to the public. The architect's drawings for the same building may not be photographed or subsequently reproduced without the permission of the architect.

For some photographers more important is the part of the exception relating to works of sculpture. The exception does not apply to sculptural works included in a temporary or travelling exhibition or where the sculpture is situated in a private garden or house. In these circumstances the sculptor's permission will be needed before photographs can be taken of their work.

For more about photographing buildings/works of architecture see Buildings Chapter 2.

Making of Temporary Copies – quite simply intended to allow technical copying as part of a machine process or transmission which enables lawful use of a work. Such copies must not have a value independent of the process.

Research and private study

This is the other fair dealing exception. The research must be for non-commercial purposes and should be accompanied by sufficient acknowledgement (although this is qualified further in the wording). Copies made for both non-commercial research and private study must be made the researcher, student or tutor on their behalf. The exception does not permit multiple copying, that is, a tutor may not make multiple copies of a print, or scan and distribute multiple copies to a group of students. This exception is likely to change in 2014. See "Coming Soon" below.

Education

There are five exceptions covering educational use. One to note is that copyright in a photograph is not infringed by anything done for the purposes of examination, provided that sufficient acknowledgement is given to the photographer.

The other educational exceptions include one for the purpose of instruction but this is heavily qualified and when combined with other educational exceptions for off-air recording and reprographic/photocopying, they currently deliver licensing schemes managed by collecting societies and from which photographers receive revenue under DACS Payback. See "Collective Management of Photographers Rights" below. The educational exceptions are likely to change in 2014 but it is hoped that these schemes will be preserved. See "Coming Soon" below.

Computer programs – this includes an exception which permits the making of back up copies to facilitate lawful use.

Disability Exception – there is currently only one exception and it applies only to Visually Impaired Persons. This exception is likely to change in 2014. See "Coming Soon" below.

Libraries & Archives – there are seven exceptions for libraries and archives, many of which are essential for the preservation of original works including photographic prints. These exceptions are likely to change in 2014. See "Coming Soon" below.

CHAPTER 1

Public Administration – there are six exceptions for public administration (e.g. parliamentary and judicial proceedings). These exceptions are likely to change in 2014. See "Coming Soon" below.

Designs & Typefaces – there are three exceptions for designs and two for typefaces. One of the design exceptions is likely to change soon with the result that it will harmonise upwards the term of protection for such designs. This will be of benefit to designers. However, while photographers are sympathetic and see this as an improvement to designers' rights, there are concerns about the impact on 2 dimensional images of 3 dimensional designs. The creation of 2-D images does not impinge on a designer's ability to protect their work in any commercial sense. The AOP's views on this and its recommendations on transitional provisions (applying to pre-existing 2-D images) can be found at http://www.the-aop.org/uploads/repeal-of-section-52-of-the-cdpa-1988.pdf

Miscellaneous & Other

There is also a range of exceptions that apply to specific uses of:

anonymous/pseudonymous works, spoken word, public readings and recitations, abstracts, folksongs, certain artistic works on public display (covered above), advertisement of sale of artistic work (covered above), subsequent works, lending of works and playing of sound recordings, films and sound recordings and broadcasts.

A Time-Shifting exception can be found among the Broadcast exceptions.

Time-shifting

On the whole, this exception is not relevant to photographers other than as consumers of television programmes. Its original purpose was to allow recording of television programmes so that they could be watched at a time to suit the viewer and to some extent it is becoming redundant.

However, it is of interest to photographers because it is a form of private copying exception. UK law does not currently permit any other form of private copying though in other European countries copyright owners are compensated for private copying through levies on machines, paper, hardware and software. This means that format shifting can be carried out as one of a range of private copying activities and an exception such as the UK's for timeshifting is not needed. It is possible that 2014 will see the introduction of a wider Private Copying exception in the UK and this will have important implications for photographers. See "Coming Soon" below.

Coming Soon

In early 2013 the Government, after several years of reviews, consultations, reports and impact assessments decided to go ahead with changes to certain of the exceptions and limitations to copyright. It was not possible to incorporate these into the exceptions described above as there are some overlaps so they are covered under this "Coming Soon" heading as a separate list.

The Government's reviews included discussions on changing from a limited number of fair dealing exceptions (see above) to a more general American-style fair use system. All the indications are that the British Government will stay with Fair Dealing. As there is considerable interest in and confusion about "Fair Use", it is discussed briefly below.

The Government also consulted on whether an additional safeguard was needed in law to prevent exceptions to copyright being overridden by contractual arrangements (contract override). It seems likely that each exception being amended or introduced in the new legislation will include provisions to prevent exceptions being overridden by contract.

There are eight areas where change is imminent. They are:

Private copying
Parody, pastiche and caricature
Quotation
Public Administration
Data analytics for non-commercial research
Education
Research, libraries and archives
Disability exception

Probably of greatest interest to photographers are exceptions for private copying and parody. Changes to educational exceptions and those for research, libraries and archives may impact on photographers, particularly as photographers currently receive substantial revenues from "secondary rights" in these areas. The disability exception may also have some implications for photographers. The "data analytics" exception will impact on publishers rather than photographers. "Public administration" is of greatest concern to journalists and "quotation" which will bring changes to the criticism and review exception is unlikely to affect photographers, so these recommendations are not covered at this time.

Fair Use

UK legislation has a large number of copyright exceptions covering a range of specific activities and only two of the current exceptions are based on "Fair Dealing". Where a court finds that the use claimed by the defendant is not covered by the exception then there is a copyright infringement. The exclusive nature of the list of UK exceptions means that there is less scope for interpretation and some would say that it is less flexible.

In the USA, most exceptions to copyright are covered by Fair Use legislation developed on the basis of US case law and codified in 1976 as S.107 of the US Copyright Act. Fair use is not itself defined, the section of the Act gives examples of what Fair Use might apply to. The Act does give four principles – purpose and character of use, nature of the copyright work, amount of the work used, effect on the potential market for and value of the copyright work – upon which fair use might be assessed.

Some argue that it is a more flexible system and therefore encourages innovation but others argue that it can lead to greater confusion, litigation costs are likely to be higher and so decisions are more likely to favour those who can afford to pursue a case.

Private Copying

The UK Government is seeking to introduce a narrow exception for private copying and which will allow format shifting, that a lawfully acquired copy of a work can be copied onto another medium or form of storage.

Unfortunately, the proposals do not currently include any provision for "fair compensation" for photographers or other rights holders. UK rights holders believe that to be wrong, given the wording of the European Directive which permits a private copying exception only with "fair compensation". The UK Government argues that "fair compensation" is factored into the original contract; rights holders, including representatives of photographers would disagree.

Even if this first principle could be agreed, Government's initial proposals are dangerously worded and do not take account of the impact of such an exception on specific categories of work such as photographs and other artworks. For example, the proposal states that a user must own a lawfully acquired copy before any private copying can take place, but a lawfully acquired photographic print can mean a limited edition print purchased in a gallery. To permit the owner to then make further prints for private use, will impact on the value of the limited edition.

In another part of the photographic market, wedding and portrait photographers rely on income from re-prints. If the printed or digital proof is lawfully acquired by the client then the photographer will have their main source of income undermined.

This type of example exists across creative sectors so Government needs to give much more careful thought to the detail of the wording for this exception. The AOP's most recent thinking on this proposed exception can be found at http://www.the-aop.org/uploads/private-copying-draft-legislation.pdf

Parody, pastiche and caricature

At both European and UK level Government and legislators are seeking ways to cover problems associated with copyright and User Generated Content (see below) and the UK has approached this is by proposing an exception for Caricature, Pastiche and Parody.

As originally proposed, the exception would cover caricature and pastiche as well as parody. However, the proposals from Government focus solely on parody. No proper analysis of pastiche or caricature has been made and greater clarity is needed on the meaning of parody.

As the proposal is for a "fair dealing" exception, it is expected that the author of any work subject to a parody will need to be given sufficient acknowledgement.

There are also concerns about how moral rights will apply to a work which is subject to parody.

The AOP's latest thinking on a Parody exception can be found at http://www.the-aop.org/uploads/parody-draft-legislation.pdf

Education
The original proposals put forward by Government went very much wider than was needed to achieve its twin objectives of ensuring that educational establishments are in a position to use relevant works for educational purposes, while rights holders continue to benefit from licensing the use of their works for educational use. The original proposals also put existing licensing schemes for educational uses, from which photographers benefit, at risk.

Research, libraries and archives
This exception will widen the categories of works to which it applies and will include photographs as well as other artistic works. The proposal will also widen the types of organisations eligible to benefit from the exception and what they can do with copies made under the exception. While it is a positive move to include museums and galleries in the exception, such institutions should be carefully defined as should the use of such copies.

Disability exception
The proposed exception will replace the existing exception (which includes licensing arrangements for visually impaired people) with an exception for disabled persons which permits them to make, or have made, accessible copies for personal use. Quite how this will work for artistic works and photographs is difficult to imagine.

Collective Management of Photographers' Rights

Collecting societies are also known as Collective Management Organisations (CMOs) and in UK copyright legislation CMOs are Licensing Bodies offering licensing schemes on behalf of more than one right owner. At last count there were 14 CMOs operating in the UK. They range from major corporations such as PRS for Music and PPL UK to the much smaller Directors UK and British Equity Collecting Society (BECS).

A CMO is normally a membership organisation, operating as a not for profit company limited by guarantee, functioning in a commercial environment, with a corresponding need to apply effective financial and managerial strategies to their business operations. Typically a CMO's operation is funded by commission income, deducted from the licence revenue they collect on behalf of the creators they represent.

As a membership organisation, the CMO is normally governed by a board of directors, which will include members and others who are appointed for their business, legal or other expertise. The business will be run on a day-to-day basis by professional employed staff. Their aim is to further the objectives laid down in the CMO's Constitution.

The CMO often licenses secondary uses (see "Secondary" Uses below) through "blanket" or collective licensing schemes. These aim to provide a practical solution to the problems associated with high volume use of copyright material where the rights of many might be exploited (photocopying for example does not just include the works of many photographers and artists, there are also many authors and publishers involved).

Such schemes tend to operate in the following way:

- terms and licence fees are negotiated in advance by the representative CMO with a body representing relevant users (e.g. a consumer organisation, body representing Universities, or local authority);
- negotiations are likely to be long and complex, to involve substantial sums of money and terms may include commitments to provide usage data, ensure compliance, etc.
- resultant revenue is paid to the CMO, or to multiple CMOs.
- each CMO must then find a fair way of distributing that revenue back to the copyright owners whose works are covered by the scheme. How this is achieved depends on the CMO's distribution policy and the availability and comprehensiveness of usage data.

What distinguishes such licensing schemes from other forms of licensing (e.g. licensing by the individual) is the scope of indemnity (that is, the guarantee to cover the rights or "insurance") provided by the CMO. In photocopying, for example, a licence that indemnified users to copy the works of some photographers, but not others, would be worthless in the same way that a television licence permitting the viewing of only parts of a programme or only some programmes would be of little use or value to viewers. Therefore, the licence offered by the CMO must cover works of all relevant creators and not just some.

DACS and Payback

The Design and Artists Copyright Society Limited (DACS) is the copyright and collecting society for visual artists in the UK. It is an independent, not-for-profit membership society open to all visual artists, irrespective of the artistic discipline in which they practice. DACS was originally formed in 1984 by a group of artists to administer and protect the rights of visual creators in the UK. DACS currently represents the primary copyright interests of over 80,000 artists worldwide and in 2012 it distributed over £9.7 million in royalties to artists and artist beneficiaries. Along with primary and secondary uses, DACS administers the Artists' Resale Right (see "Other Important Rights" below) in the UK.

In 1992, leading a group of similar organisations representing artists, illustrators, designers, journalists and photographers, the AOP mandated the Design and Artists Copyright Society (DACS) to represent its members' rights when secondary uses are licensed through collective licensing schemes. This was done with the approval of its members. Individual photographers can ask not to be represented by DACS in this way, their rights can then be excluded from any schemes in which DACS participates. While this is the photographer's choice, it will mean they cannot register for Payback or benefit financially from it.

The original aim of the mandate granted by the AOP and others was to ensure that photographers had a CMO in place to manage certain potential uses for what were then emerging technologies. Photographers at that time thought they might find themselves in a similar place to that in which composers, songwriters and music publishers had found themselves a century earlier, with the advent of recording and broadcasting technologies resulting in mass commercial exploitation of musical works and the failure of such technologies to provide any form of recompense for composers, songwriters or their publishers. PRS for Music (made up of the Performing Right Society and the Mechanical Copyright Protection Society) was created to regulate public performance and mechanical copying of protected musical works.

DACS was already receiving some small amounts of revenue from "secondary" rights for artistic works through its international network of sister societies and so with the boost from the mandating organisations it was in a position to develop collective licensing for visual artists in the UK. DACS became the UK's representative collecting society for photographers. From 1992 on it negotiated a place for photographers and other visual artists in collective licensing schemes for existing "secondary" uses.

The original challenge for DACS was at the distribution end. "Secondary" use arose from material which had originally been licensed for broadcast in the UK and in material included in UK publications – books and magazines. Similar schemes for musical works used playlists to identify rights holders, those for literary works used a combination of broadcaster licensing agreements and careful searching of TV listings or cross referencing ISBN numbers to identify their rights holders. Very little of this type of data was available to DACS and so it developed a claim based system for distributing such royalties. That claim based distribution system is called Payback and it is open to all photographers whose work has appeared in a book, magazine or on TV. More about DACS Payback can be found at http://www.dacs.org.uk/for-artists/payback

Where the visual arts are licensed by DACS under a collective licensing scheme, photographers can benefit either by becoming members of DACS, or by making a claim under Payback.

Royalties received from DACS are intended to complement and supplement the photographer's income not to replace it. By registering a claim to a share of this revenue, the photographer still preserves his or her right to control the use of their photographs in the marketplace. By supporting the work of CMOs and by asserting these secondary rights through DACS, photographers can help to generate greater respect for copyright on all levels and help to generate more revenue for themselves and for other visual artists in the future.

"Secondary" Use

More than ever, photographers must hold onto their copyright. In a market where there is less and less commissioned work and while the price for each commission and the value of individual image sales drop constantly, there is increasing demand for image resale and re-use through library sales and increased demand for access to images for secondary uses.

Many photographers have considerable first-hand experience of managing rights in their photographs or, alternatively, have arranged for them to be managed through an agent, agency or photographic library. In these circumstances, one might typically envisage the transaction between the photographer (or their agent) and another party to permit the reproduction of the photographer's work. Any specific requirements or restrictions negotiated between the parties are incorporated into the contract, or licence. This type of activity can be described as the licensing of "primary" uses.

Example A library sale or a commission for a photograph to appear in an advertisement on a poster or as a plate in a book, are primary uses.

Where a photographer's work is used without prior reference to the photographer, as part of a collective agreement, alongside the works of many other rights owners, but for a market or use which the photographer or other rights owner is unable to license for themselves, this is licensing a "secondary" use.

Example if a page from a book, including the photograph plate, is then photocopied for use in a school, this would constitute a secondary use.

All examples, whether primary or secondary use, are treated as copies or reproductions in copyright law and all need a licence if they are not to be infringements of the photographer's copyright.

The two current areas of "secondary" use which DACS administers on behalf of photographers are:

Off-Air Recording of Television Programmes

Under an exception to copyright (see above), educational establishments can make copies of television programmes, and other copyright works included in those television programmes, for educational use without permission or payment, unless there is a scheme set up which licenses this type of use and unless the category of work, in this case, photography and visual arts, participates in this scheme.

Such a licensing scheme exists. It is run by the Educational Recording Agency (ERA) http://www.era.org.uk/ acting on behalf of broadcasters and representatives of other copyright owners and its members include the Design and Artists' Copyright Society (DACS) on behalf of visual artists and photographers.

A share of the income from the ERA licensing scheme comes to DACS, which is a member of the scheme. DACS in turn pays those royalties on to individual photographers through Payback.

Reprographic Copying – Photocopying

There are a range of exceptions and limitations which apply to photocopying and the Copyright Licensing Agency (CLA) http://www.cla.co.uk/ has developed partly as a result. Originally a scheme set up by publisher and author interests, DACS has negotiated a place in the scheme on behalf of visual artists and photographers and is now channelling revenue back to photographers for photocopying and scanning in an educational context and for similar types of copying (that is, there are strict limits on what can be done with those copies) for business and government.

Coming Soon

Accountability

UK legislation covers the operation of licensing bodies (CMOs in the main) and licensing schemes and makes CMOs subject to the Copyright Tribunal. The Copyright Tribunal describes its main function as:

> *"... to decide, where the parties cannot agree between themselves, the **terms and conditions of licences** offered by, or licensing schemes operated by, collective licensing bodies in the copyright and related rights area. It has the statutory task of conclusively establishing the facts of a case and of coming to a decision which is reasonable in the light of those facts. Its decisions are appealable to the High Court only on points of law."*

That is, the Copyright Tribunal deals with issues arising from the tariffs set by CMOs and the terms on which licences are offered to users. It does not deal with complaints about how a CMO treats its members, or other rights holders, or about its standards of customer service (for users and potential licensees).

Most CMOs are registered companies and as such are regulated by Companies House and must comply with rules affecting the operation, finance and practice of companies more generally.

CMOs, as representatives of many individual rights owners, are also said to be in a dominant position in the marketplace, are treated as monopolies and must comply with Competition law.

Most are membership organisations operating under a Constitution which gives a voice and a vote to each member at its AGM and by election of members to its Board of Management, as well as through Member Charters and input into distribution policies.

Recent moves at both European and UK level encourage CMOs to operate more transparently, to improve governance and adopt principles of best practice in the form of codes of conduct.

Provision is made for collective management in a number of existing Directives but part of the latest European Commission proposal on collective management of rights http://ec.europa.eu/internal_market/copyright/management/index_en.htm concentrates upon improving transparency of governance and financial operation of collecting societies. As it has not yet been adopted, it remains to be seen how this will impact on UK legislation.

In the UK, the Enterprise and Regulatory Reform Act 2013 opened the way for Government to regulate CMOs further and has resulted in more specific legislation to be known as "The Copyright (Regulation of Relevant Licensing Bodies) 2014" and expected in the first part of 2014. Where a CMO has failed to adopt and publish a code of conduct in line with specified criteria, the Government can impose a code of conduct on the licensing body. The Government may also appoint an Independent Code Reviewer and a licensing code Ombudsman to provide a complaints mechanism. These measures also give Government backstop powers against individual CMOs should self-regulation fail.

Self-regulation is in place. The IPO (the government agency responsible for copyright) has published Minimum Standards http://www.ipo.gov.uk/hargreaves-minimumstandards.pdf with which CMOs must comply. The British Copyright Council, working with its member CMOs, has produced "Principles for Collective Management Organisations Codes of Conduct", and each CMO has since introduced a code of conduct, agrees to participate in an external independent complaints procedure and is subject to independent review. The Independent Code Review takes place in the first half of 2014 and every three years thereafter. Information on participating in that review and other information relating to the accountability of CMOs can be found at http://www.independentcodereview.org.uk/

Orphan Works

Demand from cultural institutions at a European level for the right to digitise their collections (see the Europeana project which demonstrates how valuable such projects can be http://www.europeana.eu/) led to early initiatives around Orphan Works. To digitise their collections, cultural institutions find that they must clear the rights in a great many works some of which are likely to be protected by copyright, for example, a photographic archive. It is claimed that one of the obstacles is that, in many cases, the identity of the author e.g. photographer cannot be found and even if it is, the photographer or their estate cannot be located.

The result has been an EU Directive on Certain Permitted Uses of Orphan Works http://eur-lex.europa.eu/LexUriServ/LexUriServ.do?uri=OJ:L:2012:299:0005:0012:EN:PDF was adopted on 25th October 2012 and must be implemented in the UK by September 2014.

The UK Government has also taken powers under the Enterprise and Regulatory Reform Act 2013 on introduce an orphan works licensing scheme and is coming up with its own proposal for orphan works licensing http://www.ipo.gov.uk/orphanworks-licensing.pdf. Despite regular consultation meetings between government, rights holders (including photographers' representatives) and others, the resulting proposal, in the form of draft Regulations for a UK licensing scheme for orphan works http://www.ipo.gov.uk/consult-2014-lost.pdf is, in the view of rights holders, unworkable. The draft Regulations also provide for implementation of the Directive.

Quite how the Directive and the UK's proposal will work together at a practical level is unclear.

A consultation on the UK Government's draft Regulations were published in January 2014, so the following can give no more than a quick summary of some of the issues raised by implementing the Directive and those proposed for the UK.

1. What is an Orphan Work?

The definitions being used in the Directive and in the UK Government's Regulations vary slightly. The main differences being in the detail but the basic definition of an Orphan Work is a work, where following a diligent search (the form of diligent search is specified):

- The author cannot be identified;
- If the author is identified they cannot be located.

It is not quite as simple as this, as there will also be rules relating to cases where:

- there is more than one work and one or more of the authors can be identified, but none can be located (the work then remains an orphan but only until such time as the author(s) are identified and located);

- it is not known whether the work is still protected by copyright;
- Where a work is embedded or incorporated into another work e.g. a photograph in a book.

2. How will "orphan works" be made legally accessible?
EU Directive: provides an exception to copyright (see "Permitted Acts" above) for the purpose of allowing certain organisations under certain conditions to digitise copyright protected works and make them available online.

UK Proposal: sets up a domestic scheme for licensing orphan works which grants licences to potential users.

Further issue: Does an exception, or a form of licensing which takes rights away from the photographer, weaken exclusive rights and inhibit the development of market-led solutions?

3. What types of copyright protected work are covered?
EU Directive: photographs and other artistic works are excluded from the exception, that is, they cannot be treated as orphan works unless they are "embedded" in another work such as a book or magazine or television programme which is covered by the exception. So a print held in an archive cannot be treated as an orphan work but a plate included in a book or a photograph shown as part of a television programme and which is itself an orphan work, can be.

UK Proposal: Also includes works where the author is identified but cannot be located following diligent search. The draft Regulations refer only to a "copyright work". Government's earlier fact sheet refers specifically to: "in the case of photographs", so there can be no doubt that they are included.

Further issues: Is the exception in the Directive really of value, if the digitisation of orphan works by cultural establishments excludes photographs and other artistic works? How will the difference between stand-alone and embedded photographs and artistic works work in practice? Does the UK proposal address the particular issues for photographs and artistic works e.g. lack of a credit on many individual images, the number of images in circulation, routine stripping of metadata all of which reduce the likelihood of such works being re-associated with their authors and increases the risk of them being declared orphaned?

4. Who should be able to use orphan works?
EU Directive: Cultural and educational establishments, archives, film and audio heritage institutions and public service broadcasters.

UK Proposal: An orphan licensee is not defined so presumably all forms of commercial use within national boundaries are envisaged.

5. What will orphan works be used for?
EU Directive: Subject to certain conditions, including diligent search procedures, these organisations can digitise orphan works and make them available online. Such organisations will be entitled to use orphan works to achieve aims related to their public interest mission and will be allowed to conclude public-private partnerships with commercial operators and to generate revenues from the use of orphan works to cover digitisation costs.

UK Proposal: "Specific uses" but the Government factsheet states that the licensing scheme "provides for broader commercial and non-commercial use" than the exception provided for in the Directive. With reference to the steps to be taken before a licence is granted and using photography as its example, Government says "the main use of the scheme is likely to be for unique old photographs of historical interest that are held in museums, archives and libraries, where there are no substitutes, rather than contemporary digital photographs."

Further issues for 2 and 3: The wording of the Directive raises obvious questions about how far organisations can go in making works available online, what is a "public interest mission", whether commercial operators get to keep digitised material for their own use and who determines what digitisation costs are.

Quite how the UK proposals will reconcile "broader commercial uses" with its main use for "unique old photographs held in museums" remains to be seen.

While accepting that some limited exception or licence for use of works by cultural organisations is needed, many photographers and visual artists are strongly against any form of commercial use of orphan works.

The UK also proposes to permit use only within the UK. How this will work in practice is unclear.

6. Who should be responsible for licensing orphan works?
EU Directive: No one. The Directive creates an exception to copyright (see "Permitted Acts" above) and not a licensing arrangement.

UK Proposal: The scheme will operate through authorisation a Government-appointed public body (probably an existing one) which will be responsible for verifying that a diligent search has been carried out and will maintain a register of works for which a licence has been granted. The licence fee will be held by the authorising body in case the missing photographer re-appears and unclaimed money may be used to make the authorising body self-financing,

Further Issues: The Government originally proposed a *bona vacantia* scheme run by The Treasury under which unclaimed funds eventually go to the Government. As an alternative many rights owners preferred the option of licensing though existing CMOs. Other rights owners take the view that technology itself will make the existence of orphan works a thing of the past and that online licensing (on a one to one transactional basis) will address the problem for the future.

CHAPTER 1

Extended Collective Licensing

Part of the drive towards the wider use of extended collective licensing across Europe has been a desire to see licensing solutions rather than exceptions to copyright as a response to certain forms of mass use which are of low individual value and which arise in the digital and online environment. Extended collective licensing as a solution to rights management pre-supposed CMO licensing on a one-to-many basis, rather than one-to-one online licensing which some rights owners, particularly in the visual arts and photography, believe is a better solution. This is a debate which looks set to continue but in the meantime the UK Government is acting.

Extended collective licensing originated in Scandinavia as a form of collective licensing which:

- Permits the licensing of mass uses of works and provides users with access to all works;
- Is available only where no alternative licensing model is available;
- Recognises that no CMO represents all relevant right holders but agrees that it must represent a substantial number of those rights holders whose works are used;
- Such an organisation must be approved by a public authority;
- Allows free negotiation between CMOs and users;
- Government extends the licence to cover non-represented rights holders;
- Non-represented rights holders are guaranteed fair treatment, are entitled to remuneration but may opt out.

The exception to copyright proposed for orphan works at European level has lessened the pressure for wider use of Extended Collective Licensing but the European Commission's public consultation on the review of copyright rules http://ec.europa.eu/internal_market/consultations/2013/copyright-rules/index_en.htm is likely to see it raised again.

Many of the UK's CMOs, in response to market need and with the support of a substantial number of rights holders, already offer voluntary extended collective licensing. Membership of CMOs in the UK is voluntary, and so in many sectors it is almost impossible for the CMO to enter into membership agreements with each relevant creator. Users need to be confident that they are fully protected against claims of copyright infringement if they are to be convinced to buy a licence. So UK CMOs will generally offer an indemnity to the user against claims made by members and non-members. By offering this indemnity, the CMO assumes legal responsibility for satisfying claims in relation to the use of works of non-members, provided the use was within the terms of the licence offered. The CMO then takes responsibility for ensuring that revenues are distributed fairly to the rights holder. This system has, amongst other things, made the DACS Payback scheme possible with the resulting payment of large amounts of royalties to photographers in a way that would not otherwise have been possible.

The UK Government, to help streamline rights clearances, has decided that this system is not enough and has taken powers under the Enterprise and Regulatory Reform Act 2013 to enable CMOs to apply to operate extended collective licensing in the UK, potentially for orphan works licensing purposes.

Though many rights owners take the view that the existing system works well and should be allowed to continue, placing much more stringent obligations on CMOs may make them reluctant to apply to offer new extended collective licences and impossible for them to continue with existing schemes.

Rights holders are also concerned that the introduction of extended collective licensing into the UK will reduce further the control which they have over their work, particularly if it is used for orphan works licensing. A Government consultation on Extending Collective Licensing closes on 28th January 2014. http://www.ipo.gov.uk/pro-policy/consult/consult-live/consult-2013-ecl.htm

Other Important Rights

Artist's Resale Right

The Artist's Resale Right is a royalty which arises when an artistic work, including a photograph, is resold for a minimum of €1,000 on the art market (that is, with the involvement of an art market professional rather than a private sale between two individuals). It does not apply to the first sale of the work, only the resale. The right lasts, like copyright, for the life of the photographer plus 70 years and also applies to their heirs or estate.

DACS is the default collecting society for the administration of the right and more detailed information about the right, how DACS will monitor sales of your work, how it administers the right and how to sign up for the right can be found on the DACS website at http://www.dacs.org.uk/for-artists/artists-resale-right. The Artists' Collecting Society (ACS) also administers the right and more about ACS can be found at http://artistscollectingsociety.org/

Public Lending Right (PLR)

PLR is the right for authors to receive payment for the loans of their books by public libraries. Under the PLR system in the UK, payment is made from government funds to authors, illustrators, photographers and others whose books are borrowed from public libraries. A photographer will only qualify for the right if they are named on its title page or are entitled to a royalty payment from the publisher. Where there are two or more contributors to the book the royalty is shared according to a percentage which the contributors must agree to before registering. Photographers must register their books with the PLR office to benefit.

More information on PLR can be found at http://www.plr.uk.com/allAboutPlr/whatIsPlr.htm

Rights in moving images – films

The definition of film includes all forms of recorded moving image including "video".

In the UK, the authors and first owners of copyright in a film are the producer and the principal director, each owning 50% of the rights. However, practice in the film industry is such that directors assign copyright to the producer. The reasoning is that the producer is then in a position to exploit the rights and the director receives a suitable remuneration package which often includes a royalty deal giving them an on-going interest in their work.

However, for the purpose of determining how long the copyright in a film lasts, certain individuals who are not authors or copyright owners in the UK must be considered. This is because elsewhere in the EU the rules of film authorship are different and this resulted in a compromise in the EU Directive on Term (how long copyright lasts). As a result UK copyright legislation specifies that, for the purpose of determining how long the copyright in a film lasts, it is 70 years from the end of the year in which the last to die of the following four people dies: -

a. the principal director;

b. the author of the screenplay;

c. the author of the dialogue; or

d. the composer of music specially created for and use in the film.

So any photographer wishing to use a film, part of a film or still from a film will need to check the death dates for all four of these before making the calculation.

The Publisher's Right

There are a number of misunderstandings about what rights a publisher owns in a published photograph or artistic work. The "publisher's right", as it is known, relates to the right in the typographic arrangement of a work, that is in the printed text of the book. There is no typographical arrangement of a photograph or illustration and thus there is no automatic "publisher's right" in a photograph as there would be in a published edition of a writer's work.

Publishers can and do acquire copyright from photographers. Photographers should not assign copyright, wherever possible they should license reproduction of their photographs instead.

Trade Marks and Logos
Care should also be taken when incorporating trademarks and logos into photographs, particularly where the result is commercial benefit, or the trademark is used in the course of trade, or where brands, reputations and endorsement are involved.

User Generated Content (UGC)
UGC is a general term used to refer to the many and diverse forms of content generated by users and uploaded onto the internet. Such material could be wholly created by the user, or it could be a mix of material, partly their own creation and partly someone else's.

The first raises copyright issues for the user creator in terms of how they control the use of their work and its further onward distribution and also how they deal with others who may wish to exploit such work commercially.

The second raises copyright issues both for the user and for any photographer whose material has been re-used. Photographers may also be concerned about the potential for abuse of their moral rights (see "Moral Rights" below).

A third and further issue is the commercial value which service providers, websites and content aggregation services receive from UGC and which some think should come back to both user creators and to underlying copyright owners.

It is a growing issue and such content has growing commercial value. Copyright owners including photographers should be concerned to ensure that Government does not jump to regulatory solutions before the market has had time to develop. Awareness and information on rights for user creators is an important part of that development. For user creators Creative Commons Licensing (see "Dealing with Copyright" below) may provide one solution.

DEALING WITH COPYRIGHT

Copyright has its basis in law but best practice and the negotiating skills of the photographer also have a place. In other words to successfully manage their rights, the photographer must know first what their rights are and then be able to deal in them.

Rights in practice – Assignment or Licence

Transferring ownership of copyright
The photographer may choose to transfer the ownership of copyright in a particular photograph to someone else. This is known as an assignment of copyright. The law states that such an assignment is to be made in writing and signed by (or on behalf of) the photographer, but in some cases other forms of agreement, including a verbal agreement can, in practice, have the same effect (referred to as "equitable assignment" see chapter 2 Contracts).

The alternative to assignment, and one much preferred by all creators and their representatives, is to license the use of the work. A licence permits use but does not transfer ownership of the copyright away from the photographer.

Why licences?
First it is important to know the difference between an assignment of copyright in the photograph and a licence which permits use of the photograph.

As copyright is a property right, perhaps the easiest comparison is between copyright and another more familiar property right, that is, ownership of a house. Once these parallels have been understood it is easier to grasp the principles underlying any negotiations which involve copyright.

The chart below compares the terms used and rights offered by copyright owners with rough equivalents for householders.

House	Copyright
1. A person occupies the whole of their house.	The photographer holds copyright and no-one else is granted the right to use the photographs.
2. A person rents or leases the whole house to another individual.	The photographer licenses someone to reproduce their work in any media form, in any territory or for any time period.
3. A person rents out a room or a flat to another individual.	The photographer grants a publisher the right to publish in a single edition of a consumer magazine within the European Union or The photographer licenses an advertising agency to run a 48 sheet poster campaign on 90 sites in the UK and Australia over a two year period.
4. A person sells the freehold of their house.	The photographer assigns the copyright in their work

The chart shows that rights can be divided, bundled, let for a short time, sold out and limited, however, the photographer chooses.

Most photographers would agree that it is far better in the long term, and wherever possible, to give the client a limited licence rather than a full assignment or buy out. It is, of course, for the photographer to decide which option is the best deal on a case-by-case basis.

A well known publishing and copyright lawyer once recommended: – "acquire broadly, license narrowly" and the idea of licensing narrowly makes good commercial sense for photographers too.

If, for whatever reason, a photographer must assign their copyright (in other words selling the freehold in their property), then they should recognise that, as with a house, they will have no further interest in, or control over, their photograph (other than through moral rights, see below) and there may be no further opportunity to earn from that photograph. That privilege belongs to the assignee, for example, the commissioning client.

If an assignment of copyright is necessary, then the photographer must make sure it's worthwhile – after all, no one sells their house for a week's rental income!

For photographers, the decision to assign copyright, or not, remains a major issue. Sometimes clients need an assignment (the reference to Directors' rights in a film, see above, is practice across all contributors to a film). However, in the recent past, the AOP and others worked successfully with clients to educate them about respect for photographers' rights and to develop trust between industries. This meant that photographers were, in many cases, able to negotiate licence agreements rather assignments. However, the trend is changing again. A greater awareness of the value of creative content in the digital and online environment has resulted in raised demand for assignments of copyright, for no reason other than adding to their own assets and cutting the photographer out of any future royalties from its use. (More about copyright assignments, buy outs and rights grabs is to be found in Chapter 10 Editorial Photography.)

Where is the assignment and licence located?

As the party granting the rights, the photographer should themselves write and sign an assignment or prepare the licence terms.

However, most commissioned work and any deal with a library or agency will normally include other terms and conditions for the job over which the client wants control, so clients normally provide photographers with pre-prepared paperwork e.g. on the purchase order. Though it is standardised it does not mean it is not negotiable – as long as the photographer makes the client aware of their terms in advance, negotiates before the job goes ahead and reads the small print that appears on any purchase order and other paperwork which the client issues. (See Chapter 2 on Contract Law).

Now while the law says that an assignment of copyright must be in writing and signed by the person assigning the rights (the photographer), the client's purchase order may say that the photographer assigns the right. Signing the purchase order and returning it to the client completes the assignment but not signing the purchase order, not re-negotiating with the client and still carrying on with the job also means that the copyright is assigned. This is an equitable assignment of copyright (see Chapter 2 in Equitable Assignments).

The AOP cannot emphasise strongly enough: PHOTOGRAPHERS SHOULD ONLY ASSIGN COPYRIGHT AS A LAST RESORT.

Loss of Control

The point has already been made that, through assignment of rights, the photographer will lose control of their work but this is about more than mere loss of revenue. The photograph could be used in association with a product of which the photographer does not approve, or in association with a political party or regime with which the photographer has no wish to be associated; or, particularly where models appear in the photograph, the whole or part of it could breach the contract with the model agency, leaving the photographer liable or breaching the trust between the photographer and those appearing in the photograph.

Value of Copyright

But to go back to loss of income, the fee for assigning copyright should be equal to a lifetime's use of the image in every imaginable way. Clients are rarely willing or able to pay such a fee. In any case, it is virtually impossible to calculate a fee for something which includes all forms of use including those which haven't yet been invented. The chances of a campaign becoming so successful that world wide, all media usage by the client becomes a reality, is something which is better negotiated as and when the need arises.

Example A photograph of a model in cheap jeans is commissioned for in store promotional material. The photographer charges an appropriately small fee for the photography and the "below the line" use involved. The contract with the model agency reflects the use and the fee. When the client order finally arrives (before the job) it specifies an assignment of copyright in the small print. The photographer either does not read it or fails to raise it with the client. Some years later, the agency re-uses the image in a major poster campaign for the same cheap jeans. By now the model is a well known actress and the jeans are known to be produced in sweatshops by small children, so the association between the model and sweatshop production goes viral. The photographer wonders why he hasn't been paid, the model sues the photographer for breach of contract and damage to her reputation. The agency says the photographer assigned copyright and the contract says the photographer is responsible for any claims arising from third parties (e.g. the model) used in the photograph.

It is the photographer's responsibility to ensure that rights granted to the client are clearly outlined and agreed to before a job is confirmed. It is the photographer's responsibility to ensure that they retain and maintain control of their images wherever possible.

Partial assignment & assignments for a specified period of time

It is possible to partially assign copyright. On the face of it, this may seem attractive when dealing with a client who wishes to fully acquire only certain rights in a photograph. Once again, it is not recommended because of the complications of controlling use.

Once assigned, copyright lasts for exactly the same period as it would normally, i.e. life of the photographer plus 70 years. Occasionally, clients may ask for an assignment of copyright for a specified period of time, on the basis that copyright will be reassigned after that time. It is a possibility but it begs the question, how can the photographer be sure that copyright will be re-assigned. The client's needs can more easily be satisfied by the inclusion of specific clauses in the contract with the photographer. A temporary assignment is not necessary.

Licence Agreements

Is should by now be clear that by assigning copyright, the photographer renounces all control over their work (although they may still be able to exercise their moral rights) and is no longer in a position to earn from that photograph. So what's the alternative? The alternative is to grant a licence to the user. Other copyright owners have been licensing rights to users for years and photographers, particularly successful ones, do the same.

Exclusivity

Exclusivity is important for the photographer on a number of levels.

An exclusive licence carries legal weight and enables the exclusive licensee, i.e. the client, to take legal proceedings should a third party infringe copyright in the work. This is useful for clients because the photographer, as copyright owner, may be not be in a position to pursue a breach of copyright on behalf of the client. An exclusive licence must be in writing, signed by (or on behalf of) the copyright owner, to the exclusion of anyone else, including the copyright owner themselves.

Some clients will insist on assignment of copyright because they wish to be in a position to act fast and take proceedings themselves if they find a work has been infringed, for example if their advertising photograph is being used by a competitor. By giving that client an exclusive licence, the photographer avoids the need to assign copyright and the client can sue for infringement in their own right.

Exclusivity can also be included in the details of the licence and limited to specifics, for example, for a limited time or for type of use, or over a territory of use.

Any copyright owner/photographer who wishes to use the work themselves during the period of exclusivity, for example by including it in their portfolio, should ensure that this is included in the licence agreement.

An exclusive arrangement can also be used where a client has spent a lot of money, time and energy commissioning photographs for their products and they do not want it to be used in other connections, either within an agreed time period, for particular uses, or in association with a particular type of product. For example, a client may ask that a photograph commissioned for use in a shampoo advertisement is never resold by the photographer for use in connection with other hair or beauty products.

Such forms of client exclusivity are very important for advertising photography where commercial considerations of this kind are an essential part of negotiations and the resulting agreement.

Licence Terms

The licence is given by the copyright owner, that is, the photographer, to the user or client. Ideally that licence is in writing and issued by the photographer. It is unfortunate that, far too often, such agreements are verbal or because the photographer fails to issue their own paper work it is left to the client to do so.

Licence terms normally form part of the contract along with all the other terms and conditions of business. Photographers are happy to negotiate in advance on the interpretation of the brief, style and feel of the image, even the location of the shot, choice of model, stylist and props, so there is no reason why they should not feel comfortable about negotiating the arrangements over copyright in advance too. To which, irrespective of moral rights (covered in the next section), should be added whether the photographer is entitled to a credit and to ensure control at postproduction stage to ensure their work is not excessively cropped or manipulated, if they see this as an issue. The licence terms also include exclusivity arrangements (see above) and any client confidentiality issues.

There are other basic points to be covered by the licence, and the following provide a checklist though it is not exhaustive. For more information see Chapter 9 Advertising Photography.

Term	How long does the client want the rights for? e.g. one year only or a six week trial. When does the term start?
Media	Where can the photograph appear? e.g. on the Internet generally or only on a specified website.
Quantity	Is there a limit to the copying or making available? e.g. 6 broadcasts, 10,000 books or the published circulation of a glossy magazine.
Size	Does the reproduction size need to be specified? e.g. a 48 sheet poster or on an A4 showcard
Type of use	Above or below the line advertising, editorial, educational, charity
Territory	Worldwide, Europe only, English language publication
Edition	If in a book will the licence apply only for the first edition or beyond?

CHAPTER 1

Linking the licence to payment

The law may still recognise a licence as valid even if the photographer has not been paid, unless otherwise agreed (in writing and in advance). It is always advisable for the photographer to include a term in his licence agreement which states that the licence is not valid until the photographer has been paid in full (see Chapter 2 & the appendix).

When selling library images, the photographer's licence terms should state that the licence is revoked and all rights revert to the photographer, should the client/user go out of business or into liquidation. This allows the photographer to be sure they are happy to deal with any company which takes over the assets of the liquidated company and perhaps to check that all previous usage by the defunct company has been in accordance with the licence terms, including payment.

Professional Practice and Copyright

Though professional practice is undergoing major change, most commissioned photographers are freelance and are commissioned on a job-by-job basis to complete particular pieces of work on behalf of a number of different clients. They are the first owners of the copyright in their photographs, and the agreements which they conclude and the licences which they, or their agents, issue to clients will affect their income level. That's where the similarities stop, because photographers are specialists and work in very different ways. This short section looks at ways in which those differences affect copyright and licensing arrangements and how a court might interpret those contracts and licences where there is infringement or disagreement.

Advertising Photographers

A large percentage of the income of an advertising photographer comes from the first use of the photograph, for which they are paid a fee for their time and their creativity. In the UK this fee normally includes the first use of the work for which a licence is granted, and the photographer is also paid separately for the expenses of the job.

If the first campaign is successful, the photographer may be asked to issue further licences for an extended time period or additional media, for which additional usage fees are paid by the client.

When the licence period is complete and as long as the photographer respects fully both the client's rights and requirements (e.g. agreeing never to sell a commissioned shot to a competitor of the client) and the rights of any third parties appearing in the photograph (e.g. the model), then the photographer may be in a position to earn further income from the photograph by placing it with a photographic library.

Editorial Photographers

In the past, editorial clients commissioned photography on the basis of "First British Use Only", that is, the photographer granted a licence to publish the photograph for the first time, and once only, in the UK. Now that the UK is part of the European Union, this is changing, but the principle remains the same.

Of course, any licence for online must be for worldwide use. It is difficult to limit online use by territory.

Many publishers still run in-house syndication agencies and, as part of the agreement with the publisher, the photographer may permit their photographs to be syndicated and share fees from syndication with the publisher client. Sometimes photographs will make more sales if they are syndicated alongside the article, and so the photographer will earn more this way. However, many in-house syndication agencies do not actively promote independent use of the photographer's work or prefer to wait for business to come to them. Photographers may feel it is better to syndicate their work themselves, or through a specialist picture library or agency which will be active in promoting their work to potential clients.

Stock Photographers/Library Photographers

The stock or library photography sector continues to change. For information about this see chapter 13 Stock.

Industry Entrants

Photography can be a lonely profession and photographers are vulnerable to pressure from clients who increasingly recognise the value of copyright without being prepared to pay for it. Like other creators, photographers are in most instances going to be the weaker party in any negotiation because they are dependent on their clients for work and for payment. In addition individual freelancers don't have the legal and business back up which many of their clients do.

Some clients will press industry entrants for an assignment of copyright, and though looking for ways to get into the business must be a priority for such photographers, they should be aware that in the long term negotiation, holding onto their rights and a professional approach to their business will bring respect, not just for their creativity, but for their ability to manage that business. Acquisition of such skills, tested at an early stage, is the only way to survive in the industry.

Photographers are also encouraged to join relevant trade associations, trade unions and other groups and authoritative forums for professionals. The opportunity to share experiences and problems helps to remove the feeling of isolation and provides the kind of back-up to the photographer which clients get from the companies they work for as a matter of course.

Students and Copyright

When students are accepted on a photography course, they are normally required to sign an agreement with the college. As with any other agreement, the student should read this document carefully, as it may contain an assignment of copyright covering every work that the student produces whilst at the college – even non-course work! The AOP believes that the practice of insisting on an assignment of copyright from new creators at this early stage in their career, in exchange for education which, in most cases, the student now pays for, is unfair and unreasonable. It is also a matter of concern that students are being taught poor business practice by those responsible for training in what is largely a vocational field.

It is understood that colleges want to include student work in exhibitions and promotions for the college, and even include work in brochures or leaflets. Instead of an assignment, the student should be asked to provide a licence for the very specific types of use which the college requires.

Students in college also need to work with and learn from the copyright works of other artists. This has been part of teaching practice for hundreds of years. However, with developments in technology and modern art practice, it has become increasingly easy and tempting to reproduce the works of other artists. The original artist or photographer may be prepared to accept this type of use of their work in an educational context. They will be less happy to see its continued presence in a portfolio once a student has left college. It is much more professional and much less likely to cause difficulty later if the student asks permission before reproducing the works of others.

Securing your Copyright

For information on securing your copyright when forming your own limited company see Chapter 3 Accounting.

Copyright is a property right which you can pass on to your heirs and beneficiaries via your will and with your other worldly goods. For information on the best way to do this speak to your legal adviser.

PROTECTION AND ENFORCEMENT

This section summarises the first steps a photographer should take to protect their images and provides a summary of what an infringement is, what types of infringement exist and what remedies might be available to a photographers whose rights have been infringed.

Protection

The first level of protection against copyright infringement is for the photographer to ensure an image never leaves their hands without some form of identification being attached. Anyone who subsequently receives a copy or a digital file should then be aware that it has an identifiable copyright owner. Of course, it's not quite as simple as that but it's a start!

Identifying Photographic Works

Every photographic image, whether film, print or digital file, should carry the following information:

© A. Photographer, 2014
Moral Rights Asserted
This work may not be reproduced without the permission of
A. Photographer,
Contact details

Ideally this copyright notice should appear in metadata or somewhere on the image every time the photograph is sent out. It should also be attached to images sent to clients and incorporated in some way into every piece of correspondence issued by the photographer, for example an e-mail to the client identifying the images and accompanying the digital files.

Images sent to clients or potential clients should always be accompanied by some form of e-delivery note which lists the images enclosed, states that they must not be reproduced without permission and that they must always be credited to the photographer. The photographer at least will then know who has which of their images and when the client received them.

The international copyright symbol or © does not have any specific legal status in the UK. However, its meaning is recognised and will be understood both here and in most other countries.

Websites, folio sites and blogs

Photographers now promote their work through their own websites or blogs. Photographers should always ensure that their websites, or any folio sites or blogs they subscribe to, carry proper information about copyright ownership of the images, that the information is easily accessible and that each individual image carries appropriate identifiers. With so much free content it's important that users need to be told exactly what they are, and are not, permitted to do with professional images.

Whilst it's normal practice for commercial websites to include a copyright notice in some form, it tends to appear in "credits", "disclaimers" or "copyright" sub-sections which users rarely bother accessing. If, however, the site is the photographer's own, there is no reason why this information should not appear at the point of entry or on the home page. The reason is that this makes it very obvious to any user who takes an image without permission and thus infringes the photographer's copyright, that they cannot subsequently claim they were not aware that the image was protected by copyright (see "Innocent Infringers" below).

The AOP suggests that the following be included as a minimum (other examples can be found on the websites of most major stock agencies and picture libraries) on photographer owned sites and blogs and that they do not subscribe to folio sites or blogs unless, at the very least, they carry something along similar lines.

Any photographer wanting to be really sure they are properly covered should seek legal advice on wording appropriate for their site.

Ownership & copyright

This website and its content are owned by A. Photographer.

The website, its design and its content including each and every photograph are protected by copyright and trade mark law and other related intellectual property rights.

Copyright in the photographs is owned by A. Photographer (contact details).

A. Photographers' photographs are also protected by moral rights. A. Photographer asserts his/her moral right to be identified as the author wherever and whenever his/her photographs are copied or distributed by any means.

Copyright in the website and its design is owned by A. Photographer and/or a Designer (contact details).

Use of A. Photographer's website and photographs

No part of A. Photographer's website and photographs may be copied or distributed by any means without the explicit written permission of A. Photographer. Those wishing to copy or distribute material from this website should contact A. Photographer at permissions@a.photographer'semail.com.

DRMs and Metadata

Chapter 14 (Digital Technology) covers this subject in much more detail.

The term digital rights management information (DRMs) refers to technology which allows copyright owners and/ or their agents to be identified and located. More than that, it can include everything from the data systems which CMOs, image libraries, agencies and individual photographers can use to manage rights, to the information provided when the files are accessed e.g. through Digimarc, IPTC headers. Technological protection measures include such things as fingerprinting or watermarking technology but also covers black box access for pay-for-use media, or keys for lawful access to software.

Metadata is, in its simplest sense, "data about data content" but this section concerns itself only with the fact it provides identifiers relating to the photographer and copyright owner and their contact details.

If every photographer incorporated identification and contact metadata in their digital images and if every publisher, producer and other user retained and respected that meta data then at some stage in the cross over between analogue and digital there would come a time when it would be possible to tell infringing copies by the fact they did not carry digital identifiers. Of course this would not address the problem of images which are not "born digital" and which will continue to remain available in analogue (e.g. paper and film) form but it would reduce the size of the problem and photographers will, of course, also have to find better ways of monitoring online use to identify infringing copies of their photographs.

Ideally the starting point for all this would be if an authoritative, single numbering system linked to a voluntary register of photographers and their works, existed, and if that number could be incorporated into the meta data. The register could then link the number back to the photographer, their chosen rights managers and most importantly provide a means by which contact information could be obtained. Whether this register should or could link to licensing information or systems would then be for the photographer to decide. This is basically what the PLUS Registry https://www.plusregistry.org/cgi-bin/WebObjects/PlusDB was set up for but there are other contenders. It is also what the UK's Copyright Hub http://www.copyrighthub.co.uk/ was set up to encourage.

Tampering with or removing metadata, other DRMs and technological protection devices from digital versions of photographs is illegal but, for the system to work the first step must be for the technology and any associated register to be cheap, easy to access, adopted by the majority of professional photographers and respected by their clients

Registering Photographs

There is no system for registering photographs in the UK. Copyright exists in a photograph from the moment it is created, it is automatic and it belongs to the photographer as the author in the first instance.

Any commercial service offering to register copyright, these days such services are mainly to be found on the Internet, should be approached with care. The most that such a service can offer is to register the work (not the copyright) by creative proof that a photograph was in existence by a given date, for use in legal cases where a dispute arises over which version of a photograph came first (see the paragraph on proving infringement below). However, this argument does not often arise in Court and if the photographer feels it is a useful precaution there are other ways in which to achieve it.

The simplest, cheapest and traditional way to provide such proof, is for the photographer to make copies of their photographs e.g. prints, photocopies or on CDs and send them in a sealed envelope, by registered post, back to themselves. When the envelope returns it must not be opened, it must remain sealed and the photographer should ensure that the date stamp is clear. The envelope should then be filed somewhere safe and only ever opened on the instructions of a court or legal adviser. If this mailing process is carried out on a regular basis, the photographer should also mark the contents on the outside of the envelope upon its return, so they know which envelope contains which photographs.

This method proves that a given photograph was in existence by the date on the postmark. There are other alternatives such as lodging copies in a sealed envelope with a bank or a solicitor, but these cost more.

Most photographers will feel this is an unnecessary and time consuming process as photographers tend to create thousands of images, but it is very useful for other types of authors e.g. scriptwriters. The main reason for including this information here is because photographers may have heard confusing or conflicting stories about registration and registration services. The main point to remember is that there is no system for registering copyright in the UK.

Infringement of copyright

That part of the Copyright Act which deals with restricted acts (those under the control of the photographer – see above) itemises each of the acts by defining what is an infringement e.g. copying, communication to the public, etc. and there are both primary and secondary acts of infringement.

Primary or secondary infringement?

Primary infringements are those where liability for the restricted act of, for example, copying or of communication to the public, does not depend on the infringer's knowledge of infringement.

Example A photograph is downloaded as an exact digital file from a photographer's website, it is then printed onto 1,000 T-shirts. No permission was obtained from the photographer. The original photograph has been copied first by downloading it and copied again by making it readable by the T-shirt printer and copied again on each of the 1,000 T-shirts. This is primary infringement.

Secondary infringements cover other aspects of the trade in pirated or infringing goods such as the importation, possession of, dealing with, providing the means for making, or use of premises for making unlicensed copies. For example, where the infringing T-shirts and 'art' posters are sold from a market stall, even if the market trader did not make them himself. Knowledge of infringement is required for there to be a secondary infringement.

For many photographers though, infringements are not straightforward cases of piracy.

Some ways in which photographic copyright can be infringed

1. Client or commissioner of the photographs uses the images but either fails to pay, or fails to comply with other contractual terms and where the photographer's own terms of business state that no rights pass to the client, or that the licence to use the photographs is invalid without prior payment in full to the photographer or where the client is otherwise in breach of the contract;
2. Commissioner or client uses the photographs outside the terms of the original licence;
3. Other users copy the photographs without clearing rights: –
    1. either by making an exact copy of the original;
    2. or by getting another photographer to re-take the photograph or imitate it too closely.

Negotiation and Compromise

The first two types of infringement are more often matters for negotiation and compromise than for the law. The photographer is likely to want to work with the client or at least some of the client's staff again in the future and it is possible that there has been a real misunderstanding, or a personnel change, rather than any ill intention. Most such problems can be resolved with a little pressure and patient negotiation on the part of the photographer.

Where clients fail to pay, putting pressure on the client's accounts department by using debt collection or late payment legislation will probably be quicker, cheaper and easier than arguing about copyright. Nevertheless, the possibility of a case being brought for copyright infringement is normally sufficient to persuade the client that the photographer should be paid.

Similar "client relationship" pressures also apply in the second case, where the photograph has been used outside the original licence terms, so the photographer should in most circumstances be willing to license retrospectively, at a fee similar to that charged if their permission had been sought before the reproduction was made.

Such an approach may be beneficial where other commercial users such as publishers or an advertising agency have blatantly infringed copyright but are prepared to pay a commercial rate and want a licence once they have been made aware of their error. Tactful handling at this stage may mean a new client for the photographer later.

Increasingly, there are circumstances where consumers and small-scale commercial users, who perhaps should have been aware of the copyright implications, will post and share images or add them to a website or include them in a small publication. Wherever possible, photographers should not treat such infringers with a heavy hand or attempt to charge swingeing fees. It may be better to make the user aware of the infringement and offer the chance to license or take down, or in the case of sharing ("Pin It") accept it will happen and treat it as a form of self-promotion.

Of course, cases do arise where users have stolen or pirated a photograph in the most flagrant way. Most infringement cases involving photographs are settled out of court once the infringing user becomes aware of the full costs they may incur in defending their case. Unfortunately for the photographer, if there is only a small amount of money involved,

CHAPTER 1

the legal cost and the time and energy expended on a case may far outweigh any fees or damages awarded, though this has improved with the advent of the Small Claims Track in the Intellectual Property Enterprise Court, which has been used by photographers to some effect.

Innocent infringers

Where a copyright infringer can prove they did not know and had no reason to believe that the work was protected by copyright, then the copyright owner is not entitled to claim damages. This defence is only available to infringers in exceptional circumstances, where a photograph is apparently public domain.

Seeking Advice

Copyright law is a specialist area and there are even fewer specialists in photographic copyright. The AOP and other professional associations and unions can usually make recommendations or you can contact The Law Society for a list.

Specialist legal advice does not come cheap. The cost of advice can be kept down if the photographer has used watertight contracts and licences in the first place and if they also keep other records e.g. ensuring written client approval at each stage of the (unpaid for) job. Email exchanges can often be helpful as evidence.

When approaching a solicitor for advice, the photographer should first check their hourly rate, how they would like to be briefed and ask for an estimate on the basis of that briefing, for at least the first stage of work. The photographer should realise that the work may become more complicated depending on the response from the infringer and the defence they may put forward. A solicitor cannot estimate for this at the outset. Given the limited number of specialist solicitors, before agreeing to act for you, the solicitor will need to check whether they have a conflict of interest. For example, the solicitor may be retained by the designer, publisher or advertising agency involved.

The photographer should make sure they have the basic issues quite clear in their own mind before any briefing so they can provide a clear and concise explanation of the problem. The solicitor will want to see the paperwork, perhaps labelled to show each document's relevance.

Notifying the infringer

If the solicitor agrees to act for the photographer, the first stage will probably be to write a "letter before claim" putting the copyright infringer on notice. This is something that the photographer could do and hopefully will have done in some form before seeking legal advice. However, some photographers may prefer to use their solicitor as intermediary, or may not feel sufficiently confident about what to say in their letter or may feel that a solicitor's letter carries more weight.

The purpose of the letter is to put the infringer on notice that:

- the photograph is protected by copyright and that A. Photographer is the copyright owner;
- any copying or communication to the public of that photograph without permission is an infringement of A. Photographer's copyright;
- the infringer is to cease making any further copies, making them available and distributing them;
- the infringer is to immediately provide the photographer with necessary information about how and where the photograph was obtained and how and where it has been used, so the situation can be assessed; and

to ask the user what they are going to do about rectifying the situation.

It also ensures that once the infringer has received the letter, they cannot claim, or continue to claim, that they are unaware that the photograph is protected by copyright.

Proving infringement

If a photographer chooses to pursue a case for copyright infringement, then it is likely that the court will want to address all, or at least some of the following issues:

Is it a copyright protected work?	Yes, it is a photograph and it is still within the period of time relevant for it to be protected by copyright.
Did the infringer have access to the original photograph?	Yes, the photograph is accessible on the photographer's website at this URL and could be downloaded from the internet.
Was it clear that the photograph was protected by copyright? and/or would the user be expected to know?	Yes, the photograph carried a credit. The unlicensed user was a magazine publisher and should have known to clear rights in any photograph before use. (In any event, it is not a defence to the claim that the user did not know that the photograph was protected by copyright.)
Is the person bringing the claim the owner of copyright or an exclusive licensee?	Yes, the claimant is the author of the photograph and he/she still owns copyright.
The infringer claims that their work is the original one. Can the photographer prove otherwise?	Yes, the photographer can demonstrate that their photograph pre-existed the other. It appeared on his/her website in 2009; the other was only made last year.
Is the infringing copy sufficiently similar to the first photographer's image to be a copy?	Perhaps an art director saw the image on the Internet, liked it and then got someone else to take another similar photograph. Was it just the idea he/she picked up on or can the first photographer, or an expert on their behalf, demonstrate that the second version is no more than a mere copy of the first.
Has a substantial part of the original photograph been copied?	If only a tiny part of the original photograph has been reproduced (this is a decision based on quality as much as quantity) then a court may decide it is not sufficiently substantial to be treated as a copy. On deciding this issue the court may consider previous case law.

Enforcement

Copyright infringements are actionable by the copyright owner, their heirs, or by an exclusive licensee (see "Dealing with Copyright"). They can be dealt with by either civil or in certain circumstances by criminal Courts.

It is possible for the photographer to pursue copyright infringement claims for under £10,000 through the Small Claims Track procedure within the Intellectual Property Enterprise Court. Information on using the procedure can be found in Chapter 2, "Copyright Infringement Legal Redress".

The remedies available on the Small Claims Track are: -

- Final Injunction – to prevent the infringer making infringing use of the photograph in future;
- Delivery Up – the infringing copies could be seized and destroyed or handed over to the copyright owner;
- Account of Profits – the infringer provides details of the profits they have made from the illegal copies and could be ordered to pay some or all of those profits to the copyright holder as an alternative to damages;
- Damages;
- Additional Damages – awarded for flagrant infringements.

The copyright owner does not have to prove the infringer knew the work was protected, the act of infringement is enough.

In a case where there has been deliberate infringement on a commercial scale, criminal proceedings could be considered. The photographer would need to report the infringement to the police or local trading standards office, which could lead to prosecution. Criminal intent on the part of the infringer must be proved which can be difficult in photographic copyright claims and prosecution is usually only pursued in counterfeit or piracy cases. No damages are awarded in a successful criminal prosecution, only imprisonment or fines, and in certain cases compensation.

MORAL RIGHTS

Introduction

As with copyright, an author's moral rights are a fundamental human right and recognise the photographer's role in the creation of works of intellect.

The following explains each of the moral rights as it exists in UK law, how and whether it works for photographers and how each fits in with established professional practice.

What are moral rights?

In the UK and elsewhere in Europe, moral rights are an integral part of copyright law, but they were only introduced into UK copyright law for the first time with the 1988 Act, though a right to prevent false attribution was included previously. They differ from other aspects of copyright law because they are personal to the author and are therefore not the same as the "economic" rights. That is, moral rights cannot be said to have a direct financial value. The emphasis with moral rights is on maintaining the integrity and inviolability of a work, rather than in protecting its economic value.

However, they do carry some economic value because as far as publishers, broadcasters, producers and other clients are concerned, moral rights are covered in most contracts and form part of most negotiations over terms and fees. In addition, failure to respect moral rights can damage a photographer's work and their reputation, ultimately affecting the financial value of their work. The right also has an economic value because users may suffer financial penalties if a court finds they have breached an author's moral rights.

Like copyright, moral rights can be legally enforced as it would be for an infringement of copyright (see Protection and Enforcement above) but they are only actionable by the photographer or their heirs.

Moral rights should not be confused with issues around ethics or morality (for more on these see Chapter 7 Standards and Codes)

As the moral rights are personal to the photographer, they cannot be transferred to someone else, unlike copyright which can be assigned. This means that the photographer can only exert or assert the moral rights or give them up (a waiver). No-one else (other than the photographer's heirs) can benefit from the protection which these rights afford to the work of the photographer, and it follows from this that the photographer's agent cannot manage moral rights on behalf of their photographers.

Four moral rights – key points

The Right to be Identified as the Author – the Attribution Right

Sometimes known as the Paternity Right but now more generally known as the Attribution Right.

What is the Attribution Right?

It is the photographer's right to have their name appear alongside their photograph and to be associated with their photograph whenever it appears. In the photographic world this is most easily understood as a 'by-line' or a 'credit' appearing on the photograph but the moral right is also about associating the photographer with their work in a wider sense.

What does the Attribution Right apply to?

The right applies when a photograph is published; when it is exhibited in public; when it is broadcast; or when it appears in a film.

Exceptions to the Attribution Right – i.e. are there cases where the right does not apply?

Regrettably, there is a long list of exceptions, that is, cases where the attribution right does not apply. The three which are of most importance for photographers are:

i) for the purpose of reporting current events;

ii) for publication in a newspaper, magazine or similar periodical, or a 'collective work of reference' (meaning publications such as encyclopaedias where there are likely to be a great many authors involved);

iii) to employees for works made during the course of their employment.

In practice this means that very few photojournalists are in a position to assert their moral right to be identified as the author and employed photographers do not have the right over anything created during the course of their work.

An oddity here is that before the 1988 Act was introduced, established trade practice meant that photographers were credited for work which appeared in an editorial context but for practical reasons were not for work used for advertising or promotional purposes. The effect of this exception is to turn this on its head and while a photographer may be entitled to an attribution or credit on an advertisement hoarding, they are not entitled to one on a portrait in a newspaper.

The Attribution Right must be asserted

For all authors, one of the most regrettable things about moral rights legislation in the UK is that the attribution right must be asserted in writing before it applies. In practice this is not always an easy thing to achieve and means that a statement to the effect that the right has been asserted should be written, signed and attached to the work, in whatever form it takes, by the photographer. The law states only that the form of identification on the photograph should be clear and reasonably prominent. The practice of putting the international copyright symbol, the photographer's name and the year of creation on a print is not recognised as an assertion; it should be accompanied by a statement that the right has been asserted, and include the signature of the photographer.

In practice the assertion should be included automatically with the rest of the credit on every piece of film, every print or every digital file put into circulation. In addition, it should appear in the front of every published edition in which the photograph is included, and in the copyright credits of any broadcast material or on any website on which it appears.

In cases where the copyright itself is assigned or a licence granted, the photographer should ensure that an assertion of the right is included with the assignment or written into the terms and conditions of the licence.

Where a photograph is exhibited in public, e.g. in a gallery, the photographer should ensure they are identified on the original or copy, or on the mount. According to the law this will bind anyone who comes into contact with that original or copy to the assertion, irrespective of whether it is visible or still present! There are no specific requirements as to how this type of assertion should be made. The assertion should also be made on any licence or other agreement which permits the making of limited editions of prints.

The complexities with which this right is surrounded take on an even bleaker aspect as the prospect of an exception and licensing of orphan works (see above) becomes ever more likely. A strong right of attribution would help to ensure that more photographers are associated and attributed alongside their photographs. A weak right encourages the creation of more orphan works. Photographers' representatives are now fighting for a moral right of attribution which makes the stripping of metadata from images a breach of moral rights.

The Right to Object to Derogatory Treatment of a Work – the Integrity Right

What is the Integrity Right?

The Integrity Right is the photographer's right to prevent a work being mistreated, but it is qualified by the fact that it only applies to "treatments" of the work which are damaging to the honour or reputation of the photographer.

So there are a number of tests or qualifications which a court can apply to determine whether there is a treatment of the work, and if so whether the treatment is sufficiently damaging, before they can then decide whether or not there has been a breach of the photographer's moral right.

Some of the preliminary steps taken by a Court would include those for proving infringement of copyright. They will then need to address the following issues:

Is it a treatment?	The words used in the 1988 Act are 'addition to, deletion from or alteration to or adaptation of'.
And is the treatment derogatory?	Again, the 1988 Act defines this term as 'if it amounts to distortion or mutilation of the work or is otherwise prejudicial to the honour or reputation of the author'.
Is it a distortion or mutilation?	There is no guidance in the 1988 Act and case law must be relied on.
Is it damaging to the honour or reputation of the author?	There is no guidance in the 1988 Act and case law must be relied on.

What does the Integrity Right Apply to?

The Integrity Right applies in the same circumstances as the Attribution Right.

Exceptions to the Attribution Right?

The exceptions to the Integrity Right are very similar to those for the Attribution Right.

The Integrity Right does not need to be asserted

Happily, the Integrity Right is an automatic right and does not need to be asserted.

The Right not to have a work Falsely Attributed to a Person as its Author or Director – the 'False Attribution Right'

The false attribution right existed in earlier copyright legislation, and is a right which belongs not to the author, but to anyone who wrongly has a work attributed to them. It can be useful when a photographer finds his or her name has been put onto someone else's work. This may seem unlikely, but it can and does happen.

Example a promotional publication has prepared artwork for the advertisements of two photographers and the names have been transposed under the artworks, or perhaps an advertiser wishes to use a photographer's name for endorsement value but cannot afford the photographer's fees.

The right is automatic and does not need to be asserted. It applies in similar circumstances to those outlined for other moral rights. There are no exceptions to this right.

The Right to Privacy in Respect of Certain Photographs and Films – the Privacy Right

There is a developing law of privacy in the UK, and see Chapter 2 on Privacy for more information on Human Rights.

Under the 1988 Act, the first owner of copyright in a photograph is the photographer, so legislators felt that there should be some way of controlling the dissemination and publication of private photographs, and indeed films, by unscrupulous photographers or media.

The important point to note about the wording of this moral right is that it applies only to commissions for "private and domestic purposes", for example, wedding photographs, family portraits and other forms of social photography. It is not intended to apply to photographs taken in the home of an actor or actress who has commissioned the portrait for their portfolio, or those commissioned by a lifestyle magazine of the interior of a private house with proud owner in the foreground; these are not protected by this moral right.

In practice the right means that even though the photographer is likely to be the copyright owner of photographs commissioned for private and domestic purposes, the commissioner has the right to prevent copies of the photograph from being issued to the public, or broadcast, or exhibited or shown in public – and that includes the photographer's shop window on the high street.

Duration of moral rights

Moral rights apply to the work of any photographer who was alive on or after the 1st August 1989, irrespective of whether the work was created before or after that date.

Moral rights last for the same length of time as copyright, that is, the life of the photographer plus 70 years, apart from the False Attribution Right. The False Attribution Right lasts only for the life of the person who has been falsely attributed plus a further twenty years.

Dealing with moral rights

Personal to the Author

Moral rights may not be assigned to another person or company; they apply only to the creator or their heirs. Nor can an agent represent a photographer for their moral rights, for example, by selling or waiving the rights on behalf of the photographer. The most the agent can do is try to ensure respect for their photographers' moral rights by including terms in contracts which state that the photographer asserts their right to be identified.

Consent

Regardless of the moral rights, it is not illegal for someone to do something to a photographer's work if they have the photographer's consent. That consent should normally be given in writing, but the consent can be spoken or by implication.

Waiver of Moral Rights

A further weakness in UK moral rights is that they can be waived. A waiver is normally made in writing by the photographer, but again it could be done orally, and is often seen in client contracts. Wherever possible photographers should avoid waiving their moral rights.

Photographers should ask themselves whether they really want to work for a client who expects them to give up the right to be associated with their work and why would a photographer permit the mutilation of their work to the extent that it is damaging to their honour or reputation?

Any photographer agreeing to a waiver should be very careful about its wording, in particular to the extent of the waiver, which should be very clear and precise to prevent it applying to all their works generally, or to a type of work, or to all existing or future works.

Where a waiver is required for the Attribution Right, it may be easier for the photographer to agree instead not to assert the right in that particular case. This is fairly common practice in the film industry, for example.

To prevent the photographer from being presented by their client with an unfavourable contract requiring a waiver, it is better to discuss the client's requirements beforehand and for the photographer to include the agreed terms in their contract. For example, where an advertising client wishes to manipulate an image for a particular effect. Of course, in many instances such manipulation could be seen by a court as part of normal industry practice and therefore not a breach of the integrity right.

Moral Rights in Practice

Issues which are likely to impact on moral rights such as the need for a credit, or a photographer's desire for some sort of editorial or contextual control and the wish not to have work manipulated, cropped or otherwise distorted are also matters which can be covered by contract terms. A breach of contract is easier and quicker to enforce than a breach of moral rights so it is worth covering such issues in the contract. It is better for the photographer to identify their client's needs and consent to these in advance as part of the contract

The Attribution Right does not apply unless it has been asserted in writing so an assertion should also be included in any contract or the contract could include an agreement not to assert the Attribution Right in a particular case.

If a waiver is unavoidable, then the photographer should ensure it is specific to the named photograph and in relation to the required use only. The photographer should put the waiver in writing and keep a record of it where it can be easily found.

Enforcement of moral rights

Moral rights are not property rights, and so breaches of these rights are not treated in the same way as an infringement of copyright.

Cases for breach of moral rights may only be brought by the photographer, or his/her heirs, and these are acted on in the Civil Courts only.

So far, in photography, the majority of cases have been settled out of court. Not surprisingly, photographers and their advisers have been unwilling to bring costly cases to court where the outcome is dependent on the court's interpretation of terms such as 'damage to honour or reputation' and 'derogatory treatment', and where the levels of damages are assessed on that interpretation.

Injunctions can be obtained against both anticipated and actual breaches of moral rights, and will stop the reproduction of works, or can ensure that breaches are corrected before the copies are distributed or communicated. With the Integrity Right, it is possible to prohibit reproduction or agree to the inclusion of a disclaimer in, for example, the publication, which disassociates the photographer from the treatment of the work. The photographer may also be compensated for damages, including irritation, loss of reputation and other non-monetary losses, but these can be very difficult to quantify unless the photographer can demonstrate actual damage to their career. If the photographer wins their case, then they may be in a position to recoup most of their legal costs from the infringer.

Of course, enforcing moral rights through the courts is costly and difficult, but it is important that photographers do not waive these fundamental rights. The Writers Guild, Society of Authors and groups representing other types of creators, fought hard to see these rights established in British law and continue to fight against waivers and for improvements to moral rights more generally.

A context for current legislative developments

Though not of immediate relevance many photographers are interested in the debate on legislation so this short section provides a context for the massive amount of activity on the legislative front.

What are European Directives and how do they affect photographers?

European Directives are pieces of European legislation which each Member State agrees to and then is obliged to introduce into its national law (known as implementation). The development of each Directive includes consultation, negotiation and compromise. Any policy development is normally led by the European Commission in the form of a Directorate General. For copyright it is normally DG Internal Market which takes the lead but DG Connect (formally Information Society and responsible for the European digital agenda) plays an increasingly important role. Also involved in policy development is the European Parliament, its Committees and the European Council.

The way in which the law is implemented at national level is open to interpretation. However, should a Member State fail to implement, or should it be felt that they have failed to implement correctly (normally the result of a complaint by stakeholders at national level), they can be pursued by the EU to rectify the situation.

There are now eight Directives on various aspects of copyright. So far, probably the most important for photographers has been the Directive on Copyright in the Information Society (2001/29/EC). Others cover term of copyright protection, rental and lending rights, cable and satellite re-broadcasting, protection of computer programs, protection of databases and the artist's resale right. Also relevant are parts of the Directives on the Enforcement of IPRs and on E-Commerce (which includes provisions relating to the liability of internet service providers). All these have been incorporated into UK law. There is also a Directive on certain permitted uses of orphan works, which has been adopted but which does not come into force until later in 2014.

In addition, there is a proposal for a Directive on collective management and the latest consultation on "The Review of the EU Copyright Rules".

International

UK and European copyright law is also affected by international instruments such as the Berne Convention (basis for copyright), the Copyright Treaty (dealing with technological developments), the Performances & Phonograms Treaty, the Audio-visual Performances Treaty and the Treaty to Facilitate Access to Published Works for People who are Blind, Visually Impaired or Otherwise Print Disabled. These set out minimum standards for legislation around the world. WIPO is now discussing a possible Broadcasting Treaty and a range of Exceptions and Limitations to copyright. There is also TRIPs – Trade Related Aspects of Intellectual Property which are part of world trade negotiations.

Other influences on UK law are, for example, the direction taken by American law, particularly important in the digital and on-line context, for example, the Digital Millennium Copyright Act 1998. Owing to the global nature of the internet other national developments affecting the internet and online service provision are also being followed with interest here in the UK, for example, France's HADOPI law and Canadian and Hungarian arrangements for orphan works licensing.

UK legislative activity

Coming back to the UK, there are other laws which impact on copyright. Included in the Digital Economy Act 2010 are provisions, following the lines of the DCMA and HADOPI which dealt with online piracy, including notice and take down, the role of internet service providers, etc. These provisions caused a great deal of controversy and resulted in a Judicial Review. Despite finding in favour of the provisions they are still to be implemented and rely on OFCOM to operate the provisions.

The Enterprise and Regulatory Reform Act 2013 included provisions on copyright which will be introduced through Regulations (in the form of a Statutory Instrument) which are due to appear shortly. An IP Bill, though of little direct relevance to photographers, is waiting for its Second Reading in Parliament. Perhaps more importantly a series of changes, mainly to exceptions and limitations to copyright, are expected to be introduced through yet more Regulations in the Spring of 2014. These are largely the result of the Hargreaves Review and cover subjects such as parody, private copying, education, libraries and archives.

Who in UK Government is responsible?

The UK Government Department responsible for copyright and other forms of intellectual property is the Intellectual Property Office, an agency falling under the Department of Business Innovation and Skills. Most current copyright legislation comes in the form of secondary legislation, that is, Statutory Instruments because it implements legislation coming from the European Union but some does come through in the form of Acts of Parliament, that is as primary legislation which involves considerable debate. The views of other government departments such as those for culture, education, justice, the Treasury and increasingly, the Office of the Prime Minister, have an influence on our copyright policy and resulting legislation.

CHAPTER 2: CONTRACT LAW, LEGISLATION AND LEGAL REMEDIES

GWEN THOMAS

Contract Law

Introduction

Contracts are entered into every day by people in all walks of life; negotiating the purchase or lease of any item becomes contractual, for example, purchasing a train or bus ticket enters you into a contract. Most everyday contracts are oral, but where something as important as a person's livelihood is concerned, the terms should be in writing. Peoples' minds fog; what one person understands as one thing, another person can interpret as something totally different. Write everything down; use e-mail for speed to confirm what you understood from the conversation; and keep a paper trail – confusion can be very time consuming, frustrating and ultimately costly.

Most clients use terms and conditions of business and photographers should not have to accept other people's terms whilst not being able to assert their own. Even if the client doesn't use them, the photographer should, and will be seen as using good professional business practice. Contracts serve to protect both parties and their proper use should not embarrass or impede either party.

Contracts and licensing combine the most important aspects of both standards of practice and copyright law. This section provides an understanding of these, to enable photographers to make their legal rights work for them economically, whilst ensuring that all parties' rights are respected.

Basic Contract Law

A contract is a legally binding agreement, i.e. an agreement that can be enforced by the courts, and is made between two or more persons. There must be a meeting of minds upon a common purpose to form an agreement: consensus ad idem (agreement of ideas). Absence of consensus can make a contract null and void, e.g. where both parties are genuinely mistaken as to each other's intentions. Each party must be free to consent to the contract without being put under undue duress or being induced fraudulently.

Example A photographer agrees a daily rate based on the client stating that the usage was to be a small run of leaflets; when the work was published it was on billboard posters. The client knew from the outset that the work was to be used on posters; therefore the contract was fraudulently induced.

What constitutes a contract

A contract is usually in the form of a commercial bargain: an offer, an acceptance, and a consideration (payment). The payment does not have to be a tangible amount or even the market value, just "something of value"; for example, in the wake of the 1988 Copyright Act, letters were sent to photographers by commissioning agencies which were copyright assignments and included a £1 coin. Photographers who accepted the £1 coin accepted the contract and were considered to have lost their copyright to that particular agency. Ignoring the letter and not returning the coin, could also be deemed as acceptance but, returning the coin and the letter clearly rejecting the agreement, left the agency in no doubt about the photographer's position.

Contracts do not have to be in written form, but obviously, should problems arise, something in a tangible form is easier to prove. If a problem arises with an oral agreement, the onus is on each party to prove what they understood the contract to be – if the matter went before the courts, the party that the Judge believed would be the winner (not necessarily the right party!). If the parties have worked together on previous jobs then a lot of the argument might rest on what had become "normal practice" between them.

A contract can be for anything provided it's a legal act, (it would not be legal if it involved an illegal act, e.g. child pornography) and does not need to be written in legalese – provided both parties agree to the contents.

The AOP actively encourages its members to get as much in writing as is practicably possible and, even if paperwork is not forthcoming from the commissioner, the photographer should confirm all aspects of the job in writing.

Photographer and Client – Estimate

It varies but typically the estimate would be the offer and the purchase order would be acceptance. It is important that this first paperwork gives the client an opportunity to see on what conditions they are using the services of the photographer and to ensure that the terms and conditions form part of the contract. Most paperwork is rarely posted, and usually delivered by email – the terms and conditions should be attached to the email, with the estimate, as a PDF. Alternatively, the signature at the bottom of the email could include a line linking to the area on the photographer's website, where the terms can be read and/or downloaded by the client.

If the figures on the estimate are acceptable, the client should send an order, or a telephone call made by the client accepting the estimate and consequently the photographer's terms and conditions.

Terms and Conditions

The client should be given access to the terms and conditions of the photographer, at estimate stage. All parties must be aware of the basis on which the contract is being executed. The photographer should be aware that terms on the client's order can override the photographer's terms, and so any differences between the two should be agreed before the shoot begins. The AOP has produced terms and conditions which have give protection to the photographer, these are registered with the Office of Fair Trading, and downloadable from the AOP's website. These should be included on the reverse of estimate, invoice & licence to use forms or access to them sent by email, either as a PDF, or by pointing to the relevant area in the website where they can be read. They are negotiable and if not queried by the client can be deemed as accepted. There are three slightly different versions depending on whether you are based in England or Wales, Scotland or Eire. (see appendix)

All the clauses are important, particularly the following:

2. Copyright
3. Ownership of materials
4. Usage
6. Client confidentiality
7. Indemnity
12. Right to a credit (paternity right)
14. Electronic storage.

Clause 4 – USAGE – is of particular importance with regard to payment terms, because it affords the photographer protection should the commissioning body cease trading before payment is received, and allows the photographer a chance to claim payment from the ultimate client. It also provides another avenue should payment be late and there are difficulties in being paid; the user is in breach of copyright if the work is being used whilst the photographer's bill remains unpaid, under this clause. It has been successfully used by working photographers to get money they are owed.

Client and Photographer – Purchase order

On acceptance of the estimated figures, an order should be received from the client – this is more likely to happen if you are dealing with an agency on behalf of the client, and may be in email form. This is the acceptance of the terms of the estimate, and completes the formation of the contract. If a written order is not received, but the estimate is accepted by telephone, then the photographer should confirm the conversation by email.

Written orders should be read thoroughly because terms and conditions from the client will normally accompany this document and may contradict the original instructions on which the estimate was based. Points to look out for are:

a) Copyright assignment to client
b) Moral rights waiver
c) Media use
d) Duration of licence
e) Territory of use
f) Indemnity clause
g) Syndication for editorial work

The meaning of the wording in these terms can be found on the AOP website www.the-aop.org If the photographer finds they cannot agree to any of the terms they should notify the client immediately, particularly if they contradict what was originally agreed in the estimate. These terms may override the photographer's (the last set of terms and conditions to be issued are generally the ones the contract will be based on) so it is important that if they are different and unacceptable, they are challenged. Any changes that are agreed should be in writing (email is fine); if this is not forthcoming from the client then the photographer should email the contents of the conversation so it cannot be disputed later.

Relationship with Suppliers/third parties

The photographer must develop good professional relationships with his/her suppliers. At the end of the day, it is the services which they provide that the photographer depends on.

The relationship between the photographer and each of these services is based on contract law; many of the third party suppliers will have terms and conditions, which they will supply to the photographer.

a) Models
b) Set Builders
c) Model Makers
d) Background/Scenic Artists
e) Stylists
f) Hair and Make-Up Artists
g) Home Economists
h) Location Finders
i) Retouchers
j) Agents
k) Hire Studios
l) Assistants

A photographic shoot may include any or all of the above third parties (i.e. subcontractors used by the photographer) and each will have some form of contract with the photographer; a) to d) may also have rights within the image. An indemnity clause in an order will require the photographer to indemnify the agency/client against any third party claims. This clause ensures that the client will not be responsible for problems that may arise from the use of anyone, or anything, within the image. This may be a prop, photograph, etc., the copyright in which belongs to another artist for which clearance may not have been sought. The clause may stand regardless of whether the client insisted the product was to be used, against the advice of the photographer.

Example A stylist has supplied an item for the shoot, which is an original and, as such, is the copyright of another artist. The stylist has not sought permission from the copyright owner for the item to be used in an advertising context, although the copyright owner was happy for editorial use. Another artist's copyright has been infringed as the item was used in an advertising campaign and the photographer is liable if the indemnity clause is accepted.

If possible the indemnity clause should be removed or changed to ensure liability of the photographer is limited only to those third parties or items the photographer has engaged. Ensure all third parties are aware of the use agreed with the client/agency.

The AOP's photographer terms and conditions provide for the person supplying the item to be responsible for any clearance. It is important that the client's clause reflects this to ensure the photographer does not become liable.

Models, or their agencies, license the use of their image in a similar way to photographers, in that they are paid for the exact media, territory and time period the image will be used for. Major exposure of a model's image can deplete their earning potential. A model who has been seen in many magazines or advertising campaigns will be unlikely to be used, for example, by a cosmetic company as its new face. The model agencies are therefore very careful when considering payment for the use of a model's likeness. When booking models be sure you are aware of the terms on which you are booking the model; many large agencies put the onus on the photographer to discover if the model has previously worked for clients whose products may be in direct competition with the product you are shooting. Model agencies' terms and conditions are often printed in their Agency Model Book, or on their website, and the booking will refer to these terms, so make sure you read them.

Example The model has been paid for editorial use and the client uses the shot for advertising. The model has a right to further payment; the photographer could be liable if they booked the model and the order included an indemnity clause.

Model Release Forms or other basic contracts should echo the photographer's licence, and should be copied to all parties so they all know the boundaries.

Equitable Assignments

The Copyright, Designs and Patents Act 1988 states that an assignment of copyright must be in writing and signed by, or on behalf of, the copyright owner. Unfortunately this is not the only way that an assignment can be made; many photographers wrongly believe that if they don't sign something, they haven't assigned their copyright.

Example 1 By accepting and working on an order from the client, which includes a copyright assignment, the assignment becomes a condition of the contract. With or without your signature the agency owns the copyright in equity.

Example 2 One of the rules of entry into a photographic competition is that copyright in the images entered is assigned to the competition organisers; a signature is not required. By entering the competition, knowing the rules of entry, a legally binding contract is formed and the organisers own the copyright in equity.

Equity is a system that developed over the centuries in order to qualify the rules created by legal precedent. Originally, equity was handed out by a different court from the courts that applied the law. Equity and Law are now dispensed by all the civil courts, but they remain as two different sets of rules. How this applies to the ownership of copyright is thus:

- the law says an assignment of copyright is only effective if it's signed by the copyright owner, but the contract says the client/organiser is entitled to that assignment.
- the copyright is still the photographer's at law but belongs to the client/organisers in equity.
- the photographer is still the legal owner of the copyright, but the client/organiser is the beneficial owner and is treated by equity as having all the rights of the legal owner.
- the photographer is in effect a trustee holding the copyright on behalf of the real owner.
- the photographer cannot do anything with the images as the client has sole control over the copyright.

If an order received from a client includes an assignment of copyright clause, and you have not agreed to assign copyright, it is imperative that you point this out to them. Don't ignore it; by working on it you are accepting the terms of the contract. Make sure you receive confirmation in writing, if the clause itself isn't altered, that the assignment clause is not relevant.

Legality and retrospective orders

Written contracts do not have to be signed to make them legally binding; as mentioned earlier, accepting and working on a contract, or order, can be deemed as acceptance of the terms. It is imperative that all paperwork received from any party is read thoroughly, and action taken immediately, in writing, on any parts that are not acceptable to the photographer, or are different from the original discussions on which the estimate was based. This must happen before the shoot starts.

Art orders/contracts received during, or after, the shoot are "in retrospect" and are not legally binding. As stated before, each party has to know the terms they are working on before commencement. Estimates are based on the information given, concerning territory, media, time periods, exclusivity and the photographer retaining copyright. Orders received after or during the shoot, which negate any of these areas, do not form part of the contract and should be returned to the client as unacceptable, stating that the original costs were estimated on the agreed areas of use in the initial conversation. Any agreed changes to these terms naturally affect the costs, which should then be renegotiated. Unfortunately this is sometimes difficult in practice as the Art Director may turn up, on the day of the shoot, with the art order, so photographers should make time to check through it immediately and inform the client/agency, on the spot, of any problems.

Goods in Trust (see Insurance Chapter 3)

Hire studios and stylists may also have a responsibility for the goods belonging to the photographer or their client, or which have been hired on behalf of the photographer. Check their terms and conditions to make sure any liability is not being transferred onto the photographer.

Example A room set photographer working with a stylist in a hire studio completes a shoot and the set is broken up. The stylist returns some of the goods personally, leaving the rest of the goods in the loading bay of the hire studio awaiting pick up. A number of items go missing.

Who is responsible? The stylist who was supposed to oversee the safe return of the goods, and whose job includes return of goods? The hire studio who provided the storage space and are responsible for security? The delivery company which was not on site to pick up whilst the stylist was present? Or, of course, the photographer, whose client wants to know why there is now an additional £500 costs on the invoice? Each of those suppliers should carry 'goods in trust' insurance, as should the photographer.

Suppliers should always be professional; the photographer should check their track record and if they carry insurance. If not, the photographer should ensure their own insurance covers any areas not covered by the supplier.

Privacy

Privacy is a hot potato in France, where privacy rights are much stronger and the creation and publication of images of a person without his/her consent is often unlawful. Consent must be explicit, regardless of whether the person is in a public place, as French courts focus on whether the incident photographed was a private or public activity. Just because the person is in a public place doesn't mean that anything they do there is public. In the wake of the car crash that killed Princess Diana, new legislation placed even stricter restrictions on the pictures newspapers and television stations could use. Bizarre images of protest marches, for example, have appeared with the majority of the participants faces blanked out.

Whilst German legislation has a 'right to one's own image' the law appears to seek to balance the right of privacy with freedom of speech, enabling the courts to deal with each case on its own merits.

The use of images of celebrities on merchandising is protected in many EU countries.

It is better for photographers to assume that privacy may be a problem in other countries and get model release forms signed to ensure there is no restriction on the way the image may be published. (See Annexe)

Until recently there was no actual law of privacy in the UK, unlike other EU countries and the USA, which made the UK a 'privacy haven' for many years. The little privacy protection available was in the guise of other legislation – copyright and the moral right to privacy being just two (see Chapter 1 Moral Rights). However, the introduction of the Human Rights Act has a long way to redressing this situation by incorporating into UK law the European Convention on Human Rights. The UK Government has left it to the courts to develop the law of privacy with regard to the rights given in Article 8 Privacy and Article 10 Freedom of Expression of the European Convention on Human Rights.

Article 8: Right to respect for private and family life

'1. Everyone has the right to his private and family life, his home and his correspondence.

2. There shall be no interference by a public authority with the exercise of this right except such as is in accordance with the law and is necessary in a democratic society in the interests of national security, public safety or the economic well-being of the country, for the prevention of disorder or crime, for the protection of health or morals, or for the protection of the rights and freedoms of others.'

Article 10: Freedom of expression

'1. Everyone has the right of freedom of expression. This right shall include freedom to hold opinions and to receive and impart information and ideas without interference by public authority and regardless of frontiers. This Article shall not prevent States from requiring the licensing of broadcasting, television or cinema enterprises.

2. The exercise of these freedoms, since it carries with it duties and responsibilities, may be subject to such formalities, conditions, restrictions or penalties as are prescribed by law and are necessary in a democratic society, in the interests of national security, territorial integrity or public safety, for the prevention of disorder or crime, for the protection of health or morals, for the protection of the reputation or rights of others, for preventing the disclosure of information received in confidence, or for maintaining the authority and impartiality of the judiciary.'

CHAPTER 2

This guarantees the right to pass information to other people and to receive information that other people want to give to you. It also guarantees the right to hold and express opinions and ideas.

Journalists and publishers of newspapers or magazines can use Article 10 to argue there should be no restrictions on what they write about or publish. Artists and writers can use it to defend themselves against censorship.

One of the most famous privacy cases to originally give the green light to breach of privacy claims in UK courts was the Douglas and Zeta-Jones v Hello! magazine. Douglas & Zeta-Jones took Hello! magazine to court after they published unauthorised photographs of their wedding after they had signed an exclusive deal with OK magazine. The action was based on privacy, contract and breach of confidence. The Judge found against them in their claim for breach of privacy, as he doubted that UK law had a distinct right of privacy. He stated that the UK Parliament should step in to correct this, failing that; the courts would ultimately have to do so should the Law of Confidence not provide adequate remedy. The Judge upheld their claim under the Law of Confidence (see below).

Law of Confidence

Photographers should be aware of the Law of Confidence if they are planning to take unauthorised pictures at 'secret events'. Douglas and Zeta-Jones had signed an exclusive contract with OK magazine to publish the photographs to their wedding, with the right to 'veto' what could be published. The significant part of this case is that the Judge allowed them to enforce the contract against Hello! who published unauthorised photographs. The basis of his judgment was that the commercial effect of the contract with OK was to create something akin to a trade secret. Hello! was not acting in good faith, and had clearly breached the Press Commission Complaints Codes as the photographs they bought and published were clearly obtained by subterfuge. As a result, the claimants were entitled to enforce their equitable rights in the Law of Confidence against Hello!. The Judge concluded that an important step in coming to his conclusion was balancing rights to confidence against freedom of expression. Hello! had broken their own industry's code.

The importance of this judgment is the message to publications that spoiling 'exclusives' now carries a clear commercial risk which will reduce the value of unauthorised photographs. Whilst further doubt has been placed on the existence of a distinct law of privacy, the protection granted against this type of press activity is strengthened by this judgment.

The Press Complaints Commission Code can be read on their web site www.pcc.org.uk

Another case, which illustrates the law of confidence, was a case against the Sun newspaper by Oasis. At a shoot for an Oasis album cover a freelance photographer took photographs of the scene on commission from the Sun. Noel Gallagher had arranged a scene in a swimming pool in a private club. The photographer was lawfully at the scene but it didn't mean he was free to photograph it. One of the shots, published by the Sun, was very similar to that chosen by Noel for the cover. An injunction was granted by the High Court preventing further publication by the Sun as the photographic record of the scene was intended to be confidential and so the unauthorised images were restricted by the Law of Confidence. It was deemed that by the nature of the operation and the imposition of strict security measures, the event was intended to be secret. Further, the surreptitious conduct of the Sun photographer showed the Judge that he was aware of the secrecy issue.

Advertising Codes

The Advertising Standards Authority publish codes (CAP Codes) for advertising, including the use of people in advertising and alcohol advertising. These codes are constantly updated see www.cap.org.uk/Advertising-Codes.aspx

The Data Protection Act

The Data Protection Act 1998 regulates the processing of personal data (which is, in essence, information relating to an individual from which that individual can be identified). Processing is very broadly defined and encompasses just about everything that can be done with data including simply holding it. The first principle of the Act states that personal data must be processed fairly and lawfully and in line with certain conditions, one of which is that the individual to whom the data relates has given their consent to the processing. Accordingly, it is clear that anyone holding personal data in an electronic form (therefore potentially including digitally stored images) may be "processing" such data for the purposes of the Act.

CHAPTER 2

This is an area that photographers must be alert to, given that a photographer storing digital images, without consent having been given by the subjects of those images, is potentially in breach of the Act.

There are exemptions which apply. The main one of relevance to photographers relates to the processing of personal data with a view to the publication of journalistic, literary or artistic material. There must be a belief, however, that the publication would be in the public interest. In the *Naomi Campbell* case, the Mirror published photographs of Naomi Campbell leaving a Narcotics Anonymous meeting alongside published information on how she had been attending such meetings. The House of Lords held that the Mirror was not entitled to rely on the public interest defence.

However, what is clear is that this case has not opened the way to publication in all circumstances and the law will develop on a case-by-case basis. In the *Michael Douglas and Catherine Zeta-Jones* case, the Court held that the unauthorised pictures of their wedding represented personal data and publication of them in England was covered by the requirements of the Act. Photographers should accordingly beware.

Defamation

In the UK, images of British personalities are often used in an advertising or promotional context, often humorously, and such personalities are normally seen as fair game for this sort of treatment. However, such use must still be done with care and the image of a personality should not be used in a way that suggests they endorse the product. Every individual, and not just personalities, have the right to protect themselves against defamation.

Example A photographer takes a photograph of a street scene and that photograph is subsequently sold for use in an advertisement. The advertisement implies that the individual in the photograph is a criminal or junkie. That individual may well bring a claim for defamation against the agency and client, or even the photographer.

Model Release Forms

Model release forms were originally devised as a means of establishing a basic contract between a photographer and a professional model. They were intended to permit only those forms of exploitation of the model's image which had been paid for by the photographer or their client.

Professional Models

Whilst some professional models still sign model release forms, more often that not the agreement is contained within the contract between the model agency and the photographer. This should state the rights which have been agreed and paid for and should mirror the rights that the photographer is giving their client within their licence. It is imperative that the agreement between the photographer and the model, or model agency, is relayed to the client. Should the client use the images outside this agreement, the model agency may look to the photographer for payment of this extra use. If the photographer has made the client aware of the agreed rights, they are in a better position to demand that the client pay the extra costs.

Members of the public in photographs and street casting

With the introduction of the Human Rights Act in the UK and the increasingly strict privacy legislation in other countries it is advisable to get permission, wherever possible, from the subject matter of photographs. A simple written agreement is all that may be necessary, giving the photographer permission to publish the photograph in any media for an unlimited time period. As this is a contract there must be a form of payment (consideration) – a professional print of the subject could be deemed sufficient consideration.

Failure to secure an agreement may result in restrictions on the photographer as to how and where the images can be published. This is particularly evident when the work is to be sold through a photographic library, who require an undertaking from the photographer that rights in the image have been secured. If the image is published in a country which has privacy legislation then, if a model release form has not be signed, the photographer may be open to a lawsuit in that country. For more information on supplying work to stock libraries refer to Chapter 13.

Using children as models

In August 1998 the laws that govern child employment were extended to cover child modelling and sporting activities. The purpose of this is to protect child models in the workplace and ensure that their welfare and education is not harmed.

What is the law?
The law applies to children of school age and under; they do not have to be professional models, it applies to all children. According to UK law, a child is of school age until the last Friday in June of the academic year in which he or she turns sixteen. The law applies to all paid work undertaken by school age children and to any work – paid or unpaid – undertaken by children if they have to be released from school to do it. It does not apply to children who undertake unpaid modeling work at times when they are not supposed to be at school.

For any commercial photography involving children of school age – with the exceptions above – a licence must be obtained separately for each child involved.

Whose responsibility is it?
The person in charge of the shoot or production should apply for the licence. Although this could be you, the photographer, it is more likely to be your client – the ad agency or whoever. It is not the responsibility of the model or the model agency, although reputable child model agencies will make the application for you.

How to apply
The application should be made to the Local Education Authority where the child lives. This means that if you are using two child models, who live in different boroughs, you will have to apply for separate licences to each local authority.

The application of the Act can vary from local authority to local authority: not all of them use the same procedures (although they are generally quite similar). This is potentially complicated and time-consuming, and of course not all authorities will return your licences at the same time.

Although a lot of LEAs are very helpful, be prepared for hiccups. Local authorities are usually flexible about this but technically they do have the right to refuse your application if it is late. Some LEAs only employ part-time staff to handle these licences, so be aware that you may be let down on last minute requests.

Some boroughs issue six-month working licences to child models and actors. This can save a lot of time. Once the six-month licence is in place, you only need supply basic details of your particular shoot. This can be done in a week, all being well. If you have problems getting a licence, you can raise your concerns with the Director of Education in the relevant borough. If your LEA cannot process applications within 21 days, you can also approach the Department of Health with a complaint. Be aware, that if you do not obtain a licence and the authorities are made aware of your shoot, they can turn up at the studio or location and stop your shoot, which has happened. There are also fines for not complying.

The procedure will be something like this although it may vary:

- Telephone the relevant local authority to request a licence application form (and to get advice about licences).
- They will send a form which should be completed by the applicant and, usually, the parents or guardian of the child, who will have to supply a doctor's certificate, confirming the child is 'fit and well' enough to work. More delays might be incurred if the child's parents have trouble getting an appointment to see the doctor. The charge made by some doctors of up to £60 for a certificate is a problem for parents whose child is an extra or will not be paid much.
- The sort of information required on the form includes details of the job, proof of the child's age and identity and arrangements for transport and chaperoning. Many of the questions may apply only to theatrical performances which require rehearsals, and will not be relevant to photographers. It is possible that you will have to supply a copy of or details of the contract you have with the child or their agent.
- The form is returned to the LEA for processing. Once they have all the details, they have to contact the child's school and ask for permission for them to be released to work. Some schools do refuse permission. For more detailed information on how the regulations about working hours, education, health and safety and work outside the UK apply to photographers, you should contact your Local Education Authority. The Knowledge also includes full guidelines (produced by the National Child Employment Network).

CHAPTER 2

Disclosure for people working with children & vulnerable adults

Disclosure is a document containing information held by the police and government departments. They used to be known as CRB checks (Criminal Records Bureau) but are now called DBS checks (Disclosure Barring Service) and can be used by employers and voluntary organisations to make safer recruitment decisions.

Guidance from the Department for Education and Skills requires an Enhanced level of checking for any person who comes into contact with children and vulnerable adults. This includes photographers working in schools or educational settings. The disclosures are issued by the Disclosure Barring Service (which encompasses the former Criminal Records Bureau).

It is up to the institution you are working with to request that you complete a disclosure. If you are a photographer currently working in schools or other community organisations, you may have already been asked to complete Disclosure by the School or organisation. If you have a certificate of Disclosure, this certificate is valid for the day it is processed. So the longer the time since the date on the certificate, the less reliable the disclosure is. As a result of this, the person or body that you are working with may request that you apply for another (up to date) disclosure.

Individual Local Authorities may have their own more stringent guidelines specific to the filming and photographing of children in schools and in other community organisations or facilities such as gymnasiums etc., so it is best to check with the relevant local authority what their rules are.

Schools and other organisations may have their own codes of practice so it is best to enquire directly at the place where you propose to shoot as they may have rules that go above and beyond those regulations prescribed by the Local Authority.

Information and forms can be found here: https://www.gov.uk/government/organisations/disclosure-and-barring-service

Trespass

For most photographers, only a small section of the law of trespass will ever be of interest. At present there is nothing in the law to prevent a photographer from taking photographs whilst on private property. However, the more important issue is whether the photographer has permission to be on that private property in the first place; if not they are trespassing.

Taking photographs on private property

It is important to check that there is not a restriction on photography, particularly commercial photography, in areas that appear to be public but may be owned by the National Trust, English Heritage or other institutions. If you have to pay to enter somewhere the chances are that the ticket you purchase will have terms and conditions attached to it. These are not generally printed on the ticket, or even displayed at the point of purchase, but may be referred to either on the ticket or the ticket desk. This practice puts the onus on the ticket purchaser to ask to see the terms, which may include a "no photography" clause. You may not be stopped from photographing at the time (it may not be noticed) but if the work is subsequently published and spotted by the owners of the land or building they may apply to have the images removed and try to claim any money you have made from the publication. Some require you to pay a fee; others may want a cut of the action – images to place in their own library and/or use for their own publicity. Some places allow photography provided you assign the copyright over to them!

Taking Photographs in a Public Place

Shooting in a public place, or shooting from a public place into a private place (for example standing in a public street and photographing a house and its garden), is not normally a problem and permission is not needed. Many photographers have come across shop owners, and security guards demanding they stop shooting buildings when they are on the public highway, whilst this can be disconcerting (and occasionally aggressive) taking photographs in this way is not normally illegal. It is not generally a copyright infringement to photograph a building from a public place nor is it restricted by any other legislation in the UK (see also trade marks below). Iconic, modern buildings in the UK may have restrictions on how images can be used, it's always worth checking the website of this type of building before considering any commercial use.

CHAPTER 2

If a photographer is causing a public nuisance by blocking the traffic in a public road whilst taking the photograph, then there may be other problems. This is why, when organising a shoot in a public place, it is wise to notify the local police first and stick to any recommendations they may make.

See Chapter 16 for more information

Terrorism Act

The inappropriate use of some areas of this piece of legislation by the police, in regard to photography, brought professional photographers together to demonstrate and stand up for their right to photograph in public places without interference. Section 44 of the Act was being used by police to stop and search photographers under the guise of preventing terrorism. A group of photographers calling themselves "I'm a Photographer Not a Terrorist" http://www.photographernotaterrorist.org led the way to get the legislation changed, and subsequently the section was removed.

The Metropolitan Police have issued guidelines both for Officers and people taking images or filming which can be found here: content.met.police.uk/site/photographyadvice

For more information on shooting on private property, in a public place and what the police can and cannot do see Chapter 16 Shooting on the Streets.

Permits

Parks, and particularly royal parks, e.g. Hyde Park and Windsor Park, may be private parks and a permit must be obtained before any shoot can take place in them. Similarly, owners of public monuments and private landowners will normally permit photography if asked and if a payment is made. With the exception of major product advertising, the National Trust does not charge for permission to shoot on its landscape and coastline properties, although photographers are advised to contact the National Trust Photographic Library, should they wish to take pictures of SSSI land (Sight of Specific Scientific Interest) or listed species.

Trade marks

The use of trademarks, registered in the UK, is governed by the Trade Marks Act 1994. The shooting of trademarks is not an infringement in itself, but the context in which they are used may be. Care should be taken when a trademark is to appear in an image that may be used for advertising purposes, as this could be an infringement. Trade marks would normally have to be registered in the country in which the image was to be shown, or be registered internationally, for there to be an infringement; but it would not be so easy to police if the image was placed in a picture library.

Example The Hollywood sign was used in an image advertising audio-visual equipment. The advertisement was shown in the UK. A letter was received, by the photographer, from the American company who license the rights to use the sign, demanding money and the withdrawal of the ad. It was subsequently discovered that the Hollywood sign was not a registered trademark in the UK and no rights had been infringed. If the ad had been shown in the US there could have been a claim.

NB. This case occurred some years ago; the Hollywood sign is probably now registered in all countries where registration is possible!

The UK's Trade Mark register is accessible on the Internet. More information can be found at www.patent.gov.uk

Buildings

Buildings can be registered as trademarks, although this is rare in the UK. The Eiffel Tower is a registered trademark as are various other monuments and buildings in other EU countries and the USA. Building trademark owners in the US have been aggressively pursuing claims against photographers and stock libraries and some UK building owners have been attempting the same. Threats have been made against people exploiting images of the Millennium Dome and the Church of England was even reported to have been discussing trademarking Cathedrals.

An American photographer who photographed and produced posters of the Rock and Roll Hall of Fame, whose museum and title are registered in the US as trademarks, won a landmark victory. The museum claimed against the photographer but the Judge ruled that the museum had not used images of the museum as a trade mark and neither had the photographer. People would not be buying the posters believing they were official merchandise for the museum; the US court accepted that people buy images of buildings because they like the image, not because they believe it to be official merchandise. Whilst this judgment is under US law the UK position with buildings is likely to be similar – the same reasoning was used when an attempt to trademark photographs of Princess Diana's face was made.

However, this does not mean that photographers can expect to photograph and use images of trademarked buildings – care should be taken and checks made before shooting commences. The trademark register can be checked, and clients wishing to use famous buildings for shoots should be advised to check what is and isn't allowed.

Logos

Logos may be registered as trademarks and in many cases are protected by copyright as an artistic work that may be infringed by photographing. An example of this is shown in a legal case brought by the Premier League against Panini Ltd, a company that produced unofficial football stickers. The Premier League and various Premier League football clubs sued Panini for copyright infringement, as the unofficial stickers show the Premier League's lion logo and the badges of individual clubs. Panini claimed that the badges were an incidental inclusion, which is not an infringement of copyright. The Judge decided that the club badges were "an integral part of the artistic work comprised of the photograph of the professional photographer in his present day kit and without the badge they would not have the complete picture which they wish to produce...". An injunction was granted forbidding the sale of the Panini' Football Album 2003 with stickers including the Premier League lion logo or the club badges.

Money

Strict rules govern the use of bank notes, coins and stamps in photography and illustration. The Bank of England has copyright in their notes, but reproduction is also covered by the Forgery and Counterfeiting Act 1981. There are particular procedures to be followed when seeking permission to reproduce notes, which can be time consuming and cannot be skirted around. The size of reproduction, context, positioning, and wording on the note are all taken into consideration when the Bank of England considers requests. HM Treasury's permission may also need to be gained before reproducing coins that are governed by the same Act.

Stamps

The Post Office owns the copyright in the design of British postage stamps. Applications for permission to photograph these must be made in writing, and a fee may be charged for each application received. Again, there is a strict code of how stamps may be shown, including size of reproduction, detail (no alterations), context, positioning and colour.

Confidentiality

Most contracts, received from clients, will include a clause referring to confidentiality

Advertising Photography

Every photographer should recognise the importance of client confidentiality. Problems of confidentiality arise most often in connection with advertising photography, where the photographer is working with a client on an un-launched product, which must be kept secret from competitors until the advertising campaign is launched.

The rights which the advertising client agrees with the photographer (in the licence to use granted by the photographer) normally include the exclusive right to publish the photograph for the first time.

Unfortunately there have been occasions when photographers, carried away with enthusiasm for their photographs, have sent out promotional mailings for themselves before the client's campaign has been launched. This may be commercially disastrous for the client, and it certainly is for the photographer.

Photographers should also remember that even talking about their latest shoot with friends could be a breach of client confidentiality.

Editorial Photography

Confidentiality is an entirely different issue for the editorial photographer and is more likely to arise as a matter of trust between the photographer and the subject of their photographs, and may also be contractual.

Example Nude shots of a model are taken early in his/her career when the model was not aware of the need for a model release form. The model later becomes famous and the photographer is approached to sell the shots to a tabloid newspaper. Is it acceptable, or even ethical, for the photographer to do so?

Many magazines argue that copyright in 'celebrity' portraits should lie with them, to prevent unwanted exploitation of the photograph. But when a photographer takes a portrait, they enter into a position of trust with their sitter, and a relationship exists between the sitter and the photographer, not with the magazine. The photographer is often asked to ensure that the photograph appears only in 'X' magazine and to check with the celebrity first before any further use is made of it. If copyright is assigned to the magazine then the photographer is no longer in a position to control its use.

If photographers do not respect the subjects of their photographs, or treat them fairly, then it is only to be expected that clients will insist on acquiring copyright and owning control of the photographs themselves. It is important to note that the Moral Right of Privacy (see chapter 1 Moral Rights) does not cover images taken for any commercial purpose. Photographers should be absolutely clear that this moral right only applies to photographs taken for private and domestic purposes e.g. wedding photographs or family portraits.

Risk Assessments

More and more clients are getting health and safety conscious and need written confirmation (often for their insurers) of any risks involved in the shoot and, where possible, mitigated for. Production and film companies regularly complete risk assessment forms, and many University courses are ensuring their photographic students are well versed in this area.

A risk assessment is just that – assessing what risks client personnel, models, photographic assistants, photographer and anyone else involved in the shoot (including passers by) may be subjected to. If it's a straightforward shoot you may only be looking at cables and tripods – but more complicated shoots could involve all manner of risks.

A visit to the premises (or area) where you are to be shooting together with a list of your equipment and personnel is the first step. The Health and Safety Executive have a simple booklet entitled 5 stages to risk assessment – whilst it's aimed at employers and the workplace, it simply shows what you are looking for. http://www.hse.gov.uk/pubns/indg163.pdf

A sample risk assessment form based on the 5 principles in the booklet can be downloaded here: http://www.healthyworkinglives.com/documents/2596.aspx

Passing Off

Passing off arises when a trader uses a misrepresentation to take advantage of the reputation and goodwill of another trader, and cashes in on that goodwill and reputation to the detriment of the first. Passing off can overlap with some areas of copyright law. A claim for passing off is brought in the civil courts.

In photography, deliberate passing off rarely happens; when it does, in such a visually aware industry, it is invariably found out. The photographer responsible is treated with contempt, not just by other photographers but also by clients who don't like to be made fools of.

Example A photographer puts tear sheets (images in the context of an advertisement) of another photographer's work into their own portfolio, and shows the portfolio to potential clients; or a photographer includes a brochure in his/her portfolio implying to the client that all the photographs in a brochure are theirs and not just one particular shot.

CHAPTER 2

Assisting photographers

Assisting photographers work closely with the photographer and are often given a great deal of responsibility. Their position is one of trust, which can easily be abused, mainly because they have not fully thought through the consequences of their actions.

Example An assisting photographer who has worked on a shoot as senior assistant and may even, technically, have 'pressed the button', feels that their contribution is great enough for them to claim the photograph as their own and put it in their portfolio. Of course, the client was not theirs and they were not ultimately responsible for the costs, the organisation or the creative influence. To claim such shots as their own is unacceptable practice; it may also be fraudulent.

Occasionally an assisting photographer will use a photograph taken 'off the back' of a shoot, in their portfolio.

Example An assisting photographer goes to an exotic location with a car photographer and has the opportunity to borrow the car to take some pictures independently. In this case, they should seek permission from the photographer to include the resulting image in their portfolio and from courtesy should check with the client, particularly where a product is involved. If permission is given they should also be prepared to mention both the original car photographer and the client if the shot is included in their portfolio.

Where an assisting photographer takes photographs on someone else's shoot, they should consider their image carefully and decide whether it is sufficiently different in style and technique to warrant its inclusion in their portfolio. Where there is even the tiniest bit of doubt, it should not be included without permission from the photographer/client.

Plagiarism

Within photography circles, passing off and plagiarism are often thought of as one and the same, but they are actually fundamentally different. Plagiarism is not a legal term; the correct name for it is copyright infringement and, whilst passing off is comparable to fraud, plagiarism is comparable to theft! Stealing substantial bits from the work of others, copying something from a book or photograph, and basing an image on another's, are all examples of plagiarism.

Care should be taken by all photographers when receiving a brief, particularly if it is accompanied by a copy of another photographer's image, or a sketch of an image you think you recognise. If you are told: "I want it to look like that", the alarm bells should start to ring. The resulting image may be a copyright infringement; you may be implicated legally and your reputation is unlikely to be enhanced. The instructions you are given may not appear to point towards a possible act of plagiarism – it may just be a moral decision on your part. If you feel uneasy, or are at all unsure, speak out! You could be saving your, and your client's, reputation – and possible copyright infringement legal action.

Legal Remedies

Late Payment Legislation

The Late Payment of Commercial Debts (Interest) Act 1998 as amended and supplemented by the Late Payment of Commercial Debts Regulations 2002 and 2013 allows you to charge interest and reasonable recovery costs to your clients when a business debt is overdue. This is a right that every business has regardless of the size of the company – so beware, your suppliers can also charge you if you don't pay on time! The aim of the legislation is to promote a culture of prompt payment and this legislation can help to force the arm of those who put payment off for as long as they can get away with it. – If a payment period is not set out in the contract your client must make payment within 30 calendar days of the latest of receiving your invoice or of receiving the goods or services. If payment is not received, it is up to you if you want to enforce your statutory right to interest but when the money is owed to you by a government body they must pay charges and late payment interest if they do not pay on time. A supplier and purchaser can make their own agreements regarding interest payable, however if you do make your own arrangements for contractual interest then the late payment legislation will not apply.

Under the legislation all businesses have the following rights:

- The right to claim interest for late payment
- The right to claim statutory compensation for recovery costs (currently at £40.00 for a debt under £1,000.00, £70.00 under £10,000 and £100.00 over £10,000)
- The right to claim further recovery costs e.g. debt recovery agents, if the statutory compensation is not enough
- The right to challenge contractual terms that exclude interest for late payment or compensation for recovery costs

Claiming Interest
Claims can be made as soon as the payment is deemed late as per the agreed credit period in the contract – either written or oral. If no payment period was agreed, then the default period is 30 days. However, payment terms must not exceed 60 days unless both parties agree. After this time interest can be charged.

Once payment is late you should inform your client, preferably in writing, that you will be claiming interest, compensation and any additional recovery costs under the late payment legislation. Inform them of the amount owing, when it was due, and the rate of interest being charged together with details as to whom and by what method payment should be made.

Statutory interest is charged at 8% above the Bank of England base rate, on a daily basis and on the gross debt (including VAT), but you do not charge VAT on the interest itself.

For a handy calculator; current legislation; and more information on working with the legislation visit http://www.payontime.co.uk/

Unpaid Debts – EU
If your client is resident in another EU country then there are legal procedures you can use to get the money you are owed. However, as with any legal action it is advisable to first weigh up the possible costs to yourself relevant to the amount you are owed.

There are 2 ways to collect unpaid debts from a client in another EU state:

European Order for Payment (EOP) procedure – to be used when the claim is uncontested.

There must be a contract; an agreement; or the person owing the money must have admitted they owe it, before you can use this procedure.

You must complete a form downloadable from the European e-Justice Portal website and pay a court fee which is determined by the amount of the claim. You then send the form to the relevant court by posting it or filing it electronically. Once the request for an EOP is received (and the court has checked that it has been correctly completed), the court will issue it within 30 days. The EOP will then be served on the defendant by the court. The defendant must then either pay the amount claimed or lodge a statement of opposition to the EOP within 30 days. If this happens the case will be transferred to the civil law courts to be dealt with under national law. If there is no statement of opposition by the defendant, the EOP will become automatically enforceable by the enforcement authorities of the Member State.

European Small Claims Procedure (ESCP) – can be used if the claim is contested, or not, and is for less than €2000.

As with claims for money owed in the UK, you must make all attempts (keep a written record) to resolve the issue before making a claim.

The claim form is completed in English and sent to your local County Court, in the same way as a UK debt, and there is a fee payable. Supporting documents are included at this stage. Your form will be checked and if all is OK the defendant will be sent a copy. As in the UK they have 30 days to decide if they want to pay or defend the claim.

If the claim is disputed or the defendant submits a counterclaim the court will send you the defence form and/or counterclaim, for you to comment on. Once you have replied the judge will consider the claim and may ask for more information or summons you to a hearing, which could be by telephone or video conference. The judge will usually give a decision within 30 days of the hearing or receipt of all the information.

Once you have the court's judgment you then send the judgment, and a European Small Claims judgment certificate, to the courts in the defendant's country (this may need to be translated) for enforcement.

Information on enforcement can be found here:

https://e-justice.europa.eu/content_enforcement_of_judgments-51--en.do

Unpaid debts – UK

Before resorting to court action to collect an unpaid debt, it is important to make sure you have done everything possible to get paid. Judges expect you to have exhausted all avenues, by writing and conversing with the debtor in a bid to settle the matter. This also makes you look like the reasonable party in the procedure. Keep copies of all correspondence and notes of conversations.

Issuing a claim should be your very last call and it's worth trying one more thing:

Get all the relevant information and forms and fill them in ready to make your claim. BUT before you file your claim at court, send a copy of your completed form to the non-payer (by e-mail for speed). Include a note telling them that if they don't pay up in, for example 24 hours, or seven days (depending on how aggrieved you feel) you will be sending the documents to the Court. Sometimes this will shock them into paying you without the need for you to spend money registering your claim.

As an alternative to court proceedings you could issue a statutory demand if your debt is for more than £750 and there is no dispute that payment is due to you. The person or company that receives the demand has 21 days to settle the debt or ask the court to dismiss the demand. If they do not pay you can present a petition to the court for a bankruptcy order (for a person) or a winding up order (for a company). You must do everything you can to bring the statutory demand to the attention of the debtor. You must serve it personally on an individual debtor or leave the demand at the registered office of a debtor company. You can instruct a process server to do it for you. The threat of bankruptcy usually provokes a swift response from the debtor and quite often leads to settlement. However, a statutory demand should be approached with caution if you are in any doubt that the debtor will dispute your debt. If the debtor succeeds in having the demand dismissed on "substantial grounds" you could be ordered to pay the costs of the court hearing.

Making a claim

Before issuing a claim you must comply with the Practice Direction (Pre-Action conduct):

http://www.justice.gov.uk/courts/procedure-rules/civil/rules/pd_pre-action_conduct

As set out in Annex A of the Practice Direction, you should send a final letter headed "letter before claim" to the non-payer with a clear summary of your claim and an explanation of how you have calculated the sum claimed. You should inform the non-payer that if they ignore your letter you will commence proceedings which could increase their liability for costs.

If you choose to go ahead with your case, you will need to complete an N1 form and send your claim with the court fee to the County Court Money Claims Centre, PO Box 527, M5 0BY or submit it online via Money Claim Online.

The N1 form can be downloaded from here: http://www.justice.gov.uk/courts/procedure-rules/civil/forms

Information on using the Money Claim online service is available here: https://www.moneyclaim.gov.uk/web/mcol/welcome

If your claim is complex, of importance to the general public (perhaps on a point of law) or worth over £50,000 you can commence proceedings in the Queen's Bench Division of the Royal Courts of Justice in London.

Make sure you read all the information in the leaflets and guidance notes to give yourself a good idea of what you need to do and when.

Once the court has served the claim the defendant has the chance of either paying up, directly to you or through the court, or setting out in their defence why they shouldn't have to pay. Any defence received by the court will be sent to you. If the defendant does not pay or reply, the court will let you know and you may automatically be given Judgment and you can proceed to enforcement

There are various way of enforcing payment, the one you choose will depend on what you know about your client and their ability to pay. Information on enforcement options can be found here: https//www.gov.uk/make-court-claim-for-money/enforce-a-judgment

Preparing for a hearing

The Court will send you a "Notice of Allocation" which will tell you what you have to do for the hearing. For a small claim the judge will usually give a direction that each party must file at the court and serve on the other party copies of all the documents that they intend to rely on for the hearing.

Pull together all the paperwork from your order/estimate to the final letter before claim– go through the defence and make sure you are covering all their responses to your claim within your paperwork.

Write your version of events (succinctly, the Judge doesn't want to have to read a book) referring to paperwork you have. Put the result in an ordered and labelled file. Send one copy to the court and one to the defendant. The defendant should also send you a copy of their documents. Make sure the papers arrive in good time before the date stated on the Notice of Allocation which will usually be 14 days before the hearing.

Attending the hearing

Put a day aside – whilst you will be given a time of day for the hearing the court will have a list of cases and you will be called when your time has come. Take someone with you for company, and to take notes during the Hearing (and nudge you when you forget things). Be smart, polite to the Judge and as clear as you can when answering questions (do NOT chew gum).

The Judge will ask questions regarding areas within your and the defendant's paperwork. He will make his decision and explain the reasons at the end of the hearing.

Copyright Infringement legal redress – UK

In October 2012 the UK introduced a small claims track procedure in the Intellectual Property Enterprise Court (formerly known as the Patents County Court), allowing claimants to bring copyright infringement cases, up to £10,000, to court without needing to use a lawyer.

The initial process is similar, and the claim form the same as if you were claiming for an unpaid debt (see Unpaid Debts UK).

Your final letter before claim should include copies of the infringement, with your image, and clearly state what you want them to do e.g. take down, deliver up etc. together with the figure you are looking for them to pay. You must make every attempt to settle the matter, including suggesting an alternative resolution procedure e.g. discussion and negotiation or mediation. Give the defendant 14 days to reply or, if you believe evidence may be an issue, 30 days.

If no settlement is reached, start the claim by going to: http://hmctsformfinder.justice.gov.uk/HMCTS/FormFinder.do and downloading form N1 (claim form)

On the Claim Form:

- state the facts of your case
- that you have complied with 7.1(1) and Annex A (paragraph 2) of the Practice Direction http://www.justice.gov.uk/courts/procedure-rules/civil/rules/pd_pre-action_conduct
- the fee you are claiming
- any damages (if you are claiming flagrancy)
- any interest
- that you would like the claim to be allocated to the small claims track of the Intellectual Property Enterprise Court
- a statement of truth e.g. "I believe that the facts stated in this (name the document and the date of the document) are true."

You need to make three copies – one for you, one for the defendant and one for the court – take all three to the court or post recorded delivery together with the court fee http://www.justice.gov.uk/courts/fees

Unlike the regular small claims court, the court will not serve the documents for you – the court will post two of the forms back to you, now with the court seal, (check if you go in person that you don't have to pick them up) – then post the copy to the defendant by 1st class or recorded post with the response pack. http://www.justice.gov.uk/courts/procedure-rules/civil/forms

When you have served the forms complete and file a Certificate of Service (N125) and take to the court within 21 days of serving – this is important as you use this to file for judgment if the defendant doesn't file a defence.

CHAPTER 2

The defendant has 14 days in which to acknowledge service and 42 days to file his defence at court and serve it on you. If you don't hear anything, ring the court and ask if there has been a reply, if there hasn't you can apply to enter judgment on form N227 (judgment by default).

If a defence is filed, you have the opportunity to write to the court and show why they are wrong, you have 28 days to do this. You should send a copy to the defendant as well.

The Court will now send you a Notice stating what will happen next, which could be one of the following:

- give directions on how to prepare for a hearing; or
- order a case management conference (a short hearing where the Judge will state what is to happen next)
- propose the claim is dealt with without a hearing (the Judge will decide by reading the paperwork); or
- fix a date for a hearing.

If there is to be a hearing, both parties will be asked to send all documents they are going to rely on in court, to the court and each other at least 7 days before the hearing. Witness statements are not normally required, but if you decide to prepare one this must be sent with the other documents. The defendant will be able to cross-examine you on the statement.

A hearing will generally be allocated up to a day, and heard in the Judge's room or a courtroom at the Royal Courts of Justice – it is unlikely that an expert will be allowed to give evidence, but if you really feel it necessary you should ask the Judge's permission in advance to call an expert. The Hearing will generally be informal with limited cross-examination, but there will be a chance to challenge what the other side says. At the end the Judge will deliver his reasoned judgment, and state which party he finds for.

PART 2: THE BUSINESS END

CHAPTER 3: ACCOUNTING

PAUL ROCHMAN

Introduction

Whether you plan to work alone or employ other people, running a business requires a good knowledge of all of the options open to you to be a success. This chapter aims to initiate the photographer into the world of 'how to succeed in business -and stay there'. It explores freelancing, accounting, tax, VAT, various savings and investment schemes, insurances, pensions, financial advice and mortgages, and advises on claiming benefit during the hard times.

What type of business is best for you?

Sole Trader

Most photographers work as sole traders. This is probably the simplest way to trade. It gives you the greatest freedom over your actions, and does not preclude you from taking on employees if you want or need to.

There are disadvantages to being a sole trader. You are personally liable for all your business debts, and your risk of bankruptcy, if your business fails, is greater than for traders working through a Limited Company (see below). Another disadvantage to being a sole trader is that you have no one else to share your responsibilities with.

All businesses need to understand that an invoice, say for £1,000, is not the photographer's personal money. It belongs to the business, and business costs need to be met from it before the profit element can be spent (or saved). Failure to maintain this simple discipline can end up in disaster.

Partnership

Partnerships also have unlimited liability for debts, and each partner can bind the other. The partners are jointly and severally liable for the debts of the business. This means that if one partner incurs a debt on behalf of the partnership, the debtor can recover the money from the other partners, if the partnership is unable to pay. Business partnerships should not be entered into lightly. It is crucial for there to be a proper written agreement between the partners, drawn up with the help of a solicitor. However well the individual partners get on with each other at the beginning, unforeseen problems can and do occur (death, illness, copyright ownership, pursuit of other interests, etc.). Preparation is better and cheaper than litigation.

Limited Liability Partnership (LLP)

This is a hybrid between a standard partnership and a limited company. It has the advantage of limiting your liability to the capital you have introduced into the business but it has the disadvantage of much of the additional administrative tasks of a limited company.

Limited Company

Limited companies are registered under the Companies Act and are separate legal entities in their own right. Company assets belong to the company and not to the shareholders, so if a company fails and goes into liquidation, the shareholders and directors would not normally be entitled to any of the company's assets (equipment, copyrights, etc.). These would be sold for the benefit of the people owed money by the company. The main advantages and disadvantages of a company are:

a) Liability for debts cannot normally be claimed against directors and shareholders unless personal guarantees are given. However, personal guarantees are almost invariably required nowadays by banks and other lending companies.
b) The company is perpetual, until it is wound up. It is not affected by directors coming or going, unlike partnerships which may be dissolved by, for example, the death of a partner. The company's shareholders (owners) can sell their shares.
c) The bureaucracy surrounding a company is substantial. Small companies no longer require an annual audit, but accounts have to be filed at Companies House according to a very strict deadline, or fines will result; and forms need to be completed when there are changes of directors, company secretary or shareholders as well as completion of an Annual Return.
d) A company can have its freedom to act restricted by its rules (Memorandum and Articles of Association).

CHAPTER 3

As a director and shareholder in a limited company there are two ways in which you can opt to be paid:

- as an employee, paying yourself a wage/salary with tax and national insurance paid through PAYE and/or
- by dividend, payable monthly, quarterly or at other agreed times. But note that dividends can only be paid from post tax profits. If there are no profits then there can be no dividends.

Both payment methods have their own advantages and disadvantages which would be specific to your business and advice should be sought as to which one is right for you. Dividends can of course be paid to other shareholders who may or may not be employees or directors of the company.

Copyright

If you do not take action regarding protection of your copyright, should the company go into receivership or liquidation, the copyright in "your" images becomes an asset of the company for the liquidator to sell for the benefit of creditors, not yourself.

The way to resolve this problem is to have a document drawn up, before you begin trading, to establish the ownership of copyright. This may be in the form of an assignment by the company to you; but to ensure there are no loopholes we would recommend getting the document drawn up by a lawyer. If you are already a Limited Company and have not made arrangements for copyright ownership, legal advice should be sought as to the best way to now formally assign the copyright to you. You may find that you have to buy the copyright as it has a value as a company asset, but it is worth looking into to prevent future wrangles.

Securing your copyright

If you are an employee (and sole shareholder) of the new limited company, the following should be inserted into the employment contract between you and the company. It assumes that the company will enter into contracts for your services and for the exploitation of your images. 'It is hereby agreed between (Limited Co) and (Photographer) that all copyright and other intellectual property rights throughout the world in works created by (Photographer) in the course of his employment with (Limited Co) shall vest in (Photographer).'

By having this type of clause, should the company go into liquidation the copyright and moral rights will remain with you. Naturally, you must assert your moral rights (See Chapter 1 Moral rights).

However, vesting copyright in you, means your Company has no right to deal with your work (past, present or future) without being granted a licence to do so. A further agreement needs to be written allowing your Company to licence your images.

Specialist legal advice should always be sought to ensure that the copyright is safe and that the Company can licence the work on your behalf.

WORKING AS A FREELANCER

Introduction

Tax and National Insurance are an unavoidable part of every worker's life. Employees have the advantage of the employer working out their contributions and payments every week or month; the only way the payments are usually noticed is by their absence from the employee's pay slip!

The self-employed have to give more attention to these payments because it is always their responsibility to ensure that payments are made correctly and on time. There are however, certain compensations and the figures in this section illustrate how much less a freelancer can pay, compared to an employee earning the same gross income.

This section should assist you in:

a) ensuring you are either legally self-employed or an employee and that you are paying appropriate Income Tax and National Insurance Contributions (NI);

b) contacting HMRC at the right time and by appropriate means;

c) keeping accurate and up-to-date business records and paperwork ;

d) understanding the financial responsibilities of the self-employed;

e) understanding what expenses are eligible for tax relief for the self-employed.

Self-Employed v Employed

Income Tax: Self-employment and Employment (PAYE)

Only a small minority of assisting photographers and photographers in fashion, advertising and editorial photography are employed (apart from those employed by their own owner managed companies). They receive a regular salary and tax and NI contributions are deducted from their wages before they are received. Employers also pay employer's NI contributions on the wages earn e d by the employee as part of the Pay As You Earn (PAYE) system.

The majority of the industry works on a freelance basis and is self-employed. A fee, rather than a regular wage, is received in return for providing a service and submitting an invoice. Freelancers **must be registered** with HMRC as self-employed. The old system of Schedule D tax reference numbers no longer exists. So where somebody asks you for your Schedule D number you will not have one! What you will have is a ten figure tax reference number (UTR). This reference number does not only apply to self-employed tax payers, many employed tax payers have them as well. If you have one, this reference number will usually be quoted on any correspondence you receive from HMRC. It is separate from your NI number.

Your employment status affects the Income Tax and National Insurance (NI) contributions you have to pay. It is your responsibility to ensure that you are registered under the appropriate status. The law doesn't define employment but these guidelines help:

Self-Employed Persons

- ultimately decide the course of their business;
- determine their own hours of work;
- have more than one client;
- issue their clients with invoices for which they receive fees;
- have no contract of employment (rather, they have a contract for services instead)
- receive no holiday or sickness pay;
- have to correct unsatisfactory work in their own time and at their own expense, i.e. they bear the risks of their own business;
- provide their own tools or equipment.

Employed Persons

- ultimate responsibility for the work is taken by someone else (the employer);
- have regular hours of work;
- work for one company or individual;
- receive a weekly or monthly wage (sometimes calculated hourly) and are eligible for overtime;
- work a standard number of hours per week or days per month and are eligible for overtime in excess of this;
- have a contract or letter of employment; (i.e. a contract of service)
- a re entitled to holiday pay and sickness pay.

Focus on getting started as a Self-Employed Photographer

Registering with HMRC

Once you have made the decision to set up as self-employed, the next step, as well as looking for clients, is to notify HMRC within three months to avoid the possibility of £100 penalty.

This can be achieved on the HMRC website (www.hmrc.gov.uk) by following the: "Register your Business for HMRC Taxes" link. (If you have an accountant, then he/she can register for you).

Please note that HRMC administration is constantly changing and moving towards on-line communications. In some cases it is compulsory to submit forms on-line and paper copies will not be accepted (e.g. VAT returns).

You can also register by telephone by calling HMRC on 08459 154515: Helpline for the Newly Self Employed. Be warned that there are often lengthy delays in getting through to HMRC helplines.

CHAPTER 3

Opening year tax rules and your financial year end

There are some quite complicated rules relating to how to calculate the tax during the first three years you are trading. These are known as Opening Year Rules.

Commencing trading on 6 April would cause no issues relating to opening year rules, as your first financial year end would be 5 April the following year, and would therefore mirror the tax year.

Many new businesses will commence trading part way through a tax year. In such cases, the new business will be subject to HMRC's Opening Year Tax Rules, unless their accounting date is 31st March (or 5th April).

For instance, if you commenced trading on 1 October 2013, and set your first accounting period to be 30 September 2014, you will be taxed on your taxable profits generated between 1 October 2013 and 5 April 2014 during the tax year 2013/14.

During the following tax year (2014/15) you will be taxed on your taxable profits generated between 1 October 2013 and 30 September 2014. In essence you will have been taxed twice on your taxable profits generated during the first six months of trading (to 5th April 2014). This "overlap profit" as it is known can only be refunded once you cease trading, or if/when you change your accounting date.

It is possible to change your accounting reference date (the date you make your accounts up to), but an accounting reference period must not be less than six months long or greater than eighteen months long.

When commencing trading, it is recommended you discuss the opening year rules with your accountant in order to ensure the best tax outcome for you.

Guidance on accounting records

As a self-employed freelance photographer, possibly the last question on your mind is "Am I keeping the correct accounting records?".

Maintaining good accounting records on a regular basis will take up some of your time, but will almost certainly save time and costs in the long term. Promises of sorting all the paperwork "next year when I really start earning" are never realised and create many more problems and much bigger bills than would have originally been the case. Failure to notify HMRC of liability to pay tax due and on time will lead to substantial fines and interest penalties. HMRC can potentially fine taxpayers for poor record keeping.

It is recommended the following records should be maintained as a minimum:

- A business bank account separate from your own personal accounts;
- A sales invoice list to record all sales invoices raised by you **and dates paid**;
- A file of purchase invoices paid through your bank and a spreadsheet or computer records of your purchases.
- A bank receipts list/spreadsheet to detail cash, cheques and bank credits received from customers;
- A cash payments list/spreadsheet to detail cash paid to suppliers;
- A petty cash list/spreadsheet detailing all those small items you will pay for on behalf of your business, quite often from your own money.
- A spreadsheet of business payments made by credit card. (NB. The more credit cards you use, the more work needs to be done to produce accounts. Try to use only one credit card for your business transactions).

Writing up your records on a regular basis needs to be a discipline to avoid future problems. Most self-employed people will look to write up their records every week, or as a minimum once every month. This can be done on using a spreadsheet program such as Excel or you can use a commercial software package, but you do need to understand what you are doing as it can take a long time to find and correct mistakes and HMRC now issue penalties of up to 30% of tax due in cases of carelessness. Should you decide on keeping computerised records it is recommended you discuss your requirements with your accountant and possibly use a freelance bookkeeper or bookkeeping bureau to do this for you. If you do decide to use a bookkeeper you should always ensure that you use somebody recommended to you. Good bookkeepers are thin on the ground, but there are plenty of poor bookkeepers around! It is a good policy to use a referenced filing system (normally a number sequence), and to record the number in your accounting books. This will enable you to locate invoices with ease.

You must include the name of the customer or supplier, the invoice number, your reference for filing, the net amount, VAT and gross amounts, together with the date the invoice was raised. Similar details should be kept for cash payments and receipts, for instance cheque numbers should be recorded.

There are computer packages around to help maintain your accounting records, but these require a similar amount of detail to be entered. The golden rule is to keep all receipts and paperwork regardless of how your records are maintained.

Zooming in on an Accountant

There is no legal requirement for you to hire an accountant if you feel you have sufficient knowledge of maintaining accounts and the relevant tax regulations. However, for most people starting out in business on their own it is recommended that you consider seriously the benefits a qualified accountant can bring to you.

An accountant does not need to be expensive especially if you maintain good accounting records. Indeed, through their knowledge of the complicated tax system, completing self-assessment tax returns and your accounts, most good accountants should free you from administrative chores and may be able to recommend ways to reduce your overall tax burden.

Tax and National Insurance payments are part of the law and cannot be avoided. Developing a professional relationship with a qualified accountant who is familiar with the industry, and who understands fully the expenses which are eligible for tax relief can save you money and should also be able to provide you with good commercial advice.

Visualisation of the Tax Benefits for the Self-Employed

From the accounting records kept, as described above, it will be possible for either you or your accountant to draw up a set of accounts detailing accurately your income and expenditure, assets and liabilities and cash incomings and outgoings.

HMRC will look to tax you on your trading income from being self-employed. This is your income less your expenditure adjusted for certain disallowed expenses and other allowances. Income and expenditure is not the same as the cash you have received or spent, for instance you will be taxed on jobs you have completed and/or invoiced within your financial year even where your customer has not yet paid you.

It is possible to earn up to £9,440 (for the tax year 2013/14) before tax is deducted from your income.

The table below indicates the different amounts of tax payable under self-employed and employment. It is based upon a freelancer earning £25,000 profit after deductible expenses, and an employee earning £25,000 salary.

	Tax	National Insurance	Total Tax Deducted
Employee	£3,112	£2,070	£5,182
Self Employed	£4,664*	£140	£4,804
Difference	£1,552	£1,930	£378

* Includes class 4 national insurance collected via income tax payments.

National Insurance Classes

In 2013/14 employees pay class 1 National Insurance at a rate of 12% on earnings between £149 to £797 per week. Earnings above £797 per week attracts national insurance at a rate of 2%.

Self–Employed workers pay two types of National Insurance, Class 2 and Class 4. Class 2 is a flat rate payment of £2.70 per week and will normally be collected via direct debit or a monthly, quarterly or six monthly bill. Class 4 is at a rate of 9% on earnings above £7,755 but below £41,475 per year, and at a rate of 2% on earnings above £41,475. Class 4 is based upon the taxable earnings of the freelancer and will be assessed on the tax return and paid with income tax.

Class 3 National Insurance is voluntary for both the self-employed and employed and is a flat rate of £13.55 per week. It will help to protect rights to future benefits.

Some clients require freelance subcontractors to pay Class 1 contributions as employees, although their earnings are usually assessed for Class 4 contributions. This often happens to photographers who are commissioned to do stills on a movie or a commercial, where they will be working with technicians in a union. However, it is possible to get a refund on some contributions if the combined NI contributions exceed certain limits. Again, should such circumstances exist for you, please contact either your accountant or discuss the issue with the NI Contributions Office – part of HMRC.

It is possible to get a Class 2 exception certificate if your net income is less than £5,725 in the tax year ending 5 April 2014 by completing form CF10, 'Application for Exception from Liability for Class 2 Contributions' in leaflet CA72, 'NI Contributions: People with Small Earnings from Self-Employment'.

People who have been self-employed for over one year will be asked for accounts evidence to show that sufficiently little has been earned and that there is eligibility for exception. It is not necessary to send accounts details if you have been self-employed for less than a year and it is estimated that earnings will be low enough to be entitled to NI exception. If earnings then exceed the £5,725 limit the regular annual contributions of £140.40 will have to be paid.

However, you should bear in mind that not paying Class 2 National Insurance may preclude you from claiming benefits.

Processing your Self Assessment Tax Return

Each UK taxpayer is responsible for assessing his or her own tax. Under the PAYE system, most employees will not have to do anything, especially if they are basic rate tax payers.

All self-employed freelancers will be required to complete a self-assessment tax return. The key dates for completing this form are:

31st October following the end of the tax year in question for the submission of a paper return or 31st January following the end of the tax year for the submission of a tax return online.

You can find a great deal of advice on the HMRC website giving details of How to Complete Your Tax Return. However many self employed people prefer to use an accountant to do this so as to free up their time to concentrate on their profession.

The Self Assessment Tax Return comes with notes (downloadable from the HMRC website) giving details of how the form should be filled in, and may re q u I re up to nine additional schedules requesting further information (depending on the relevance of those schedules to the taxpayer concerned). For instance a tax payer who is self-employed and also employed will be required to complete the standard form, an employment form and also a self-employed form. A standard penalty of £100 is levied if the tax return is submitted after the 31 January largely regardless of circumstances, which increases to £10 a day if the tax return is still outstanding after 30th April.

Established businesses (no longer under the opening year rules mentioned above) will be assessed on a current year basis. This means that they will be taxed on the trading profits earned during the accounting period ending in the tax year.

For instance, a business with an accounting reference date of 30 September 2013 will be taxed on any profits made during the year from 1 October 2012 to 30 September 2013. The tax liability will relate to the tax year 6 April 2013 to 5 April 2014 as the accounting reference date falls within these two dates.

Tax is payable on the 31st January following the end of the previous tax year (5th April). If the Tax liability is more than £1,000 a further 50% of that liability is payable at the same time on account of the following year's tax liabilities and a further 50% is payable on the 31st July. The balance is then due 31st January after that together with another payment on account and so on... If profits are falling tax payers can appeal to have payments on account reduced. This appeal needs to be prepared carefully as if you have no grounds for making an appeal you risk substantial penalties. Always liaise with your accountant with regard to making appeals.

Example Calendar of Tax Due Dates where Trading started 6 April 2013

Payment Date	2013-2014	2014-2015	2015-2016	Total
31.01.15	£1,200.00	£ 600.00		£1,800.00
31.07.15		£ 600.00		£ 600.00
31.01.16		£ 200.00	£ 700.00	£ 900.00
31.07.16			£ 700.00	£ 700.00
31.01.17			£ 500.00	£ 500.00
Total Due	£1,200.00	£1,400.00	£1,900.00	£4,500.00

Many people struggle with their Tax Returns on their own and will often require assistance from an accountant. Again as indicated above, accountants are not necessarily expensive and may save you both time and money in terms of the tax you are required to pay. Taxation is a complicated subject and it is difficult for individuals to stay abreast of the ever increasing tax legislations and rules.

Prizes, Awards and other Income

Prizes and awards related to your profession, and particularly awards you have entered for, are normally taxable income. For example, a golfer or snooker player would pay tax on prize money as well as appearance money. Any such prize should be entered on your Tax Return. However, a prize given to you by a third party, and for which you did not enter, would not normally be taxed (e.g. Booker Prize).

As a self-employed photographer, you may be in the position where you have your own studio. Renting the studio to a third party should be classified as rental income rather than profits from trading as a professional photographer. The benefit of rental income is that it does not attract National Insurance Class 4 contributions.

Artists Averaging – Royalty Income Only

Photographers may be able to benefit from tax legislation designed to help creative artists with fluctuating royalty income. The legislation allows the results of 2 consecutive years of trading to be added together and averaged over those 2 years. The purpose of this is to reduce the possibility that any tax free allowances, lower rate tax bands, and basic rate tax bands remain unused.

Small Limited Companies

Many photographers and other freelance professionals trade through a limited company. In recent years it has become beneficial to do so where trading profits make this cost effective (as there are additional accounting and other costs to be taken into account – and quite a substantial amount of bureaucracy).

Under the Companies Act 2006 it is possible for a person to operate a one person company with a sole director/shareholder. The director is automatically an employee of the company and can pay himself/herself a small salary up to the threshold for PAYE/National Insurance and then take the rest of the profit from the business by means of dividends which are not subject to National Insurance. This way the saving can be substantial.

A simple example:

		Company	
	Sole Trader £	All Dividend £	Salary & Dividend £
Profit	30,000	30,000	30,000
Less all tax and NI	(6,254)	(6,000)	(4,450)
Net Disposable Income	23,746	24,000	25,550

As mentioned above one of the main pitfalls is that there is a lot more paperwork. In addition to the director's personal tax return, the company has to submit a corporation tax return and information on the company has to be made available to the public at Companies House (the Registrar of Companies). There are very strict deadlines for submission of information etc. and hefty penalties for being late – even by one day.

If you are considering forming and operating a limited company you should not do this without fully discussing the implications with your accountant.

Currently Corporation Tax for small companies is 20% and this is payable 9 months after the company's financial year-end. For small companies the profit limit is £300,000. After that profits are taxed at 24% with a reduction for profits up to £1.5 million This percentage is dropping year on year as the government wants to align the two rates and also wants the overall rate to be competitive of that of other EU Countries.

However tax is not the only reason for incorporating (becoming a limited company). A limited company does offer some degree of protection in litigation. However where banks lend to limited companies (for example to finance asset purchase) they almost invariably want personal guarantees from the company's directors/shareholders).

Value Added Tax (VAT)

Introduction

Value Added Tax is a form of indirect taxation on most everyday transactions. It enables the Government to collect revenue from individuals without directly taxing their income. It is not a tax on turnover, fees or profits, but a tax on consumer spending, collected by HMRC on behalf of the Government.

It is important that any person in business should understand how VAT affects their income and expenses, and the legal requirements for VAT registration and payment. This section will define the differences between voluntary and compulsory VAT registration and will clarify those goods and services on which VAT must be charged and on which VAT can be reclaimed.

Do I need to register for VAT?

Compulsory Registration

As soon as a photographer's turnover (total invoices raised) exceeds £79,000 (current compulsory level from 01.04.2013) in any twelve month period or if they think their turnover will exceed £79,000 in the next one month, they have no choice but to register, by law, with the VAT office within 30 days. Registration must be online via the HMRC website. The twelve month period test is a rolling test, and therefore will need to be checked each month to ensure the total invoiced amount during the previous 12 months has been under the threshold. Registration will not be required if the photographer can show or indicate to the satisfaction of HMRC that the turnover for the forthcoming 12 months will be below £77,000.

Voluntary Registration

Even if turnover is less than £79,000 (for 2013-2014) in any twelve month period the photographer can voluntarily become VAT registered.

Advantages of being VAT Registered

The main advantages of being VAT registered, should you be below the compulsory threshold are:

i to give the impression that the business is better established than may be the case;

ii) enables you to recover VAT on the expenses charged to you by your suppliers. This reduces the costs borne by you on purchases. If you are not registered for VAT, an item you purchased for £100 excluding VAT, would cost you £120.00, whereas being registered for VAT you could reclaim the additional £20.00 back, unless you are on the flat rate scheme;

iii) enables you to reclaim VAT on equipment purchased.

Disadvantages of being VAT Registered

i) Accounting for VAT may take up additional time, and would have to be charged on all items sold through the business.

ii) Any clients who are not registered with HMRC will find a VAT registered photographer's fees and costs more expensive because they will be unable to reclaim the VAT on their invoices.

Notifying HM Revenue & Customs

Whether registering for VAT is compulsory or voluntary, it is necessary to inform HMRC using a VAT 1 form which should be downloaded from the HMRC website by following the links: www. hmrc.gov.uk. HMRC will then inform you of your VAT registration number when they issue you with a VAT 4 form.

VAT Rates

The standard VAT rate for the majority of goods and services is 20 percent. In simple terms, if you invoice a customer £100 for your services before becoming VAT registered, on registration you will invoice the customer as follows:

Goods and services	NET	£100.00
VAT	20%	£ 20.00
Total		£120.00

Other rates of VAT also apply. For example certain items have reduced rate such as domestic fuel, some are zero-rated (children's footwear), and some are exempt (for example insurance). A full list of all these are available in the HMRC VAT Guide 700, Appendix A.

Accounting for VAT

In general the difference between the amount of VAT you charge your customers (known as Output VAT), and the amount of VAT you have incurred through purchases from suppliers (known as Input VAT) will be paid by you to, or refunded to you from, HMRC.

Depending on the net value of the sales you make to your customers (net being before VAT), there are different methods of accounting for VAT:

Flat Rate Scheme (Optional)

Where you make taxable sales excluding VAT during a year of less than £150,000, you can opt to join the flat-rate scheme.

Those using the scheme will need to total up all their sales including the VAT charged (Standard rate + Reduced rate + Zero rate + Exempt sales), and will then apply the industry standard percentage. For photography this percentage is 11 percent.

The advantage of the scheme is to make calculating VAT easier – you will not need to recover the actual input VAT on purchases as this is taken into account with the flat rate percentage. You will still need to charge your customers the normal VAT percentages, however you will retain the VAT collected from these customers. You have to apply to HMRC to join the flat rate scheme and details are on the HMRC website. The scheme is not completely straightforward. Generally you don't reclaim any VAT you pay on purchases. However you may be able to claim back VAT on the purchase of assets (not services) costing more than £2,000 each. Once you join the scheme you can stay in it until your total annual business income is more than £230,000. During the first year there is a discount on the amount you have to pay over to HMRC.

There are however substantial disadvantages using the scheme for certain traders and these are detailed on the HMRC website – or you should discuss with your accountant.

Cash accounting scheme

Businesses with turnover excluding VAT of £1,350,000 or less can opt to join the cash accounting scheme. The scheme means that VAT is only paid over or reclaimed from HMRC once you have received payment from your customers or made payment to your suppliers. The main benefits of this scheme is that it is better for your cash flow purposes as you will only pay the VAT once you have received the cash from your customer. Accordingly, if some customers never pay your sales invoice you receive instant bad debt relief as no money has been paid by you to HMRC.

The main disadvantage is that this system is often more difficult to administer as you need to keep a detailed record of the cash payments from customers against the invoices raised for the customer. It is necessary to charge VAT on invoices as normal under this system. Should your annual turnover exceed £1,600,000 excluding VAT you must inform HMRC and you will have to leave the cash accounting scheme.

Annual accounting

Using annual VAT accounting, you make 9 monthly or 3 quarterly interim payments through the year. You only need to complete one VAT return at the end of the year when you either make a balancing payment or receive a balancing refund.

Standard system

This is the most common system for accounting for VAT. The basic rule that triggers the need to pay VAT to or reclaim VAT from HMRC is known as the tax point. For the majority of goods and services, the tax point is when goods are made available or services are performed, unless they are invoiced and/or paid for earlier, in which case the earlier date is the tax point.

All entries (sales and purchases) made on the VAT return each quarter will be based upon the tax point. **It is therefore irrelevant when customers pay you, or when you pay your suppliers**, unless this happens to be before the date on which the goods were supplied or an invoice was raised.

Submitting a VAT return

A VAT return is normally submitted on a quarterly basis. The return is known as a VAT 100 form. HMRC will normally email you to remind you to submit your VAT return online by the due date. In general the due date is seven days after the month following the month of your VAT quarter. E.g. If your VAT quarter is to 31st March your VAT return needs to be submitted on line by 7th May. Your VAT will then generally be collected direct from your bank three days later. (In this example, 10th May).

Invoicing and other VAT issues

It is a legal obligation for all VAT registered traders to have their VAT number shown clearly on their sales invoices. In addition, VAT at the appropriate rate must be shown as a separate item. Invoices must be in strict sequence with no gaps, otherwise the suspicions of HMRC will be aroused when a VAT inspection occurs. Cancelled invoices should be kept, as should credit notes.

It is simpler if the VAT return date matches the business's financial year, so that the annual turnover and VAT account can be checked simultaneously. It is easy to change your VAT return dates. Accounting records need to be kept for a minimum of six years.

VAT and trading abroad/Export of Photography

Some confusion exists concerning VAT and the export of photography abroad, whether it is advertising or editorial work, or whether it is shot in, or produced for a client in other EU countries or worldwide.

However, the VAT office has been satisfied on a number of occasions that exports of photographic services almost invariably consist of the supply or assignment of copyright and/or licences to use photographs. The VAT Act -1983, 3 Schedule 1 (Section 7), states that 'Transfers and assignments of copyright, patents, licences, trademarks and similar rights' are all treated as 'supplied where received'. Therefore, VAT is not applied to invoices for work for a non EU client, even if shot in the UK.

Sales to the EU can cause potential VAT problems. You can only zero rate your supplies if your EU customer is VAT registered in their own country. In these cases, their VAT number must also be quoted on your invoice. You should speak to your accountant before you invoice your first EU customer. VAT registered businesses selling to the EU must complete quarterly online EU VAT Sales Lists and you should request these from HMRC. These returns only need to be completed for quarters in which sales are made to EU clients. Please note that there are penalties for failure to follow the rules in submission of these returns.

Bookkeeping

Introduction

Whether computerised or handwritten, well managed and up to date books of accounts can quickly provide you with information about how well your business is doing, as well as satisfying the tax authorities and keeping accountancy costs down!

Many photographers contract their main bookkeeping to specialised bookkeepers, either directly, or via their accountants. This has the advantage of removing the worry of having to do the work themselves when other business is more pressing (as well as ensuring that VAT Returns are ready on time). The main disadvantage, particularly to the photographer just starting out, is cost. However, if you get (and heed) advice from your accountant, you should be able to maintain your own accounts books in a straightforward way.

Basic needs

Rather than keeping manual books you should maintain your bookkeeping records either using Excel spreadsheets, or there are many good and simple computer accounts packages around that will keep all the information you need, showing what you've spent and where you've spent it; who owes you money and how long they've owed it; give you all the information for your VAT return; and may even provide the information you need to fill in your self assessment form for HMRC. Ask your accountant for a recommendation – if you have the same system (or a compatible one) you may save even more money on accountancy fees! If you prefer to keep manual records then you will need the following:

- A business bank account separate from your own personal accounts;
- A sales invoice list to record all sales invoices raised by you and dates paid;
- A file of purchase invoices paid through your bank and a spreadsheet or computer records of your purchases.
- A bank receipts list/spreadsheet to detail cash, cheques and bank credits received from customers;
- A cash payments list/spreadsheet to detail cash paid to suppliers;
- A petty cash list/spreadsheet detailing all those small items you will pay for on behalf of your business, quite often from your own money.
- A spreadsheet of business payments made by credit card. (NB. The more credit cards you use, the more work needs to be done to produce accounts. Try to use only one credit card for your business transactions).

Good sales and payments records will show who owes you money, enabling you to keep an eye on slow payers. Records of your purchases paid by cheque and through your bank and cash all need to be kept meticulously, with suppliers' bills, both paid and unpaid, filed properly.

Don't throw anything away! All books and records should be kept for up to eight years, depending on when your accounts period starts. The authorities can impose large fines if records are lost or destroyed. Good advice from your accountant before you start can save you money on accountancy fees later on, as well as giving you peace of mind, knowing that bookkeeping is one less thing to worry about.

Credit Control

Poor credit control can result in failure of a business and possibly bankruptcy. Your clients often cynically look on you as a cheap form of finance. Most photographers don't charge interest, unlike their bankers, so by delaying payment for a long time people who owe you money can actually cost you a lot of money (see Chapter 2 for legislation on charging interest).

Chasing payment

Credit control is something you need to tackle early on in the life of your business and the policy you adopt needs to be stuck to. Your credit terms need to be stated clearly on the bottom of each invoice (e.g. Terms Net, 30 days).

Your sales records and bank statements need to be checked monthly against payments received and statements should be sent on a regular basis to clients who have not paid their outstanding accounts. These statements should be backed up with telephone calls to the accounts departments of the companies concerned.

Photographers dealing with advertising agencies and publishing groups should not fear treading on the toes of their clients as the creative departments usually have little to do with the accounts departments of these organisations. You need to find a contact name in the relevant accounts department and if necessary harass that person until your overdue account is settled. Daily telephone calls can work wonders. If you shout louder than the next person you are more likely to get paid, if only so that they get rid of the nuisance (you!). If you have used the correct paperwork, including terms and conditions (see Appendix) the use of your image is dependent on your being paid; the client could be in breach of copyright.

What to do if they don't pay

If an account becomes seriously overdue, you should consider the threat of legal action. This can prove expensive but many photographers use a specialist firm of solicitors who will issue a very effective chasing letter for (currently) only £2.00 + VAT. The solicitors concerned claim a 70% success rate just for these letters and this can be an effective and inexpensive option. If payment is not made then one needs to consider further action.

Debts of up to £5,000 can be pursued through the small claims division of the County Court; £5,000-£15,000 (if a hearing is likely to last less than a day) can be claimed through the fast track County Court system, and debts of over £15,000 (or if a hearing is likely to take more than a day) through the multi track County Court system. These last two County Court proceedings usually require legal representation so you also have to weigh up the time costs involved.

You can threaten an individual who owes you more than £750 with the prospect of bankruptcy and, via a solicitor, commence bankruptcy proceedings. You can also threaten a limited company with the prospect of having it wound up. A formal letter on these lines, particularly from a solicitor, ought to have a pretty salutary effect.

Another option is the issue of a written Statutory Demand which involves the completion of particulars dependant on the nature of the debt and if your debtor is a limited company. Further details can be found on the Insolvency Service website. NB. Issue of a Statutory Demand can involve substantial legal costs.

You may be trading very successfully, but if people are not paying you for the work that you do, you cannot pay your suppliers or your own living expenses. You would not expect your suppliers to tolerate you not paying them.

Opening Accounts with Suppliers

Paying cash on delivery for all business purchases is not advisable business practice, and you will therefore need to open accounts with major suppliers.

To open an account you will usually first need to obtain an application form. This will ask for your name, address, length of time trading, etc., as well as for two trade references, your bank details and the amount of credit required (your supplier will double this amount when seeking trade references as you will always owe him for both the current and previous month's purchases). The trade references you give should be organisations you already have credit accounts with. If this is your first account, give a personal reference, but make sure both your name and your business name are quoted on the form.

Many suppliers include, as part of their application form, a declaration or reference to their Terms & Conditions of Sale; by signing the application, you agree to abide by these terms. The terms cover the supplier's obligations, liabilities, payment terms, penalties and other areas, which ensure suppliers are legally protected against pretty well everything. These do not normally present a problem but should always be checked very carefully before signing.

Borrowing money

Most businesses have to borrow money at one time or another, for example, to finance a new piece of equipment or a large job where payment is likely to be received after costs have been incurred. Often a short term bank overdraft can be arranged, but always ask first. If you overdraw without permission you are less likely to be successful when you want more substantial finance. You also run the risk of being asked to close your account and will be charged a penal rate of interest.

Companies supplying equipment, motor vehicles and so on, are often keen to offer finance because they get commission from the finance company who provide the money for the transaction. Interest rates on such transactions are often, but not always, higher than the rates charged by banks.

Banks are the natural source of finance; both short and long term, and are often the best place to go. If you feel that your business is likely to require a lot of services from your bank you should consider developing a relationship with your business manager. This can sometimes be complicated as personnel at banks are moved from post to post often at short notice and you need to ask how long the person you are dealing with is likely to be in place. If a bank knows a great deal about your business it is more likely to be helpful. Some photographers invite their business managers to shoots to impress them with what they do and what is involved with regard to equipment etc. Most bank managers think of commercial photographers just as high street photographers who do weddings and portrait photography only and are not aware of what is involved in modern commercial photography and the cost of up to date technology.

Cash in your pocket enables you to negotiate better terms with the equipment supplier, reducing the overall cost of the transaction. The down side is that banks often demand a great deal from borrowers – particularly new businesses – and they still have a long way to go before they shake off the commonly held opinion that they are heavy handed. Except for small sums, banks often want security, such as personal guarantees for loans.

They also want to see accounts to back up claims of business viability. Cash flow statements and detailed business plans are often required by bank managers before they will consider a loan.

Business Plans

A business plan is a projection of how you think your business will develop in the future. It is normally split into trading years (twelve month periods) and covers any period from one to five years depending on its purpose. In the context of sole traders, it should also include a summary of personal expenditure so that the business profits and cash flow can be related to domestic circumstances. The object of a business plan is to calculate in advance what your financial requirements might be during the next twelve months and to enable you to plan your cash flow and expenditure sensibly, thus being pre p a red for problems before they arise.

When preparing a business plan, the best advice is to stick to the rule 'what in your heart of hearts do you really think will happen'. If you are over-optimistic on fees, or reduce your expenses unrealistically to show an improved profit for any reason, you will only lead yourself into cash flow problems; your bank manager will lose confidence in you and you may end up spending money which you do not have.

Most major banks publish booklets and on-line advice spelling out what they want from your business plan. These booklets are very detailed and sophisticated in their scope and offer much advice and help, as well as showing you how to present the information they require before deciding to lend you money.

Factoring

Factoring is a way of turning your sales into cash before your clients pay you. In practice you borrow the bulk of each invoice you issue. Factoring companies are often subsidiaries of major banks. Factoring (or invoice discounting) companies buy your unpaid invoices as they arise and pay you up to 80% of their value, with the balance, less administrative and finance charges, being paid to you when your clients pay their invoices. They also advise on credit risks and potential bad debts. They want to see a turnover in excess of at least £50,000 and an established trading record. Their service is designed to improve cash flow, but they can be expensive.

Factoring companies will not normally deal with new businesses. Factoring should only be considered as a last resort, and a factoring arrangement should not be entered into without first discussing it with your accountant.

Leasing and Asset Finance

Borrowing money so as to pay cash for a piece of equipment may result in obtaining a good discount, thereby reducing the financial cost of the deal. Leasing or hire purchase may be a suitable alternative, and homework needs to be done before a decision can be made. The main points to be taken into consideration are:

- The cheapest cost of borrowing money to pay for equipment.
- Your ability and desire to provide security.
- Cash flow and tax considerations.

As with other financial decisions, if you are unsure check with your accountant before entering into any agreement.

Hire Purchase

Hire purchase is an agreement whereby goods are hired to you over a period. At the end of that period you then obtain ownership of the goods for a nominal sum. You can claim capital allowances (depreciation) for tax purposes, based on the cost of the goods.

Lease Purchase

A lease purchase is a commercial form of hire purchase and not a form of leasing. In both cases, hire and lease, the interest costs are a tax allowable business expense.

Contract Hire or Leasing

Contract hire or leasing is usually for a fixed period and the hire cost is high reflecting the capital cost of the asset. The hirer retains ownership throughout, and the hire costs are again a tax allowable business expense. HP and leasing companies normally carry out rigorous checks into credit worthiness before entering into an agreement, but they do not normally require any security. You need to check the APR interest rate of the different types of deal before you sign any agreement. Your accountant should be able to help you if required.

Remember that, in the current economic climate, salesmen will exert a lot of pressure on you to take their 'deal'. Their commission is high, and business is slow. You have to live with what you agree, so don't be pressurized into signing something you are not sure of.

CHAPTER 4: INSURANCES

Williamson Carson Ltd

Introduction

Photographers usually deal with one insurance agent or broker and have all their required policies on one annual schedule to make administration simpler. Insurance and Liability are essential to every business and it is important not to avoid what is a legal requirement. To do so can incur much greater penalties in the long run. It is also important to consider those optional and advised insurance policies outlined below. However, it is too easy to calculate just the costs of these and not what is at stake if cover isn't arranged. A lack of or inadequate cover can affect more than just the photographer's finances, but also the lives and income of people working with them.

When starting as a photographer or assisting photographer, it is a legal requirement to have certain insurance and liability protection. Others are not compulsory, but are recommended because of the financial protection they provide. Photographers should be aware of the distinctions, so they are able to anticipate the point in their career when it is necessary to get cover from these policies. There are fundamental differences between voluntary and legally

Required insurance and liability policies:

i) liability provides protection against claims made by other people (or companies) against a photographer, and will cover any payment awarded against the insured, in or out of court.

ii) insurance policies can protect virtually anything including individuals, income, premises, equipment, film, portfolio, car, home or personal possessions, from accident, damage, loss or theft, and claims are not usually dependent on a court decision.

This section will provide details on different voluntary and compulsory general insurance covers and those policies specific to professional photography practice.

Employer's Liability Insurance

All employers must, by law, have Employer's Liability Insurance. The definition of an 'employee' in this case is often unclear and this may cause confusion, but it is generally understood to be anyone working under someone's 'care, custody and control', whether or not a fee is being paid for the person's services. This can include:

- a person under contract of service or apprenticeship;
- a person employed by labour-only sub-contractors;
- a self-employed person;
- a person hired to, or borrowed by, the insured;
- a person undertaking study or work experience.

Employer's Liability protects the photographer from any claim of death, bodily injury or disease to an employee arising during a job. If action is taken by an 'employee' who has suffered, say, injury, and the court decides that the photographer was negligent and therefore liable, Employer's Liability will meet the costs of the action and also the compensation. However, if they don't have a valid policy they will be liable for all costs, fees and compensation and face prosecution for not having Employer's Liability.

Optional Insurance Policies

Public Liability Insurance

Public Liability Insurance is not compulsory, however hire studios and locations will almost certainly require Public Liability. Policies will protect a photographer from a situation where the photographer's proven negligence causes:

- loss or damage to property;
- disease, death or injury to another person (third party injury)

Example A photographer is shooting on location in a busy street and a member of the public trips over a lighting cable and injures themselves and decides to seek compensation from the photographer. A court would have to decide whether the accident was caused because of the photographer's negligence (was the shooting area sufficiently cordoned off? Were the cables secured properly to the ground? etc.) and whether the claim against the photographer is justified. If the photographer does not have public liability cover, they will have to meet the costs of defending an action and the additional costs of lawyer's fees. Public Liability means that all costs are handled by the insurance company, no matter what the outcome of the claim.

CHAPTER 4

Professional indemnity insurance

Professional Indemnity Insurance is considered essential protection for all professional practices in today's litigious climate. Photographers are at risk in the same way as other professional practitioners to claims arising from professional negligence. Incidents of an apparently minor nature could ultimately result in substantial court awards and £300 legal costs. Cover enables you to reduce the financial effect of such claims on your business, and protect your livelihood. The cover can be comprehensive and include your liability at law for the following essential features:

- any neglect, error or omission by you, your employees or agents;
- infringement of property or contract rights;
- libel, slander, defamation or violation of copyright law;
- dishonesty of employees or agents.

And in addition:

- fees and expenses which a client would have paid to you, but for your mistake;
- additional costs incurred by you to rectify a mistake;
- the costs of replacing lost or destroyed films, photographs and documents;
- legal defence costs.

It is impossible to estimate how much these claims could cost, but any commercial dispute is likely to be expensive, and substantially more will be involved if solicitors are engaged or if you have to re-shoot a large job.

Exclusions

There are very few exclusions with Professional Indemnity Cover, however you cannot cover a claim arising from circumstances of which you were aware when you took out the policy, and you will be asked to make a specific contribution to each claim. Cover can only be granted to independent photographers (including partnerships and limited companies) and not to employees. Employees should be protected by their employer's policy.

Equipment Insurance

Most insurance brokers can provide insurance for loss, theft or damage to a photographer's equipment, but a firm which specialises in the film, TV and photography business is usually recommended, because it will probably have a better understanding of your business needs. A complete list of all the insurable items should be submitted to the insurance agent with accurate information or current replacement values. Where items of equipment are obsolete, the nearest equivalent should be found to avoid under-insurance. These figures should be updated annually so that equipment is adequately covered. Policies can be arranged to protect equipment for:

- Studio only
- UK only
- UK and Europe
- Worldwide

Photographers are able to expand the cover if they are shooting outside the area normally covered, and pay an additional premium. If a photographer has to do this more than twice in a year, it is usually cheaper to upgrade the policy at the renewal date to include the additional area(s) on a permanent basis. Some equipment policies automatically cover theft from the photographer's car, but individual policies may specify that cover is only during daylight hours or that the car should be fitted with a 'suitable' car alarm. However, some policies will exclude theft from a car altogether, and so policies should be considered very carefully to ensure that all the provision is suitable. Details should always be checked and nothing should be assumed.

Re-Shoot Cover

With the cost of photographic shoots increasing all the time, consideration should be given to insuring the re-shoot of work either on an annual or job-by-job basis. The main elements of a re-shoot cover are as follows:

1. *Non Appearance:*

Cost to re-shoot following the loss of photographer or anyone essential to the shoot who is in your original budget.

2. *Negative/digital:*

Cost to re-shoot following loss of or damage to exposed film or digitally generated images.

3. *Extra expenses:*

Cost to re-shoot following loss of or damage to essential equipment, props or location.

Re-shoot policy can also include hired equipment, props, sets and wardrobes, cash, liabilities and so on.

The time and money invested in putting together a student portfolio is multiplied many times during the development and maintenance of a professional photographer's portfolio or 'book'. A portfolio will often be out of the photographer's or agent's care, custody or control and the personal and commercial value that it holds should be insured for. Most photographers pay an additional premium on their equipment insurance to cover their portfolios against loss, damage or theft. If you consider the times that a book will be with a courier or will be carried in the street or on public transport, insurance is essential. However, be aware that portfolio insurance only covers the cost of remounting a new portfolio and not the cost of re-shooting the lost or damaged transparencies.

Portfolio Insurance

The time and money invested in putting together a student portfolio is multiplied many times during the development and maintenance of a professional photographer's portfolio or 'book'. A portfolio will often be out of the photographer's or agent's care, custody or control and the personal and commercial value that it holds should be insured for. Most photographers pay an additional premium on their equipment insurance to cover their portfolios against loss, damage or theft. If you consider the times that a book will be with a courier or will be carried in the street or on public transport, insurance is essential. However, be aware that portfolio insurance only covers that cost of remounting a new portfolio and not the cost of re-shooting the lost or damaged transparencies.

Goods In Trust (props, sets & wardrobe)
Goods In Trust is a voluntary insurance policy which protects photographers against damage to props they have hired or borrowed. In the same way that Employer's Liability covers any person working under a photographer's 'care, custody & control', Goods In Trust provides the same protection for props and items temporarily under the photographer's care, custody and control.

These 'temporary' products and props cannot be covered on the studio contents insurance, nor on Public Liability policies. Many companies and freelance people in the industry should have Goods In Trust cover, whether they are stylists, home economists, design groups, advertising agencies, or any person/organisation that may be temporarily entrusted with someone else's property. In the case of a photographer, this is loosely referred to as 'props, sets and ward robe'. Goods In Trust does not cover camera and lighting hire equipment; these are usually insured when the hire fee is paid, according to the hire agreement (the only exception to

this is the insurance of hire studios, which are covered by the photographer's Public Liability and not Goods In Trust).

Goods In Trust is usually an addition to the photographer's studio contents insurance and is arranged to a limit agreed between the photographer and bro k e r. Usual cover is for a specific amount and the photographer is able to organise additional cover for items that go over this limit, such as a car or an expensive prop specially made by a model-maker. It is a common mistake for a photographer to think that Public Liability cover will always protect them against damage to another person's property, caused by their negligence, during the course of a job.

However, special circumstances of props and locations must always be considered and accounted for, before the day of the shoot.

Example 1a — A photographer is on location in a stately home and is photographing an interior shot. They walk backwards, knock a valuable vase from a pedestal and smash it.

Possible Outcome — The vase was not in the shot and would probably be covered under Public Liability Insurance.

Example 1b — A photographer is on location in a stately home and is shooting an interior which features many valuable porcelain vases in situ. They knock one from the pedestal and it smashes.

Possible Outcome — The vase was intrinsic to the shot and was therefore a prop. The photographer would not be covered under Public Liability but would have to make a claim on Goods In Trust. Negligence does not have to be proven in court before the insurance company will pay.

It is a common mistake to assume that Public Liability will provide cover for this situation because damage was done to another's property. However, anything that is featured in or is intrinsic to the photograph is considered to be a prop and therefore any damage would have to be claimed for under the photographer's Goods In Trust policy.

Example 2 — A photographer hires a mirror from a specialist hire shop and arranges the invoicing and a courier to collect it. The mirror is collected by the courier company and taken to the photographer's studio. While the courier is closing the van doors, a member of the public walks into the mirror and damages part of the frame.

Possible Outcome — This is more difficult to resolve and it would be up to the insurance companies to decide who was ultimately responsible for the damage. However, if the photographer or the courier had Goods In Trust insurance, no liability would have to be proven and no decision would have to be made by the court, and it can be left to the insurance companies involved to resolve the matter. The Goods In Trust policy should cover the replacement value of the mirror and frame.

Policy Excesses
All policies will vary but it is important to check the excess that is payable. An 'excess' is the amount the insured must contribute to a claim before any payment is made by the insurance company and applies to most insurance policies.

Motor Insurance Additional Premiums

Motor insurance is of course mandatory, however, there are certain additional voluntary premiums that should be considered if the vehicle is used as part of the business.

When photographers require an assistant (or any other person) to drive any business vehicle, it is the photographer's responsibility to provide adequate insurance cover for the occasion.

Alternatively, an assisting photographer may obtain cover so that they are insured to drive any vehicle for business or pleasure, so that they are certain of being covered. This can be expensive, so they should always check the insurance status with the photographer before they drive their vehicle. Don't take risks with motor insurance and don't make assumptions about cover.

Weather Contingency

With escalating production costs, Weather Contingency Insurance is becoming increasingly popular with some photographers' clients. This cover indemnifies the photographer and his/her client against interruptions to and abandonment of shoots in exterior locations. Cover is usually for unreasonable photographic conditions, which can include rainfall, high winds and poor light. It is possible, at certain times of the year and in certain overseas places, to insure against lack of sunshine if sunlight is essential for a particular production. The costs are high, however may be reduced by including a specified period of time before a claim can be made, for example two hours of rain before the interruption becomes claimable. It is normal practice to include weather insurance as a specific item in the budget, thereby passing the cost on to the client. Be aware that ten calendar days are needed, from the date on which the photographer issues an order for cover, before Weather Contingency Insurance comes into effect.

Personal Accident Insurance (PAI)

Employees who have a contract of employment and pay Class 1 NI contributions are given protection at work from the National Insurance (Industrial Injuries) Act. In the case of an accident or injury which prevents them from being able to do their job, they are eligible to claim benefit until they are able to resume work. However, self-employed people do not receive the same protection unless they make their own provision and arrange cover with Personal Accident Insurance (PAI).

PAI differs from liability indemnity because it does not depend on the discretion of a court and proof that negligence caused the injury or accident. Most PAI policies will also provide cover for:

- 24 hours a day
- Worldwide (unlike liability cover)
- Death and Capital Benefits
- Temporary or total disablement.

But the small print should always be carefully checked. These terms mean that, even if a photographer is on vacation or working in the UK or abroad, at any time of the day or night, and suffers an accident which results in them being unable to work, they will receive payments until they are able to work again. The following points should be borne in mind:

i) PAI does not always cover sickness.

ii) PAI does not cover existing on-going injuries (e.g. photographers frequently suffer back-problems) and the policy should start before any such complaints occur.

iii) Most PAI policies have a 7-day policy excess, although some may be longer. This means that they must be unable to work for more than a week (or longer) before a claim can be made.

iv) PAI will only provide compensation if loss of earnings can be proven (i.e. an official art order confirming a job or, for an assisting photographer, a statement from the photographer saying that they had been booked for a job which injury prevents them from being able to do). Alternatively, the previous year's earnings may be taken into consideration.

v) If someone is involved in a 'hazardous activity' and an accident occurs, this may invalidate the PAI claim. Some policies will cover leisure skiing, but competition or racing events are excluded. As a general rule, any dangerous sport should be checked with the insurance company in order to consider whether extra cover is necessary.

CHAPTER 5: PENSIONS, SAVINGS, INVESTMENTS AND MORTGAGES

Sentinel Independent Financial Advisers

Introduction

The following information is supplied for guidance purposes only and in no way constitutes any form of recommendation. It is based on our current understanding of existing tax and financial services legislation which may be subject to change in the future. The reader should also note that the value of investments can both rise and fall.

Pensions

With tax relief of up to 50% on contributions, and the facility to take a portion of the eventual benefits tax free, pensions are the most tax efficient investment format available in the UK. However, with the ever contracting State pension scheme, the importance of ensuring adequate personal provision for retirement is ever greater.

Since the introduction of personal pensions in 1988, there is much greater flexibility available in respect of how contributions can be made, what investments can be held, and when benefits can be taken. The maximum contribution is governed by an annual allowance.

For tax year 2011/12 onwards. The maximum personal contribution is **£50,000, subject to a limit of 100% of Earnings. Employers can contribute greater amounts in certain circumstances**. This may be increased over the longer term. If the annual allowance is exceeded a tax charge is normally payable.

However, from tax year 2011/12, it is possible to **carry forward** unused **annual allowance** from the previous three tax years to allow pension savings of more than £50,000, without triggering the tax charge.

There are strict rules governing how carry forward works:

- Unused annual allowance can be carried forward to the current tax year from the **previous three tax years**.
- It is only possible to do this once the current year's annual allowance has been fully used up.
- The unused annual allowance is used up starting with the earliest year first.
- The person has to have been a member of a registered pension scheme for the carry forward year in question.

All contributions within these limits qualify for tax relief at your highest marginal rate. All individuals make pension contributions on a net of basic rate tax. Higher tax relief must be claimed against profits/income.

Contributions can be made either on a monthly basis or as a lump sum, annually or individually. For those who have an erratic income profile, it is difficult to estimate what your likely profits will be and therefore what your pension contribution should be. Equally, the availability of a lump sum to make a contribution at the year end is not assured. The use of a combination of regular and single contributions is usually the best solution.

Personal Pensions can, in certain circumstances, be used as a repayment vehicle for a mortgage in place of an endowment, ISA or capital & interest. This enables you to gain advantage from the tax efficiencies available. Up to 25% of the fund accrued at retirement can be taken as a tax free cash sum and it is this that may be used to repay the mortgage. The other 75% of the fund is then used to provide an income in retirement. The high level of tax efficiency that pensions offer enables two tasks – loan repayment and retirement provision.

Although pension contribution levels tend to be driven by tax mitigation, it is essential to ensure that the eventual benefits are sufficient to meet your income needs in retirement. Estimates of benefits produced by particular contribution rates can be a useful guide if appropriate estimates of fund growth and inflation are used. It is particularly important to review your pension provision on a regular basis (annually is recommended) to ensure the level of accruing benefits is in line with your expectations, taking into account the level of contributions being made, the economic environment, investment returns being achieved and the level of investment risk you are prepared to accept.

For many people, their pension fund at retirement is their second largest asset after their home. It is therefore essential that the investment strategy is correct. Investment funds covering the whole range of risk profiles are available, from low-risk 'with profits' funds to higher risk/potentially higher return funds, investing direct into worldwide stock markets. Whilst higher risk funds are an acceptable part of the portfolio when you have in excess of 10 years before retirement, consideration should be given to a transition to low risk investments as retirement approaches.

For the more sophisticated investor with large pension assets, a Self-Invested Personal Pension provides a high level of personal investment control. Direct holdings of equities selected personally or with a stockbroker, can be held, as can commercial property, including your own business premises.

When selecting which company you should use as your pension provider, it is essential that you assess the charges they levy, their quality of their administration and flexibility, and their performance prowess. The difference made to your eventual benefits by using a high-charging and under-performing plan is enormous.

SAVINGS & INVESTMENTS

The creation and effective investment of capital is of particular importance to those in business on their own account, be it for the short term purposes, such as meeting an impending tax liability, creating a financial safety-net, or a specific medium term purpose such as school fees planning. There are several investment formats that offer tax free status to the investor. Use of these could boost the overall return on your capital.

National Savings Certificates
National Savings Certificates are available on either fixed interest or index-linked, 5 year rates. An investor can buy up to £15,000 of each issue. A reduced interest rate is applied on early exit.

ISAs – Individual Saving Accounts
ISAs were introduced to replace Personal Equity Plans (PEPS). They have evolved over recent years into a competitive format offering a very wide investment choice, from low risk, e.g. guaranteed and corporate bond funds, to high risk e.g. Emerging Market Equity funds. Up to £11,280 can be placed into a Stocks and Shares ISA (2012/13) and a new plan can be effected each financial year. Regular savings schemes start from as little as £50 per month.

Having utilised your tax exempt savings allowance where appropriate, further investments can be made potentially tax free by using one of the investment formats whose growth is taxed as capital gains. Each individual can make gains up to a limit each year, (£10,600 for 2012/13) without liability to tax. Investments of this type include:

Unit Trusts
Types of funds available are similar to those for PEPs and ISAs, although no maximum investment applies. Sums of more than £10,000 are usually best held as part of a portfolio with several diverse holdings.

Investment Trusts
Broadly similar to Unit Trusts, although different types of share are available, such as geared Capital Shares or Income Shares.

Regular savings schemes for both Unit Trusts and Investment Trusts start from £50 per month. For investors with larger portfolios and higher incomes, there are several other areas offering tax mitigation for higher rate tax or roll-over relief for capital gains. These include:

- *Permanent Interest Bearing Shares (PIBS)*
  A fixed-interest Building Society stock.
- *Enterprise Investment Schemes (EIS)*
  30% income tax relief on the first £1,000,000 invested (Tax relief will be limited to the amount of income tax paid). Growth on the EIS is usually free from capital gains tax as long as the investment has been held for at least three years. Also the ability to defer a capital gain into the EIS, thus deferring the payment of capital gains tax can be beneficial.
- *Venture Capital Trusts (VCTs)*
  30% income tax relief on the first £200,000 invested (Tax relief will be limited to the amount of income tax paid). Exempt from capital gains tax on disposal of the shares and tax free dividends.

Using offshore investment vehicles can be efficient for managing the tax position on capital for higher risk taxpayers, although the plan charging structures is often higher.

Having invested in several of the formats listed above, it is essential to ensure that the risk profile of your portfolio as a whole matches your expectations.

Income Replacement

The revision of the State Invalidity Benefit structure, and in particular the end of mortgage benefit after 12 months, has highlighted the need to ensure that, should you be prevented from working due to illness or injury, you receive income at an appropriate level.

Permanent Health Insurance will provide an income in this event, up to a maximum of 60% of our Net Relevant Earnings. You can elect for a time delay between the beginning of the illness and the payments starting of 4, 8, 13, 26 and 52 weeks – the longer this deferment period, the lower the cost of cover. The interim period should be covered by capital reserves or work-in-progress. Payments continue until you are able to return to work or you reach your elected retirement age.

With effect from 6th April 1996, all benefit payments from these schemes are wholly exempt from tax.

Great care should be taken to ensure that any policy you effect will pay out in the event of your illness or injury preventing you from practising as a photographer, not on the basis of 'any' occupation.

Critical Illness Cover

Whilst Critical Illness contracts are no substitute for an Income Replacement contract they are very useful for creating capital to repay the mortgages and loans and provide for a change in life-style in the event of diagnosis of a serious illness such as cancer, heart disease or a stroke. Where Income Replacement pays for non-life threatening illnesses and injuries, conversely, Critical Illness benefit can be received at a time when you are still able to work but perhaps would rather not.

Financial Advice

The Financial Services Act of 1986 created two distinct forms of financial adviser.

- The Tied Agent or Company Representative, who is limited to using the products of the Insurance Company or Bank for whom they work;
- Independent Financial Advisers, who are subject to regulations designed to ensure that they advise you on the best products available, across the whole financial market place, to meet your needs. Solicitors and accountants who offer financial advice can only do so on this basis.

In theory, an independent adviser should be able to save you money by finding the best rates for life insurance or income replacement, and by ensuring that only the most cost-effective providers are used for pensions, ISAs, etc.

A good financial adviser should be able to offer you consistent advice over a number of years and in sympathy with your other advice, such as your accountants and solicitor's. The most effective way to choose an adviser is either in conjunction with your accountant or a colleague who has experienced the advice given by the firm in question over a reasonable time period.

Many accountants and solicitors have ceased to provide direct advice due to the time commitment required to meet the qualifications necessary in addition to their own work.

All advisers are obliged to inform you of the costs and charges associated with the recommendation they make, and Independent Financial Advisers are happy to work on a fee basis similar to accountants.

The selection of an adviser capable of delivering high quality advice on pensions, investments, lending and insurances, without too much impact on your time, can be of enormous advantage if the right adviser for you is chosen.

CHAPTER 5

Commercial Lending

The purchase of a commercial property, such as a studio, on a freehold or long leasehold basis, can not only make you money as an appreciating asset, but can also help your cashflow if the loan is structured properly, relative to renting an equivalent premises.

Loans of up to 75% of property value are available on owner-occupied premises; however, in the circumstances where you are purchasing the freehold of a property on which you hold a short lease, a higher percentage can be borrowed

When approaching a potential lending source, it is essential that you show your finances are in harmony with the lender's requirements and that you have a clear idea of how you want the loan structured. Lenders are looking for ability to service the loan; so items such as current rent can be added back into your profits in most cases. The greater the ease with which the loan servicing can be met, the more competitive the interest rate you will be offered. Short and long term fixed rates, together with discounted and variable rates normally charged at base rate plus a margin, are all available alternatives.

The use of your pension scheme to purchase a commercial property offers several advantages. Firstly, you are able to utilise your current pension fund as a deposit (the balance subject to limits, being borrowed in the normal way) and, secondly, all rental income and any growth in property value are not subject to tax.

This facility has long been available to those trading as a limited company via a Small Self-Administered Scheme, but is now available to sole-traders/partners using a Self-Invested Personal Pension.

Residential Mortgages

Although residential mortgages are available on every high street, it is difficult to know which are the best options. With building societies, banks and centralised lenders all active in the market, the choice is wider than ever.

Which type of scheme is the first choice to be made, whether you want a fixed or discounted rate or perhaps a 'cashback'. A fixed rate, where the rate of interest charged is set at outset for a predetermined period, provides stability and security. If however you feel that interest rates are likely to fall, a discounted rate or tracker rate may suit you better. You may then pay interest at a rate lower than the standard variable rate, without any concessions, but receive a cash sum following completion. This can be between 3% and 5% of the loan amount. Another factor in the choice of scheme is how long you are likely to remain in the property. Most schemes, whether fixed or discounted, may include a substantial penalty for redeeming in the early years.

The next decision is how the mortgage is to be repaid. This can be on a traditional capital and interest (repayment) basis, or interest-only, linked to a suitable repayment vehicle. This could be an Individual Savings Account, an endowment policy, or part of your pension fund. It is essential that professional advice is taken at this point. In most cases, life assurance is recommended.

The various costs associated with a new mortgage must be taken into consideration. All purchases of over £125,000 attract stamp duty at 1% of the purchase price. Valuation and survey fees must be paid, and possibly an arrangement fee from the lender. If the mortgage required is over 75% of the valuation, an additional charge known as a 'high lending charge' could be payable.

There are still very few lenders who really appreciate the requirements of those who do not have standard salaried employment. Whether someone is self-employed, a director of a limited company, or employed on a short term contract, income is likely to fluctuate over the years. Flexible and sympathetic underwriting is often required – fortunately a number of lenders will look at your ability to pay rather than just applying standard income multipliers.

A plethora of Mortgage Payment Protection policies have recently been launched by lenders but the small print must be examined carefully. The policies are aimed primarily at employees and so are unlikely to provide adequate protection to the self-employed.

CHAPTER 6: DEALING WITH INCOME & CAREER PROBLEMS

Ella Leonard & John Cole

Introduction

If your career is going through a low or if you need to change your approach, then this section on Claiming Benefit and the following one on Life Coaching may be for you.

Claiming Benefit

As a self-employed person you are allowed to seek help from all sources that are there for the employed. This means, contrary to popular mythology, that you are allowed to sign on and get housing benefit if things fall flat and/or hard times come thick and fast. It may be for only a few weeks or months that you need assistance; it may be for a couple of years, but, whenever the problems start to arise, it is essential to deal with them immediately.

What help is available?
There are varying amounts of income support available. Depending on whether you are single or married, between 18-24 or over 25 these amounts will vary. You could contact your local Citizens Advice Bureau or take a look at the following website which is the Governments site

http://www.direct.gov.uk/en/MoneyTaxAndBenefits/BenefitsTaxCreditsAndOtherSupport/BeginnersGuideTo Benefits/DG_4016266

Support is also available with National Insurance contributions, which are normally credited in full during the period of signing on. Note that the NI contributions are specifically the stamps that all employed people pay on a weekly or monthly basis (see section on Tax NI & VAT). They are different and separate from the NI deductions that are calculated on your annual tax returns. In addition, there are support structures for council tax payments and housing benefits and, where applicable, for child support where not already claimed. These three areas provide essential support in areas that are often the most worrying in terms of stress and insecurity. To know that they are there allows certain pressures to be lifted at a time when there is so much else to cope with. Any benefits you are entitled to will be subject to meeting statutory requirements.

If you do not exceed more than 16 hours work a week, you are automatically eligible for benefits. If you work less than 16 hours a week (two working days) whilst you are signed on it will not affect your benefit, but you are obliged to declare the hours that you work (i.e. are employed). The amount that you are paid for this work does not affect your right to claim benefit. However if the amount you earn and declare is greater than the weekly benefit, then you are not allocated benefit for that particular week. The amount earned by the work does NOT roll over week by week. The amount that constitutes earnings is the net income from the job, thus, if the job has heavy expenses, these do not constitute earnings.

You are able to draw council tax relief immediately you sign on and apply for housing benefits, whether it be mortgage relief or rent paid. If you have a mortgage that was taken out prior to October '95 the new laws about relief payments do not apply.

Full details of all benefits are available from any Social Security office and local DHS offices can supply full details of Housing benefits and Council Tax help. Also check www. dwp.gov.uk .

How long does it take?
Your benefits will be calculated the date you apply and are registered. At present the DHS and Benefits offices take around a week to 10 days to process the applications. Housing benefits can take a little while longer, but everything is back-dated to the day that you apply. The important thing to do is to apply as soon as possible; be patient with the system and keep a record of names and times of conversations with all those that you deal with.

Mortgage Relief

With every mortgage the interest is generally paid in full. So if you have an endowment mortgage the majority of the monthly payment is met, with a repayment mortgage the interest alone is paid. For the first 39 weeks of benefit, the amount paid towards the monthly rent or mortgage is nil. Thereafter the interest is paid at 100%. There is a limit to the amount on which interest is paid on and at present this figure is £100,000. In either case, an approach to your mortgage company to let them know of the difficulty in maintaining the payments will universally be met with understanding and a sympathetic ear. As long as they can see something coming in, they will be helpful. Even if your mortgage is with your bank, do not be afraid to deal with the relevant department. It does NOT jeopardise your standing or position with the bank. There are plans to decrease the payments of housing benefits but these apply to mortgages taken out after October '95. The local benefits office will clarify the present rulings.

Exemptions from Social Security Benefits

You will be ineligible to claim for Social Security Benefits if:

- you or your partner work more than 16 hours a week. However this may not affect you being able to get housing support.
- if your savings are over £16,000. The amount of savings held by your partner is also considered and included in these amounts.

What to expect when signing on

Use every opportunity to look for work while you are signed on and be pro-active. This means visiting all of your existing contacts, looking for job opportunities in the press and using every possible source. Ultimately the term 'actively looking for work' means that the end goal is being in full-time employment. A three monthly interview must be attended at your local employment office where you will need to show them that you are "actively looking for work". These meetings are specifically there to help and advise you – show them you are serious in your quest and they will continue to be helpful.

Life Coaching – John Cole

Bringing Clarity to Your Life
Life coaching is about bringing clarity to your life. Clarity about what you want and what you need. Clarity about what's important, urgent and fundamental to you. Clarity in all you think and say and do. It's as simple as that.

Socrates, arguably the first life coach, summed up the true essence of life coaching over two thousand years ago:

> *"Real understanding comes from within. It cannot be imparted by someone else. And only the understanding that comes from within can lead to true insight."*

How can life coaching help you as a photographer? It can help you keep on track or indeed change track. It can help you assess where you're going and how you're going to get there. Coaching can, in fact, help you gain clarity about any aspect of your career. It doesn't really matter what the issues are – money, time management, change of direction, motivation, running a business, assisting, digital, self promotion, relationships (personal as well as professional), or personal health – the list is limited only by the needs of the individual. The two questions I constantly ask my clients are, 'What do you really want?' and, 'What do you need to do to achieve it?'. With those two questions as a starting point, I use a wide range of coaching tools:

non-judgemental listening, incisive questioning, curiosity, acknowledgement, responsibility, encouragement, reframing, a sprinkling of gentle humour and my two favourites: common sense and empathy.

I challenge clients to change self defeating, limiting beliefs and begin working on a pragmatic program that moves them forward to their goals. In short, how to be happy.

> *"I believe that the very purpose of our life is to seek happiness. That is clear. Whether one believes in religion or not, whether one believes in this religion or that religion, we are all seeking something better in life.*
>
> *The very motion of our life is towards happiness."* *(The Dalai Lama)*

It is important to understand that life coaching is not therapy. Life coaching is for people who are stable and grounded, yet feel stuck and want to move forward in their lives. Therapy often deals with the past, whilst coaching is focused on the present and future.

Life coaching is most definitely not "This year's essential accessory...", as one newspaper recently called it. Life coaching is a tool to add to your camera bag, like a filter or knowledge of Photoshop. If used as a fashion accessory, then it is exactly that, a glittery bauble. If used with intelligence and commitment, this powerful tool can change your life.

Nelson Mandela, like so many great people, was a natural life coach, as he demonstrated in his inaugural speech:

> *"Our deepest fear is not that we are inadequate*
> *Our deepest fear is that we are powerful beyond measure.*
> *It is our light, not our darkness, that most frightens us.*
> *We are all meant to shine as children do.*
> *We are born to manifest the glory of God that is within us.*
> *It is not just in some of us; it is in everyone.*
> *And as we let our light shine, we unconsciously give other people permission to do the same. As we are liberated from our own fear, our presence automatically releases others."*

Life coaching is not magic. In fact, it's hard work and demands perseverance and emotional courage. But if you are willing to make the commitment, then the results are indeed magical.

CHAPTER 7: STANDARDS, MARKETING & REPRESENTATION

Standards & Codes

Gwen Thomas & Janet Ibbotson

Introduction

Marketing yourself and being marketed by others can be the difference between success and mediocrity. As a photographic business you need to be seen and presented in a way that puts you on a par with others. The way you conduct your business is equally important, knowing what to expect and what is expected of you in a business full of photographers vying for commissions can give you the edge you need to succeed.

Standards & Codes

Sustaining a living as a photographer requires an applied knowledge of general business practice and also an understanding of standards specific to the photographic industry.

Standards and codes of practice are necessary in an industry where a small business deals with large corporations and are intrinsic to making a business out of photography. Establishing good business ethics from the first commission gives a photographer the same standing and respect extended to large companies. To have everyone working to the same standards gives photography a strong voice and the respect it deserves. The following codes may appear to emphasise the business of an advertising photographer, but the basic principles apply to all areas of photography.

Portfolio presentation

Portfolio cases should be distinctive, workable and well marked. Bigger is not better – a large, unwieldy portfolio is difficult to courier and less likely to be hauled up the stairs. Delivery should be accompanied by a delivery note with special tabs being kept on any original work submitted. Photographers should always have insurance for their own portfolios even though a folio and its contents are the responsibility of the client/agency from the time it is delivered to them until it is returned to you or your agent. The portfolio is covered by their 'goods in trust' insurance. Remember, however, that if you or your agent send the book in speculatively, and then it is lost, they may not liable, as they did not request the book – you offered to send it in.

The portfolio should not be used by an agency in a 'pitch' unless representing the photographer. A pitch is when the agency is attempting to win a client's business for a specific product and presents a possible campaign using visuals. Permission must be given by the photographer before work is used for pitching and a fee may be charged for this.

Compiling a Portfolio

The content of a book depends entirely on what field of photography you are in but there are general rules. Less is more so do not be tempted to present every piece of work you have ever done and if you haven't done much, don't pad it out with work that doesn't do you credit. Be happy with every shot you have put in your book – if there is any doubt in your mind don't put it in. If your book is called in for a job that falls out of your field don't be tempted to submit work that is not relevant or good enough. This can be detrimental to you, consider ducking out of sending a book altogether if you know it is not right or good enough for the job. And it is not only creatives who view your book. Personal work will impress creatives but if the book is seen by a less visual person, often the client, they may need the reassurance of seeing commissioned pieces. If you are going to blend personal and commissioned work make sure it flows smoothly – if it doesn't, then consider splitting your work into different portfolios. Having another person look over your portfolio will give you a fresh perspective, it is very difficult to be subjective when it is your own work.

Working out your fee

There are no standard fees in photography and it is recommended that the client's budget is established before pricing of the job begins. Photographers' fees, or day rates, need to encompass not only their creativity, experience, specialisation and uniqueness, but also the tools of their trade. These include the cost of running a studio (heat, light, phones, full-time assistants, insurances, etc.), equipment purchases and maintenance. Location photographers will still need to maintain a base/office and this should be included. Work out all these amounts over a year and divide the total by the number of anticipated working days; this figure will represent the minimum fee required before charging for personal expertise. Editorial fees are generally set by the commissioning magazine (see Chapter 10 Editorial for more info).

CHAPTER 7

Pre-production/experimental & speculative photography

Some shoots may require extensive planning, location finding, model casting, pre-production meetings or consultations, and detailed quotes. Fees may be charged for these pre-production costs and should be agreed with the client in advance.

When the client doesn't t know what use the finished work will be put to, they may commission on an experimental basis. Recommended trade practice is to charge a fee of 50% of the normal day rate plus expenses. The work should not be used by the photographer, client or models unless all parties agree. Any use by the client must then produce the other 50% of the fee. Agreements must be reached with any third parties involved in the shoot (eg. set builders, models, and stylists) with regard to payment, and re-negotiations may be necessary, particularly with models, if the work is subsequently used by the client.

Any work done on this basis for less than 50% of the fee is called speculative photography and is unethical, but a minimum payment of expenses should be claimed by a photographer who chooses to work on this basis. If the work runs, a full fee plus expenses should be paid.

Bookings/Art Orders (See chapter 2 for information on contracts)

Bookings can be oral or written, provisional or confirmed. If a photographer already has a provisional booking by another client, the first client should be given the opportunity to confirm and that booking should be honoured. Oral bookings should be followed up by an official art order from the agency/client, before the shoot begins, stating the following:

i) Client, product and agency

ii) Photographer, Art Order No., and date

iii) Format

iv) Agreed fee, Base Usage Rate (see Part 3 chapter 9 Advertising) pre/post production fees

v) Media, territory, exclusivity & time period

vi) Expenses

Editorial commissions are generally made at short notice, but where possible the photographer should email the magazine a confirmation of their conversation, as orders will not normally arrive before the shoot starts. Where possible, request an art order to be emailed before the job commences.

Expenses and advances

Photographers are entitled to request up to 100% of reasonable estimated expenses in advance of large-scale shoots, payable by the first day. On large scale overseas shoots commanding large up-front expenses, the photographer can expect to have the advance paid at least one month prior to commencement of the shoot.

Reasonable expenses should be agreed with the client, and are additional to the fee. They should not exceed the amount stated on the official art order. If, during the shoot, more expenses than agreed are required, the client contact (often an art director/art buyer) must be kept informed as they are incurred. Extra expenses are often at the request of the client, but approval should still be confirmed. Approval from the client should be sought at all times when purchasing props, etc. outright.

Model fees

Model fees include fitting, rates for additional usage and agency commission; model agencies charge 10 – 20% on top of the model's fee, so make sure this is in the budget. Child models require a casting fee. Where possible the client should pay the model agencies direct, but the booking of the models is generally done by the photographer on behalf of the client, although in some circumstances the agency/client will book the models direct and the photographer acts solely as a liaison for casting. Model fees are very specific to the usage, and care should be taken that this usage is the same as the photographer.

Insurance (See chapter 4 for more info)
The cost of insurance policies including goods in trust, public and employer's liability and loss/damage is normally reflected within the photographer's fee. Clients have the option of refusing to pay extra insurance premiums, eg. weather insurance. When a shoot is weather dependent, the client should be given the option of taking out weather insurance. This insurance is optional and can be costly, but its importance should be stressed.

Labour/Subcontractors
Fees for stylists, hairdressers, make-up artists, location finders, set builders and freelance assisting photographers are all payable by the photographer and should be itemised fully and agreed with the client in advance.

Studio & equipment
Basic facilities are generally included in the photographer's fee, but, dependent on the type of photography, hire studios and special equipment may need to be itemised and charged for separately.

Props
The cost of hiring or purchasing props should be itemised, together with any insurance necessary for prop hire. If a stylist has been budgeted for, ensure that the stylist's time and any expenses incurred in securing props has been agreed with the client.

Transport and travel
Transport could include transportation of props and personnel, location vehicles, accommodation, subsistence (meals), and carnets. Carnets are usually necessary when equipment is being taken out of the country, and are basically a listing of the equipment being taken into other countries outside Europe. In countries outside the EU, that country's taxes will have to be paid on equipment where a carnet has not been completed. Carnets and advice are available from the London Chamber of Commerce or can be arranged by a number of companies specialising in obtaining visas and arranging carnets. Mileage is generally charged at RAC or AA current rates, and figures are worked out on the cost of keeping a car on the road over a year. Up to date mileage rates can be found at www.theaa.com/motoring_advice/running_costs/

Cancellation
Cancellation is when a shoot has been confirmed and is then abandoned and not re-booked. Cancellation fees are due only on confirmed bookings. The photographer will have booked time out to complete the work and may have turned down other work on the strength of it. Time will have been spent arranging assistants, models, equipment etc, so the photographer's time should be paid for. Ensure your terms and conditions state that you reserve the right to charge a cancellation fee – this can prevent argument later as it becomes a term of the contract, and not just industry practice. Any expenses already incurred should also be claimed.

General industry charges are as follows, but photographers may have different variations, (all days are working days):

Shoots of 2 days or less duration:

Within 2 days	100% fee + expenses
3 – 6 days	50% fee + expenses
7 days or over	25% fee + expenses

Shoots in excess of 2 days duration:

No. of shoot days or less	100% fee + expenses
Twice No. of shoot days	50% fee + expenses
Excess of twice shoot days	25% fee + expenses

Editorial work is more difficult for calculating cancellation fees, due to the short time span between commission and shoot. Very often the only payment will be actual expenses incurred, but some of the fee should also be claimed for.

Postponement

Postponement is when a new date is given and confirmed, and fees may become payable to cover costs and inconvenience, but are at the photographer's discretion. However, expenses incurred which will have to be paid out again for the new shoot, should be paid in full.

Bookings dependant on weather conditions should be discussed with the client prior to the shoot, weather insurance can be taken out by the client and the premiums paid by them. Recommended trade practice is that 50% of the photographer's fee plus all expenses are payable on postponement due to bad weather.

Rejection

A representative of the client on the shoot, normally the Art Director, accepts or rejects the photography on behalf of the company. If they are present throughout, they will have seen the set, given and taken advice on the presentation of the subject matter and lighting, been shown how the final shot will look, and the final images chosen. Acceptance by this representative is taken that the shoot has produced the agreed images and the photographer has kept their side of the bargain and completed their side of the contract. If no representative is present, then it is generally taken that the photographer's judgement is final.

CHAPTER 7

Rejection after the shoot

If no representative of the client was present, and a portfolio of the photographer's work was seen before the commission, then rejection of the work after the shoot, on aesthetic grounds, is not acceptable. It could be presumed that no direction from, or on behalf of, the client gives the photographer the final say, and that the expertise of the photographer is sufficient. If the client's representative attended the shoot and accepted the photography on the day then, rejection after the shoot on aesthetic grounds is equally unacceptable. The photographer should be paid in full and should not be expected to subsidise any expenses of the shoot. Should a re-shoot be negotiated, new fees and expenses should also be negotiated.

Rejection of work on technical grounds

Work may be rejected for the following technical reasons:

i) Technical failure by the photographer or any service for which it was agreed they were responsible.

ii) The photographer has not produced the details or effects as specified in the brief.

The photographer should be given the opportunity to re-shoot at their own expense. If a re-shoot is not offered or accepted, no fee is payable and any expenses paid in advance should be refunded.

Any rejection of work should be made within a maximum of 10 days from the date the images are delivered to the client.

Non use of accepted work

Work that is accepted, then not used by the client, should be paid for in full. Photographers' licences give the client the right to use the work, it is the clients choice if they decide not to use it.

Liability of work/materials

The photographer is responsible for the safety of the image files until they are delivered to the client. Loss or damage, prior to delivery to the client, would involve a re-shoot at the photographer's expense. Insurance can, and should, be taken out to cover the shoot through all its varying stages. Public and Employer's liability insurance should be held by every photographer (see chapter 3 The Business End).

Paperwork

Estimate *(see appendix for an Estimate template)*

Photographers do not normally "quote" for a job because it is impossible to give a firm figure and a quote is binding. Estimates are based on the information/brief originally supplied by the client and should include the following:

- Agency and Advertiser or Client
- Photographer
- Job description
- Media use/territory/time period
- Right to a credit

- Exclusivity
- Fees (to include the original use)
- Expenses
- Base Usage Rate (see chapter 8 Advertising)
- Contingency (10%)*
- Terms and Conditions

* The contingency figure allows 10% to cover any unforeseen costings, enabling the client to allow for a possible extra charge over the estimated figure up to a maximum of 10%.

Invoice (see appendix for an Invoice template)
Invoices should follow the same format as the estimate, but without the contingency and less any advances paid.

Correct and precise details with regard to the client, dates, and order numbers will help to ensure fast payment and are vital should the invoice not be paid and legal action for recovery required.

Licence (see appendix for a Licence template)
The terms of the licence should have been negotiated at order and estimate stage and is what the fee has been based on. The layout of the licence is more specific than the estimate and invoice and should clearly show:

- Agency and advertiser or client
- Agency/client order No.
- Photographer job No.
- Date
- Photographer and agent
- Specific media (not just 'advertising'!)
- Particular country and language
- No. of years
- Exclusivity clause
- Description of the image/s
- Right to a credit

The licence period is deemed to start on the date of first insertion (when a campaign is first shown/magazine edition is first published) and the time period agreed would start from this date and not the date of the licence. The licence must be in writing and signed by the photographer. A copy should go to the agency on behalf of the photographer and an additional copy should accompany the invoice.

NB. The estimate, invoice and licence (above and illustrated) specify the words 'Agency and Advertiser'. Where the client is a Design Group, or there is no middleman, substitute the wording as appropriate. For specific information on editorial commissions see chapter 10

Model Releases (see appendix for samples)
It is important when using any models, whether professional or not, that the use the image is to be put to is understood by all concerned. Model Release Forms should be used and clearly define the fee, territory, time period and media. Copies should be given to both the client and the model. Large model agencies advise their models not to sign releases, and so in these cases ensure the booking/confirmation form, given by the model agency, states the correct use as agreed.

The agency/client must be informed as to how, where and when the model agency will allow the model's image to be used. Should the client use the work for a different purpose than originally agreed, the model agency will look to the photographer for extra payment. Where possible, further usage should be negotiated by the client directly with the model agency and it is strongly advised that photographers do not get involved. Usage fees for models are dependant on the amount of exposure the model's image is to receive. Extensive exposure of a model using a particular brand will narrow their market for further work with other brand products and re-usage negotiations may be based on this fact. The client is best placed to agree extended use.

Work placed with a stock library should normally have paperwork showing that the models, whether professional or the general public, have agreed to the image being used. Laws of Privacy exists in almost every other country, but not in the UK, so care should be taken when using members of the public in any image used for advertising purposes (see chapter 2 Privacy). Stock libraries generally don't like accepting work that does not have clearance by the people within the image (see Chapter 13 Stock Photography). If they do accept them then the use they can be licenced for will be curtailed and the images should clearly show 'not model released'.

Payment

Payment from the agency is expected within 30 days from the date of the invoice. Invoices should be submitted promptly and interest can be charged on overdue accounts under the Late Payment of Commercial Debts (Interest) Act 1998 (see chapter 2). If an invoice is not queried within 10 days it can be deemed as accepted.

Social Media

Simon Leach

The actual profitability gained through using social networking media is difficult to quantify for most photographers. Many will tell you that although they cannot directly attribute financial gain to their social networking efforts, there does seem to be a gain in terms of profile; awareness of both the photographer and their work, when social media is utilised effectively.

Like any other portal for your work, with social media you need to focus. Do not try to spread yourself too thinly or try to cover too many bases. You need to decide why you wish to use social networking and what benefit you hope to gain from your efforts. Are you wanting to stay in touch with agency creatives or client contacts when they change company? Are you wanting to tell everyone about your latest project? Or do you want to post general photographic interest items to show a wider knowledge of the craft or industry? Do you want a social network to be the outlet of your thoughts and ideas? Or is it there to drive more traffic to your own website? Generating more hits and aiding search ratings as a result?

Remember social networking sites are not the end to all your marketing worries they are just another tool, which you must learn to understand and control, if you are going to make them effective for you. How they are effective can also depend on your market and who your buyers are. Try to consider seriously who you are wanting to attract and what content they may find most appealing. Creating a buzz around your personal projects or edition print sales will obviously require a different strategy to connecting with and gaining the trust of those commissioning internationally based industrial shoots. Social networking done properly and effectively will also be time consuming and require new content at a reasonably prolific level. You need to choose the particular medium you wish to try and you need to be pro-active in terms of keeping it refreshed on a regular basis. This is certainly likely to be more regularly than perhaps your own web site or print portfolio, although there can be some variation to your personal preference, as always consistency is highly recommended both in terms of regularity and of content posted. By being consistent you can enhance 'the Brand' which is you and your work and your followers will develop a firm understanding of what they can expect from you.

Which ever route you choose, blog, networking, photo-sharing, there are some simple rules which you should apply to all.

Read carefully the terms and conditions. Make sure you understand them and take note of whether there are any differences in the way they treat words, stills or video content. Remember these terms will change at intervals, so review them when changes are notified and make sure you are happy with how the site managers control your content.

Consolidate the outlets you have to a number that works for you. Although you can trial different sites for personal preference, you should consolidate quickly to a number that you feel able to maintain and that you feel are an outlet to your chosen market. You should not waste to much time on vague hopes of success and you do not want to build up to many followers on a site which you cannot practically maintain longer term. Remember that some sites will need more work to keep fresh and interesting than others, but ultimately a badly maintained site can actually be worse than no site at all. Be careful not to fall into the trap of opening every account possible during a quiet week only to forget them when you are busy the next.

Finally always be careful about uploading, posting or re-posting information on others, even when this has been posted elsewhere first. Remember that you can be held legally responsible for information or opinions you make public about other individuals or companies.

Photographers and Agents

Niall Horton Stephens

What an agent does...

As a photographer you need to decide whether or not an agent can provide something that you cannot provide yourself… you know you can take good pictures, but can you do that and still handle every other aspect of your career?

So what does an agent offer? They probably provide some or all of the following:

- An understanding of the contemporary marketplace and an advisory role with the goal of creating the most marketable portfolio (and digital portfolio) of work, via editing of existing material and encouraging creation of new work. A good agent should have a feel for where a particular portfolio has weak areas and ideas on how to plug these gaps. They will know what the market trends are, who the competition is and what they're shooting, and should plan to give your career longevity. They will also get blunt feedback from folio showings that viewers may be reticent to give to the artist themselves. As the creator, you may in any case be the worst judge of your own work.
- A good idea of what markets to promote your work in and access to those markets. Many agents target ad agencies as potential clients. They should know who best to approach, have access to them, and ideally have existing (good) working relationships with those people.
- An understanding of the different marketing tools available and an ability to pursue various routes to put the photographer's work in front of potential clients. This might be via personal portfolio presentations but should also include web presence and marshalling mail-outs and e-cards.
- All of the above deal with the really big thing, that is getting work through the door! However, once an enquiry comes in, the agent should, in cahoots with the photographer, follow up in a professional and timely fashion providing sensibly pitched estimates and plans of work. They should understand different areas of the market to pitch realistic, achievable fees and of course offer guidance on all aspects of usage, copyright and best working practice throughout the project from inception to completion. Of course where negotiation is taking place it is much easier for an agent to negotiate for you as a third party, than when you negotiate for yourself and are "put on the spot". For example, the agent has the luxury of saying that "they will have to revert to the photographer" whereupon a considered strategy can be put in place.
- Some agents will get involved with all aspects of the production of commissioned projects, some will not, but a good agent will be involved enough to help maintain and nurture the relationship with the client whilst ensuring that the project runs smoothly and changes to brief etc. are reacted to in the appropriate matter. Where issues arise the agent will advise how best to deal with them. They may not always take the photographer's side and may on occasions argue the client's case in areas of contention, both in the interests of fair play and protecting reputations all round. This is in the interests of maintaining a satisfied client that will return again. Sometimes the benefit of having an agent is to keep certain tough conversations away from the creative process – leaving the photographer free to be… creative!
- An agent provides their reputation and the reputation of their whole roster of other artists and uses it to enhance the reputation of the single photographer – the sum total hopefully greater than the separate parts. Commissioners like the reassurance that working with a good agent provides. They will believe that the agent has preselected the photographers that they represent from a much larger number and that they are prepared to stake their own reputation on those photographers. They know that the agent cannot deliver a shoddy job in a relatively small, incestuous marketplace where reputation is everything; the agent cannot afford, for their own sake and for the sake of all their artists, to tarnish this reputation.

Will an agent want me? Do I need an agent?

So, we've established the benefits of having an agent, but will an agent want you and do you need one?

Put simply, if an agent thinks that they can sell you, they will want you. Accordingly, to find your agent your prospects will be improved if you are already marketable, if your work has direction, cohesion and potential commercial appeal. It is not a bad thing to pigeon-hole yourself in order to gain a toe-hold in the market. A master of one area is easier to sell than a jack-of-all-trades. Remember that you are selling yourself as a person too. You need to show the agent that you have the right attitude, drive and energy without being overbearing: a team player with a "can do" attitude. Your agent will invest a lot of their time and effort in you and will therefore want to know that you will be there shoulder to shoulder with them, providing new folio material, shooting tests and cultivating relationships with clients.

There are different kinds of agents, so do your research and find one that's a good fit. For instance, some agents deal exclusively with the fashion world, some only pursue ad industry work and others approach design, corporate and editorial clients. The agent's website is a good place to start. You can see if there is a gap in the agent's existing stable that you would neatly fit in to. It's not necessarily a bad thing to overlap a little with one of their other photographers as sometimes a couple of talents working in a similar area can attract client enquires along the "street of tailors" principle. A new agent may be looking to build their stable, may not have many other photographers on the books and as a result have more time to devote to you. On the down side they may not have the depth of knowledge or the contacts that a more experienced agent would. If you join a more established agency you may be joining a group of ten plus other photographers. Although it may be harder to get the individual attention, a thriving, buzzing business is often more visible in the marketplace and a high level of project traffic often generates further new work. Success breeds success! Many London based agents are members of PhotoAgentsLondon, which has an established best working practice (published on their website).

When approaching an agent, it's an audition. Have a good web link that you can send in as a first step and when following up with a phone call don't be surprised if the agent can't spend much time talking to you; they get lots of enquiries. Rest assured though, if your work is interesting and shows promise you'll be noted. Good agents are always pleased to look at web links and like to keep abreast of new talent. They will get back in touch if something has clicked and once your work has "broken the ice" you can use your personality to sell yourself. The agent will want to gauge how personable you are going to be for their clients to work with and how well you are likely to deal with meetings and behave on shoot. When you're working with a client, the agent is staking their reputation on you. Of course, how the agent is perceived will reflect on you too; they are the first contact point when your work receives an enquiry and a potential client is buying in to the agent as well as you, so it'll help if they are liked and respected. If the agent feels you're not quite ready to launch on to the market they may offer to give one-to-one folio advice and want to keep in touch. This can be a helpful opportunity worth making the most of. It is not unusual for an agent to punt a new talent towards an appropriate client enquiry even before a formal working relationship is established.

Do you really need an agent? In truth, there's not necessarily anything that they do that you can't do yourself. You can market yourself, you can seek your own work, you can show your work around town, and you can produce and negotiate your own shoots. None of this is rocket science and there are plenty of photographers that do it themselves. In fact it's a very good way to understand what the market is really like, and if you do seek an agent later, the fact that you have this experience and have already begun to carve yourself a profile may well be an incentive to take you on.

Practicalities

So you've got an agent, you've worked together to structure the folio, promotional material has been printed, you're on the agency website and the folio is doing the rounds, but there's no work coming in! Well, don't necessarily blame the agent. The adage "Rome wasn't built in a day" is true here. It does take a while to establish new work in clients' heads, often requiring several folio showings and a demonstration that the work is moving forwards, growing and worthy of a client's attention. If after some time the work still isn't shifting then maybe some reassessment of the balance of the portfolio is required in context of client feedback. Sometimes work can look good but doesn't sell! Is anything else wrong? Are you providing the new work that is the lifeblood of promotion? Your agent can't just show the same client the same work over and over again. A lack of new work does not just leave your work standing still – it causes it to move backwards! Remember that an agent has done the key part of their job by getting your work in front of a client when there is a commission in the offing. Thereafter, it comes down to whether or not your work is preferred over the other photographers that are being considered. You will rarely be the only contender.

Work considerately with your agent. Neither party should play the blame game, but do work together to analyse your current standing. Be a team player. Nothing creates ill feeling and mutually diminishes reputation than bad-mouthing behind each other's backs. It's not a bad idea to have a contract as it forces both parties to address all sorts of issues and establish levels and areas of responsibility. PhotoAgentsLondon have a standardised contract which covers most of the contentious areas... who's going to render invoices, who pays for folio transport, who pays for promotions, how many portfolios are going to be created, who is going to maintain and insure the folios, what are the commission rates, is there a retainer fee, what territories will the agent act for the photographer in, will the agent deal with all commissions or will they exclude editorial work, what are the contract severance terms, etc., etc. Not all agents work in the same way so it's best to get everything clear.

Remember, you're in it together – it's a marriage! For better, for worse, for richer, for poorer.

CHAPTER 7

Collecting Societies

Design & Artists Copyright Society

Introduction

This section describes the role of collecting societies, how they can help photographers to manage certain of their rights and how photographers might benefit from this. In the UK, the Design and Artists Copyright Society (DACS) undertakes this function on behalf of visual creators including photographers.

Many photographers have considerable first-hand experience of managing certain rights in their photographs, (or *artistic works* as they are known under copyright law) or alternatively, have arranged for them to be managed through an agent or photographic library. In these circumstances, one might typically envisage the transaction between the photographer (or the photographer's agent) and another party to permit the reproduction of an artistic work the photographer has created. Any specific requirements or restrictions negotiated between the parties would be incorporated into a contract, known as a *licence*.

This particular area of activity is generally known as licensing of *primary* uses. But there are also circumstances which lead to the *secondary* use of artistic works, enabling further or multiple copies of a work to be made without prior reference to the photographer.

For example, the reproduction of an artistic work in a book constitutes a primary use. If the same reproduction were photocopied, this would constitute a secondary use. Both acts of reproduction are restricted by copyright law and as such need to be licensed by the copyright owner in order to become permitted acts.

Photographers have therefore looked towards a solution which composers, musicians and authors have known about for many years: the *collecting society*.

What is a collecting society?

Collecting societies are not a new phenomenon. They have long existed for composers and publishers of music, who, in the early years of the 20th century, were concerned that the advent of broadcasting and recording technologies would result in the mass commercial exploitation of their work without any recompense to the creator of the original work. The Performing Rights Society and the Mechanical Copyright Protection Society (now joined and known as The Music Alliance) were created to regulate public performance and mechanical copying of copyright music. In more recent times, recording companies and performers have benefited from legislation guaranteeing them income from radio broadcasts of recorded music.

Collecting societies are normally not-for-profit enterprises, although they operate within a commercial environment, with a corresponding need to apply effective financial and managerial strategies to their business operations. Typically, collecting societies are funded by commission income, which is deducted from the licence revenue they collect on behalf of the creators they represent. Most societies are membership organisations, governed by a board of directors, which will include members, and others appointed for their business, legal or relevant expertise. The business will be run on a day-to-day basis by a professional employed staff, aiming to further the objectives of the society's Memorandum and Articles of Association.

In recognition of the global marketplace in which creators participate, collecting societies operate internationally through a network of related societies, bound to each other by reciprocal agreements, which allow each society to represent the members of another society within its own territory. This arrangement ensures that the members of each society in the network are represented globally whilst offering the consumer a convenient and comprehensive point of access to many creators of copyright material.

What do Collecting Societies do?

Licensing

Members will typically join a collecting society in order to have all or some of their copyright administered by the society. Typically, the society will be thus mandated to negotiate licences for primary uses with consumers wishing to use the work on behalf of individual members. The consumer pays a fee to the society, from which it deducts commission, and passes on the remainder as a royalty to the member. In buying the licence, the consumer purchases "peace of mind" in the form of an indemnity provided by the society. This guarantees that permission has been granted by the member entitling the consumer to use the work and thus protects the consumer from an infringement claim.

Collective licensing

It is generally recognised that whilst primary uses can be licensed transaction ally on behalf of an individual photographer, it is not usually practical to licence secondary uses in the same way. In the photocopying example, the sheer volume of photocopies made every day renders the negotiation of a transactional licence for every act of copying nonsensical, yet some form of licence is essential if the consumer is to be persuaded to respect copyright and pay to use copyright material.

Licensing of secondary uses often takes place through collective agreements or blanket licences. These licences aim to provide a practical solution to the problems associated with high volume use of copyright material where the rights of many might be exploited (in photocopying, authors and publishers have rights in the books and magazines copied in addition to photographers and other creators of artistic works). Blanket licences usually provide the consumer with permission to make a variety of uses of the material on behalf of all the creators whose rights are potentially affected. Blanket licence fees and terms are negotiated in advance by the representative collecting societies with consumer representatives (such as trade associations). Negotiations are typically long and complex, and may involve substantial sums of money. The resultant revenue is then shared out amongst the collecting societies, and commission is deducted before the money is further distributed by each society amongst its constituents.

What distinguishes blanket licences from transactional licences is the scope of indemnity provided by the society. In photocopying, a licence that only indemnified the consumer to copy the works of some photographers (such as those who are members of the society) but not others would be worthless, in the same way that a television licence which permitted viewing of only parts of a programme but not others would be. Therefore, the collecting society has to offer a licence that covers the works of all creators within their repertoire whether they are members or not. Membership of collecting societies is normally voluntary, and it is almost impossible to represent 100% of the repertoire through collecting society membership agreements. All the same, consumers need to be completely confident that they are fully protected against claims of copyright infringement if they are to be convinced to buy a licence. Thus, the society will generally offer an indemnity to the consumer against claims made by members and non-members. By offering this indemnity, collecting societies assume legal responsibility for satisfying claims in relation to use of the works of non-members, provided the use was within the terms of the licence granted to the user.

Where artistic works are licensed collectively under blanket licence schemes, photographers may stand to benefit and it is worth considering joining a collecting society. In this regard, the activities of a collecting society complement the professional practice of photographers. By registering a claim to a share of blanket licence revenue collected, the photographer still preserves his or her right to control the use of their work in the normal way. In supporting the work of collecting societies, and asserting their rights photographers can help to generate greater respect for copyright, strengthen the negotiating position of collecting societies and thus help to generate more revenue for visual artists.

For information on Extended Collective Licensing see Chapter 1, Copyright.

Collecting for the Visual Arts

The Design and Artists Copyright Society (DACS)

The Design and Artists Copyright Society Limited (DACS) is the copyright and collecting society for visual artists in the UK. It is an independent, not-for-profit membership society open to all visual artists irrespective of the artistic discipline in which they practice. DACS was formed in 1984 by a group of artists to administer and protect the rights of visual creators in the UK, and currently represents the primary copyright interests of over 36,000 British and international artists. DACS issues individual primary licences on behalf of its members for the primary use of artistic works, subject to the authorised consent of the artist (or artist's heirs) concerned. A further 16,000 visual artists also mandate DACS through 15 professional organisations to represent their rights when secondary uses are licensed through blanket schemes. There are currently four photographers' organisations that mandate DACS in this way: AOP, British Institute of Professional Photographers, Chartered Institute of Journalists and National Association of Journalists.

The blanket licence revenue negotiated and collected by DACS is then distributed to members and non-members (including photographers) through the DACS's 'Payback' scheme.

CHAPTER 7

What is Payback, and how does it benefit photographers?

Payback is the name of the annual distribution of the licence revenue DACS collects for secondary rights uses. DACS collects this revenue from a range of sources where rights have been subject to secondary use in addition to the photocopying example already described: cable re-transmission of terrestrial television broadcasts, reprographic copying (photocopying), off-air recording of television programmes by educational establishments and other similar schemes. During Payback 2002, over half a million pounds was available to visual artists, including photographers with a valid claim. A photographer or other visual artist need not be a member of DACS to make a claim to Payback for a share of the revenue DACS collects.

DACS's distribution policy has been formulated with the direct participation of the various mandating organisations and DACS is committed to ensuring that its distribution practices have the credibility provided by the involvement and continuing endorsement of the various constituencies it represents. DACS has advertised Payback campaigns in a range of publications, and on its website, and is continually monitoring the media for more opportunities to reach photographers and others with the message that money is collected on their behalf, and they should claim it. Photographers who have not made a claim for their share of Payback income before should let DACS that they wish to do so, in order to receive details of future Payback campaigns via the DACS website http://www.dacs.org.uk/for-artists/payback.

Artists Re-sale Right

The Artist's Resale Right was introduced in the UK in 2006, and may entitle you to a royalty when your work is resold by an art market professional. An art market professional is defined as someone "acting in the course of a business of dealing in works of art". In practice this includes galleries, auction houses and art dealers, but in general it excludes museums and private individuals. The right doesn't apply to all sales. You're only entitled to a royalty if the following conditions are met.

Sale Price	An artwork must sell for €1,000 or more to qualify for a resale royalty. As the threshold is given in Euros we use the exchange rate on the date of sale to work out the threshold in Sterling.
Type of Sale	The Artist's Resale Right only covers works sold on the secondary market with the involvement of art market professionals; it doesn't cover works being sold for the first time. Sales between private individuals or between a private individual and a museum are exempt.Where an art market professional is using a web-based platform or service such as eBay or ArtBank to conduct their sales, then a royalty is due providing the sale satisfies all other qualifying criteria.
Type of Artist	You must also be a national of a country in the European Economic Area (EEA). If you have dual nationality, for instance if you are American but also hold a British passport, you may also be entitled to a resale royalty.

For more information see http://www.dacs.org.uk/for-artists/artists-resale-right

Enforcement of the law

The 1988 Copyright Design and Patents Act (as amended) provides for a number of civil and criminal remedies in respect of unlawful reproduction of copyright works, and it may be open to an individual (or the collecting society to which the creator belongs) to pursue infringements of copyright through the courts. Most collecting societies take protection of their members' copyright very seriously and will aim to promote compliance and take steps to remedy the unlicensed use of members' works.

The Act also provides the consumer with the right to refer a collecting society to the Copyright Tribunal if a licensing scheme it operates is considered to be unreasonable or in breach of competition law. Collecting societies cannot themselves refer consumers to the Copyright Tribunal and must rely on the Small Claims Court or the High Court to take legal action against a consumer.

Regulation of collecting societies

Collecting societies are usually registered companies and as such are regulated by Companies House and the Office of Fair Trading and are subject to all legislation affecting business practice. The Department of Trade and Industry is the Government ministry with responsibility for the copyright industry, and the Patent Office is the department within it that deals with copyright matters.

Increasingly, collecting societies are being encouraged by the European Parliament and by the British Government to operate transparently and to adopt business practices that enshrine the principles of best practice. The British Copyright Council has introduced a voluntary 'Principles for Collective Management Organisations Code of Conduct' which has been widely accepted and recognised. However, there is no statutory body that directly regulates the conduct of a society or the scope and the terms of any licences it may offer.

Other activities of collecting societies

In addition to licensing the use of their members' works, collecting societies often undertake a range of other activities. Many seek to promote and protect copyright in other ways such as through educational work, and through lobbying around legislative developments at national, European and international levels. Some collecting societies provide an advice service for their members, and other services such as professional insurance policies and membership benefit schemes. Some collecting societies also set up trust funds or grant giving bodies to distribute licence revenue, which has not been unclaimed or cannot be distributed. Such funds normally aim to benefit the constituency represented by the collecting society: for example, the Performing Rights Society Foundation provides grants to fund new music.

Unions and Associations

Gwen Thomas

Why join?

As individuals, photographers often find it difficult to have their voices heard – unless they are in the unique position of being able to refuse work when the contracts they are asked to work under are untenable. Without a way of networking with others of a like mind, they can become isolated and oblivious to the fact that the problems they may be facing are not unique to them.

This is just one of the reasons for joining an association or union who are in a better position to negotiate, lobby and set standards. Most of these bodies specialise n a particular area of photography and are able to advise, protect, promote and educate in their particular fields. There is no rivalry between the bodies, most sit on committees together to pool their knowledge and speak as one voice when the need arises – as it did when the Copyright Designs and Patents Act 1988 was being debated by the legislators.

The associations and unions mentioned below represent photographers and other creators in the visual arena, if you search the web you will find others, but these are the main bodies:

CHAPTER 7

Association of Photographers (AOP)

The Association of Photographers was first formed in 1968 as the Association of Fashion and Advertising Photographers and is one of the most prestigious professional photographers' associations in the world. The Association's aims remain the same today as they were more than 40 years ago: to promote and protect the worth and standing of its members, to vigorously defend, educate and lobby for the interests and rights of all photographers, especially in the commercial photographic industry.

The Association brings professional photographers together and provides a sense of community that is simply unavailable anywhere else. We promote the highest levels of achievement and we lobby for our members' interests at all levels.

Membership is open to:

Professional Photographers, Assisting Photographers, Agents and Students. http://www.the-aop.org/

Association of Illustrators (AOI)

The Association of Illustrators (AOI) is a not-for-profit trade organisation promoting contemporary illustration and maintaining industry standards. Established in 1973 the AOI has worked successfully with businesses and colleges to increase the standing of illustration as a profession and improve commercial and ethical conditions. With a membership that includes freelance illustrators, agents, students and colleges the AOI continues to support and educate future generations at every stage of their career.

Membership	AOI services include an advice line for contracts and pricing, an extensive pricing survey with rates of pay across all sectors, portfolio advice, and a wide range online advice and resources in the members section of this website.
Campaigning	The AOI actively campaigns to maintain and protect the rights of our members through the Pro-Action Campaign and Liaison Group, the British Copyright Council, the Creators Rights Alliance and the European Illustrators Forum.
Varoom! and VaroomLab	The AOI publishes a quarterly Magazine, featuring articles and editorial on current illustration practice. The AOI is the founder member of VaroomLab, a forum for academic enquiry and debate on illustration set up in partnership with a number of leading Universities.
Exhibition and Events	A regular programme of talks, seminars, training events, partnership projects, education programmes and exhibitions for students, illustrators, commissioners and the general public.

AOI Illustration Awards	The AOI is the producer of the UK's only jury selected international illustration competition celebrating the work of new graduates and professional illustrators.
Publication	The AOI publishes a range of titles including The Illustrator's Guide to Law and Business Practice and contact directories for commissioners in the editorial, advertising and publishing sectors. http://www.theaoi.com

British Association of Picture Libraries & Agents (BAPLA)
Members include the major news, stock and production agencies as well as sole traders and cultural heritage institutions. A substantial percentage of images seen every day in print and digital media is supplied by BAPLA members.

BAPLA's core objectives:

- Represent picture libraries and agencies of all sizes and types.
- Encourage best practice within the industry.
- Lobby at UK and international level to ensure the core principles of our industry are protected.
- Develop and deliver solutions on 21st Century copyright.
- Channel the knowledge and expertise of the wider picture community.

BAPLA is steered by an elected voluntary Executive Committee of seven officers, supported by two permanent office staff, a freelance senior lobbying consultant and a number of subcommittees. Our work is funded by membership fees and in return we are dedicated to supporting our members by providing day-to-day business support and by representing our industry on a national and international level. www.bapla.org

British Institute of Professional Photography (BIPP)
The British Institute of Professional Photography (BIPP) is an internationally recognised qualifying organisation with over 100 years of experience in supporting and networking photographers. We have over **3,200** members worldwide, covering every discipline of photography. The core aims of BIPP are to train, qualify and support professional photographers. We offer a challenging qualifications structure, a full programme of training courses and events and a number of preferential deals on useful products and services. We also work with a number of colleges, including the Defence School of Photography and the College of Policing to ensure the future of the professional photographic industry. One of the key areas of our work is representation, we represent professional photography to government and industry.

BIPP is a not-for-profit organisation, run by photographers, in conjunction with a small Head Office team. Our Advisory Boards, Board of Directors (elected by our Members) and all Regional Committees are run by volunteers, who give their time freely. **www.bipp.com**

Broadcast Entertainment Cinematograph and Theatre Union (BECTU)
BECTU is the UK's media and entertainment trade union; sectors covered include broadcasting, film, independent production, theatre and the arts, leisure and digital media. The union represents staff, contract and freelance workers who are based primarily in the United Kingdom. The key aims of the union are to: **protect jobs; increase membership; win new recognition agreements; improve pay and conditions of service, including pensions.**

- BECTU provides a wide range of services to its circa 25,000 members, including: Negotiating pay, conditions and contracts with employers
- Personal advice and representation for individual members
- Advice and representation on health and safety
- Benefits and services for BECTU members
- Training support and courses
- Networking events and career development opportunities
- Union journal, Stage Screen and Radio, published six times a year.
- Website designed to improve access to the union's advice and support.

The union is financed entirely by individual subscriptions from members. Membership is voluntary, and anyone working or seeking employment in the sectors covered by BECTU can join online www.bectu.org.uk

Chartered Institute of Journalists

The Chartered Institute of Journalists is the oldest professional body for Journalists in the world. It was founded – as the National Association of Journalists – in 1884 and six years later was granted its Royal Charter by Queen Victoria, to protect and serve those employed in the field of journalism.

The Institute combines the role of professional society with that of a trade union – known as the IoJ(TU). The Institute's union section protects its members' interests in the workplace and campaigns for better conditions for working journalists.

The Institute's professional side is concerned with the standards and ethics of the media, the protection of journalistic freedom, training and administers the Institute's many charities.

The International Division has members in more than 30 countries who joined to be members of the senior professional organisation of journalists and who support the Institute's principles of honest reporting, independence and being apolitical. **http://www.ioj.co.uk/**

Editorial Photographers UK (EPUK)

EPUK was founded in 1999 by a small group of photographers who wanted to create an email group to address business issues affecting photographers working in the UK and Irish markets.

Inspired by the original Editorial photographers email discussion list, EPUK has informal links with other photographic organisations such as the Association of Photographers (AOP) and the National Union of Journalists (NUJ) and the PLUS Coalition. However, EPUK remains an independent organisation. Everything EPUK does is produced by full-time photographers working in their spare time. EPUK's moderators work behind the scenes making the list run smoothly, as well as vetting membership, writing website articles and working with other photographers groups.

All photographers working for the UK or Irish editorial markets are welcome to apply for membership. EPUK is entirely free to its members, although we occasionally ask for voluntary donations to go towards covering the running costs such as our server, domains and software. EPUK is generally funded by hosting other lists, and by website promotions and advertising.

The main EPUK list works via email discussions. Say you want to ask a question about a magazine's rates, or a newspaper's record of rights grabs: you put your query in an email to the list address. That then gets sent out to each of EPUK's 1000+ members, each of whom can reply, and their reply is then posted to all EPUK members in return. Because of the speed of our servers, this pretty much happens in 'real time', so you can get an answer very, very quickly. In a typical day, there will be usually be six or seven topics being discussed, with around 30 emails. http://www.epuk.org/

Institute of Medical Illustrators (IMI)

The Institute of Medical Illustrators was founded in 1968 to bring together the several disciplines of medical illustration, and since that time IMI has set and maintained standards for the profession. We represent Clinical Photographers, Healthcare Designers, Medical Artists and Clinical Video Producers both in the UK and internationally. For its membership, IMI provides a rich network of fellow professionals, working together to improve and develop medical illustration by means of conferences, courses, resources and regional meetings.

IMI introduced the first Diploma in Medical Illustration in this country and in conjunction with Glasgow Caledonian University, this was validated as the first BSc in Medical Illustration in the world. In partnership with Westminster University we developed the first and only BSc (Hons) in Clinical Photography. Post-graduate courses in clinical photography and healthcare design have also been developed with Staffordshire and Cardiff Universities. Qualified members are entitled to use the letters MIMI after their name.

IMI provides its members with the umbrella of a Code of Professional Conduct and a Continuing Professional Development scheme, which guarantee employers well qualified and up-to-date staff. The Fellowship of IMI is the advanced practitioner grade and is a prized distinction, demonstrating outstanding professional achievement. IMI has negotiated full registered status with the National Register of Medical Illustration Practitioners for all its qualified

Members who, since 1st January 2001, are entitled to use the letters RMIP after their names. IMI's major refereed publication, the Journal of Visual Communication in Medicine, is widely recognised as the leading European publication in the field, while IMI News, its sister publication, carries up-to-the-minute reports of current activity.

At a National level, IMI constantly campaigns to improve recognition of the profession and is the principal body named by the Department of Health for consultation by Trusts on matters concerning Medical Illustration. IMI is an active member of the Committee for the Accreditation of Medical Illustration Practitioners (CAMIP) and is working with that body to seek national registration of all medical illustrators. IMI will continue, unashamedly, to promote its standards to government, to employers and to potential Members. Without a doubt, IMI membership and qualifications provide a solid foundation on which to build a successful career in medical illustration. http://www.imi.org.uk/

Master Photographers Association (MPA)

Established in 1952, the Master Photographers Association is the United Kingdom's only organisation for qualified and professional photographers.

The MPA offers members a variety of membership benefits, including education, qualifications, informative regional meetings, national seminars, business building promotions and marketing support.

All qualified members adhere to a strict Code of Conduct and have undergone qualification to at least Licentiate standard. Established in 1952 the MPA has promoted true professionalism in photography for 60 years, the UK's qualifying body for full-time professional photographers. Each must have undergone a rigorous assessment of their work – and only then do they appear in our Online Directory. http://www.thempa.com/

National Union of Journalists (NUJ)

Founded in 1907, the NUJ is one of the biggest journalists' unions in the world. The industry has never needed an active and strong union as much as it does now.

- The National Union of Journalists is the voice for journalists and journalism.
- The NUJ is an inclusive union and represents a broad range of media professionals.
- We strive to improve the pay and conditions of our members and protect and promote media freedom, professionalism and ethical standards.
- The NUJ is an active union – our members take part in campaigning and negotiating to ensure we are properly rewarded for the skilled work we do.

The union is represented in towns and cities all over the UK, Ireland and parts of Europe. NUJ members work together to improve living standards and working lives. They work across the media – as staffers, casuals and freelances. Members work in broadcasting, newspapers, magazines, books, in public relations and in new media. Our members are linked to journalists and trade unionists throughout the world. Together we're stronger and we can make a difference.

The NUJ rules state that "[t]he union shall consist of journalists, including photographers, creative artists working editorially in newspapers, magazines, books, broadcasting, public relations and information, and electronic media; or as advertising and fashion photographers, advertising copywriters, editorial computer systems workers..."

The NUJ represents journalists working in a broader variety of roles than the ONS category – our members also include photographers, producers, presenters, website managers, content providers, advertising copyrighters, designers, social media officers, bloggers, podcasters, press officers, communications officers, photo and video journalists. Some of our members working in magazines, books, PR and communications don't call themselves journalists but they are still members of our union. http://www.nuj.org.uk

Picture Researchers Association (PRA)

The PRA encourages active picture researchers, picture editors and picture managers to join. There are three categories of membership depending on experience. We offer members:

- Information on where to find pictures, copyright advice, and other resources from the vast amount of knowledge our membership has built up over the years
- PRA Forum – accessible by paid- up members only
- Members Area – List your experience & contact details
- Job vacancies – Permanent posts are mailed to our membership when we are notified about them. Full & Introductory members can obtain freelance engagements through the PRA Forum.
- Photography Focus: A showcase of a leading editorial photographer
- Agency Focus: A showcase of new, unusual and specialized sources
- News: Industry; Copyright; Film & Footage + an on line news feed (accessible on line or via RSS feeds)
- What's On: Events & Forthcoming Exhibitions
- Social Networking (Twitter, Facebook & Forum)
- Careers advice and information
- Information Technology Advice
- Montage Magazine – ebooks/back issue

Anyone wishing to employ an experienced freelance researcher can do so by emailing the freelance register: or searching our membership list for a member with the appropriate skills. If you need to discuss your project in more detail, send an email via our contacts page – marking your subject: Freelance Project

This service and any specific advice required by the client, prior to engaging a PRA member, is offered confidentially and free of charge.

You can also enquire regarding an expert researcher/photobuyer for your project. The PRA is happy to provide advice to other professional organisations and individuals, although services to our members have priority. http://www.picture-research.org.uk/

Royal Photographic Society (RPS)

The Royal Photographic Society is an Educational Charity promoting both the art and science of photography. Membership is open to all, whatever level of experience or knowledge. No qualifications are required to join, just a passion and love for one or more of photography's myriad of genres, technologies and applications.

Most of our members join to further their own photography and to embrace the challenge of working towards our world recognized Distinctions (LRPS, ARPS and FRPS) and Imaging Science Qualifications (QIS, GIS, AIS and ASIS).

By attending Society National, Regional and Group Events, our members enjoy unparalleled opportunities to share knowledge, meet and learn from other photographers and to develop their photographic interests and skills.

Open International Print and Projected Image Exhibitions are held annually alongside an Audio Visual Festival and members' exhibitions.

The Royal Photographic Society is well respected for its outstanding achievement in Education. Although the majority of its work focuses on supporting and organising practical workshop and lectures it also organises community projects and work in schools and colleges.

Our internationally renowned Awards are presented annually, recognising the highest achievements in all fields of photography – Albert Watson HonFRPS and Annie Liebovitz HonFRPS being recent Centenary Medal recipients.

The Society has a long and proud History, established as The Photographic Society in 1853 in the pioneering days of photography, it became Royal by decree in 1894 and in 2004 it was presented with a Royal Charter. The Society's Collection of priceless photographs and historical items is now housed at the National Media Museum, for the Nation. http://www.rps.org/

Fighting your corner in the wider market

British Copyright Council (BCC)

Founded in 1965 and incorporated in 2007, the British Copyright Council is a not-for-profit organisation that provides a forum for discussion of copyright law and related issues at UK, European and International levels. The BCC is independent, receives no government funding and is the only organisation of its kind in the UK. We aim to provide an effective, authoritative and representative voice for the copyright community. We represent those who create, hold interests in or manage rights in literary, dramatic, musical and artistic works, films, sound recordings, broadcasts and other material in which there are rights of copyright or related rights; and those who perform such works.

Copyright and related rights provide creators and performers with a means of earning a living, as well as being an important tool for those at the business end of the creative and cultural industries.

- We inform and represent our members, and promote the effectiveness of and respect for copyright. In the UK the BCC is consulted by government departments, agencies and regulators.
- We follow copyright developments in the European Union and are an NGO Observer Member of the World Intellectual Property Organisation.
- We maintain links with similar bodies in other countries.
- We encourage members to review and debate proposals for legislative change in the field of copyright and related rights. Discussions on specific issues take place either in the full Council or in delegated Working Groups. From these discussions the Council's views are developed and further member consultation takes place before final approval.

The Council responds to proposals or consultations initiated by the British Government, Directorate Generals of the European Commission or Parliament and at International level by the World Intellectual Property Organisation (WIPO). However, we also respond to papers produced by other interest groups and are pro-active in making recommendations and urging action on Government and other policymakers.http://www.britishcopyright.org.uk/

British Photographic Council (BPC)

The British Photographic Council exists to protect, develop and promote the rights and interests of photographic image makers, those involved in the distribution of their work, and the bodies that represent them in the UK. The Council represents these view to the Government, the European Commission and other relevant bodies either directly or through or with the co-operation of other bodies with similar aims. It also exists to improve and encourage best practice nationally and internationally on matters relating to the use of photography, and the employment and commissioning of representing photographic image makers and the distribution of their work.

The British Photographic Council is an umbrella body, and its board is comprised of representatives from its member organisations. http://www.british-photographic-council.org

Creators Rights Alliance (CRA)

The Creators' Rights Alliance brings together the major organisations representing copyright creators and content providers throughout the media -- particularly, television, radio and the press. CRA's member organisations represent an important section of our cultural and economic resources. Their work is at the heart of the media in the information technology society, which is vital to the future of the economy.

The CRA campaigns to confront growing abuses of creators' rights in all media, particularly newspapers, magazines and broadcasting; defend and improve the intellectual property rights of creators belonging to the member organisations; Promote greater understanding of creators' intellectual property rights within the industry and among the public. http://www.creatorsrights.org.uk/

Pyramide Europe

Pyramide Europe was founded, and took its name from, a meeting held in the Pyramide of The Louvre in 1989, when the founding members signed a declaration of ten items of fundamental legislative importance to photographers – the Manifesto of the Pyramide. This manifesto binds Pyramide, and encompasses the rights of creators with regard to their copyright and moral rights.

With its headquarters in Finland, Pyramide is a European Economic Interest Group and as such is invited to present evidence (written and verbal), comment on draft papers, then white papers on legislation. Within Europe, Pyramide currently represents over 75,000 creators. Each nation or national group has its own Pyramide, which in turn is a member of the European organisation. In the UK it is Pyramide UK and Ireland, which encompasses the main visual arts organisations.

It is imperative that photographer's voices are heard at European level –harmonisation of legislation through out the Union begins at the Commission. If photographer's needs are not addressed at the first presentation of evidence and throughout the Commission process then rights will be dissipated. Once the process of evidence and papers is finalised a draft directive is issued to the member states and each member state must then encompass the directive into it's own legislation. Within Pyramide Europe each country keeps the others informed as to the passage of the legislation within each country, and help is given to any country that needs it.

An added bonus to being part of an EU wide network is the help each member country will give to others –should an individual countries member have a problem within another country there is either an association, union, lawyer or photographer to lend a hand. http://www.pyramideeurope.com/

PART 3: MAKING A LIVING

CHAPTER 8: THE JOURNEY

How to be a Student

Phil Haynes

When you are at university or college you think you know it all. Your top of the class, having a great time and everyone inside of your social walls thinks you're the next "big thing" The problem is you actually know nothing.

University is a good laugh and about making friends but there is much more to it than that. In this chapter I will try and outline a few of the many things I have realized since graduating.

I feel I was lucky as the course I attended was taught in an old fashioned way with modern techniques, I'm not sure this is common. Most places today want to mass-produce fashion photographers and fine art photographers to exhibit in galleries. The problem is due to people realizing how financially incorrect the world is those opportunities are like golden eggs. Of course there will always be the exception, the odd student with undeniable ability to create, shoot, retouch whilst tweeting and connecting to the mass social media and creating their own online persona. But in my opinion they are a rarity.

So lets start with the basics whilst trying not to be patronizing.

Take full advantage of all the free gear and studio space you are offered. At the time I know it's hard as you would rather be festering in your bed or out chatting up the opposite sex, but that won't pay the bills. Even if you feel you are using the studio and equipment lots, your probably not. What time does your university open and what time does it close? That is your window. Use every minute of it, because it's likely most of the other students on your course won't be. But when it gets to the assessment times they will start to get scared and frantically use it. Except you will already have been using it, been experimenting, been expanding your student book and most importantly building friendships with the studio technicians and people in charge of letting you hire out the equipment.

The very same people that will let YOU stay later, help YOU more, let YOU borrow more, and will push more opportunities YOUR way. Yes this is pure favoritism but this is how the world works. If you work your socks off giving it everything then these technicians and tutors will give it back as they can see a bit of themselves in your personality. If you're lazy then no one will bother because you don't bother. You could be just a student number, a financial figure, but if you want more than try hard and make the effort and then you can be whoever you want to be.

There are loads of assisting photographers and photographers, but only a handful of amazing ones. These aren't the hardest jobs in the world, but it is simply he or she who wants it most will get it. Simple as that. Work hard and you can have it. It is not about being rich, privileged or lucky. Just hard graft. You make your own opportunities in life and this industry is no different. If you submerge yourself within your passion you will get good at it and allow yourself the best chances to succeed.

So now you're paying attention because of the harsh realism of my opening section we can begin to focus.

When you are in the studio try using everything. Not all at once, but try it all. You might know the obvious difference between a bare head and a gridded head but what is it actually doing. Think of the science behind it. Photography is about science and I wished I had paid more attention when I was at high school, as now I have had to go back in my spare time to relearn about electricity and light waves. Try reading a book called Light, Science & Magic. Its cheap as chips from amazon.co.uk and is I think a must have. It's not a piece of literacy genius, it won't suddenly change your morals but it will make you stop being stupid and actually look at what your doing and how your actions will effect the image your working hard to craft. Effectively allowing you to solve the problems before you quicker, and that is all photography is about...Problem solving.

Try shooting the same shot with different lenses, we all think we know what we want to create but the subtle differences between some lenses or focal distances can make or break a great shot. Don't be lazy.

University is the same as every other year of your life in education. By that I mean in every year there will be the clichés. The cool ones, the quiet ones, etc… ignore all of these concepts and grow up a bit. Yes these people are your friends but when you graduate you probably won't see them again. EVER. So have a laugh but just get on with it, so many of my year are now either unemployed or in rubbish jobs they hate and are in upward of £20,000 worth of debt. Don't be like them, what's the point of wasting all that money just to be in a worse position than before you started.

Its easy for me to say in retrospect the importance of using facilities but now when I want to shoot a test I have to beg, borrow, or even pay for gear and it is certainly not cheap. Not when you need specific gear for certain effects or ideas. You might feel like at university/college you don't receive anything for your money but photography is one of the few courses where it costs loads to have equipment. So use it, but treat it with care. There is nothing worse than having a £15k camera sitting on the shelf because some fool broke it.

I don't want to talk directly about assisting as your main income but it is something that needs to be mentioned, as it is very important. Wherever you're studying, look into local photographers and contact them for work. Start off small with local press and wedding photographers, so you can find your feet, then work up to more established photographers the more you learn. I found working for press and wedding photographers really helped me, as they have to work so quickly under some intense pressure. There is no second chance for them, they have to get it or their kids won't be eating. They will teach you the ways to talk and flirt your way into people giving you just a couple of minutes of their time for you to get the shot. They are usually also the guys that are really good at modifying their kits to get what they need from it as well as being good business managers.

Hopefully your tutors will be telling you that being a photographer is a very hard and lonely game to be involved in. They wouldn't be lying if they did tell you, as an assistant it is no different. Your self-employed working for others in a freelance capacity and no one is there to protect you. As an assistant it is long day after long day. Cuts, bruises and plenty of ruined clothes go alongside ruined relationships and social lives. You have to be willing to give your all because if you don't then the next person who has been hammering on the door will and you will be out and forgotten. So yes university is fun, but it is the initial step into a career path that can be full of glory and money. You will get the chance to travel, meet famous people and get fed like a king on shoots, but you have to be there on merit.

When I was at university my tutor was a right old bastard. Or so I thought until I began to understand why he was like he was. To an outsider it could appear he was bitter and angry towards youth, but in fact he was frustrated with the system. The school system that took somebody who had a glorious record for teaching people to go off and gain work within the industry and reduced them to someone who ended up taking early retirement. This man changed my life by teaching me to grow up and understand the harsh realities that this industry throws up. He always had this wall up that separated himself from the students. I hated it and I fought back and pushed myself, harder and harder. Then I realized it was all done on purpose so I wouldn't be lazy, instead I'd try to reach my potential. What was the point in making out that the world was smelling of roses when all around us there was and still is, professional photographers and others related to the industry going under? If there were thousands of students graduating then he was making sure he tried his hardest to make them worthy of employment.

So this tough bastard, he was a right tough nut to crack. He never had a good word to say about my work just criticism. But his skill was to give constructive criticism, real world ideas and thoughts that came from experience. We worked on real briefs that were based around commercial ideas. He taught me to be whatever sort of photographer I wanted to be, but most importantly he taught me how to make money from my work and that is the single most important thing I learnt at university. If you cannot make an income from your work or how you contribute to a larger piece of work then you will fail. It is not about being rich (which we would all secretly like) it is about being able to live off your career choice.

Listen to people's advice and look at ways to apply it to your own work or ways of thinking, it might not always be right but be prepared to be criticized and aided in ways to improve. Keep an open mind and you're already on the right track.

Again look at the people around you and question how they are affecting you, both good and bad. They aren't always going to be around. So get your head down and work hard. The good times will come I promise you.

Working as an Assisting Photographer

Conor Masterson

Introduction

What I am going to write about is the early stages of being an assistant, some of the working practices and what is expected from you when you are involved in a shoot. It is based on my experiences as a fulltime and freelance assistant from the time I left college in 1992 to 2000. In that time I have worked as an assistant, a commercial photographer in Nottinghamshire, and an advertising photographer in London, which I feel informs my perspective from both sides of the camera bag

Making Contacts

The first step is to contact the photographers you want to work for. Ideally make an appointment to meet them. It can take a while to get an appointment but persevere and be polite. We have all been in your position and a pleasant phone manner can eventually get you through the door. Ask to show your portfolio. A lot of photographers like to see your work even though it actually isn't relevant to what you will be doing. At your stage as a beginner, any chance you get to show your book and get feedback is invaluable. Working on a shoot is such an intensive situation it is vital that you get on. The photographer is looking for someone who is bright, on the ball and enthusiastic.

First Jobs

If you are straight out of college you will be expected to be able to manage digital files on a Mac or PC. Managing will include the ability to download, backup and check quality for images captured. You must also have a basic familiarity with lighting. Be honest about what you do and don't know; it's not the critical part of the interview and you can learn quickly what you don't know. Absolute honesty and a good attitude to learning is what they are looking for.

If you are a beginner you may want to volunteer to work for free at first so that at least you will get experience of being in and around a shoot. Soon you will be able to say that you have helped with lights, file management, painted a background and so on. These can be tricky skills; even painting a background has to be done immaculately with no streaks or cross strokes, so the sooner you can say you have some relevant skills the sooner you will have a value on a shoot. Days, weeks or months later you will get that first phone call to ask you to assist on a shoot. This can come from a variety of sources: the photographer, his main assistant (who may be your only regular contact throughout), his producer, or perhaps an assistant to his agent. If you are new to assisting it is unlikely you will be asked to take on the responsibility of being the sole assistant, however if it is a simple job you may be chief bag carrier and lighting grip.

I'll mention money now because this is where it should be discussed – before the work commences. The rates of pay for an assistant in England are a contentious issue. Most photographers will pay even a beginner, others will ask you to work for nothing because of your lack of experience and they know you want to learn.

This decision is yours and, as mentioned, the sooner you can explain what experience you do have, the sooner you can start to move up the ladder. Discuss this thoroughly before the job.

There is value to everything you can do and in reality you will be hired in a role to do what you are capable of.

If you feel that your experience warrants more money, then put your case forward. I have worked in the past with assistants whose maturity has been a real bonus on the set despite their lack of technical experience.

Regarding rates of pay. I suggest you phone up a few assistants on the AOP list and ask them what the going rate is. As a rule there is a variation in pay, from editorial photography at the lowest to advertising at the highest. I cannot stress enough how important it is to learn how to represent yourself and sell your skills to be paid properly. Unfortunately, throughout your career as a photographer and assistant, you will always be asked to work for less than your day rate and it is up to you to explain the value you are offering for this price.

Inevitably you will lose work because of this but do you really want to work for a client who does not want to pay you for the work you will do? There are a lot of photographers out there, grateful for a good assistant, who will pay the going rate. On the other side of the coin, some photographers respect a good and savvy assistant and know their worth.

What to expect

It's important to realise that you are entering into a pressured environment where a lot of time, effort and money is going into the shoot. Everyone is there to achieve the images and, crucially, make money; this is their job. Sounds patronising in print, but it's an essential concept to grasp.

The other realisation is that you are there to work. Your main role ideally is to do everything so that the photographer is free to concentrate on the image he is producing. Obviously you want to learn for yourself, but this is far and away secondary to your position as the assistant photographer who soaks up the workload in the day and maintains everything from the bins to the fingerprints on the lens. The advancement of your career is of absolutely no interest to anyone there at the shoot and nor should it be. If you are not thinking about the shoot and how you can help get the job done, you are a distraction and a hindrance. Leave your best clothes on the rack, roll up your sleeves, and be prepared to get covered in dirt and paint.

There are some golden rules and ways to behave that can keep you on the straight and narrow:

- If you are not sure about anything, ask. This is a good reflection on you. It means you are paying attention and you want to get it right. No one expects you to know a lot so they are happy to explain it to you at your beginning stages.
- If you do something wrong or might have done something wrong, say it and say it immediately, before anything is changed. This is vital. A good analogy for a shoot is a series of problems that need to be solved, eliminating all the things that go wrong. Lights and cameras have a habit of letting you down when you don't pay attention to the basics. Simple mistakes do a lot of harm e.g. manually focusing the still life camera without realising the autofocus is still on … turning the modelling light off on a flash and not the head itself…
- You must treat everything that happens on the shoot confidentially. You will be present at some very sensitive stages of the job and overhear things that are not meant for your ears. Any discussions regarding the shoot between anyone on the shoot, especially the photographer and client, must be treated with the greatest of respect and not passed on to anyone outside of the shoot. You will find that it is a very small industry, full of sensitive, creative and highly-strung people with a lot of pressure on them, and no-one will appreciate you telling others about their working practices.
- Remember at all times that you are in a privileged position. You are on the shoot by invitation to work. Bear this in mind if you are tempted to take out your camera and take photographs. It is easy to forget this if you are going to a glamorous location or a foreign country that you might never normally travel to. Be thankful that you get to experience the place but do not expect to be taking any photographs at all. Never take photographs while working without first asking.

Clients on set

This is an awkward one when you are young and hungry. You will be on the shoot with someone who commissions photographic work and your natural impulse is to corner them with your portfolio and tell them all about your wonderful outlook on imaging and why they should be commissioning you as a promising up and coming talent. All of these approaches are completely out of the question; there should be no suggestion that you are anything other than an assistant, there to work for the photographer. Never forget your position and overstep your privilege to be there. What you will find is that, over time, you will begin to work with the same clients and begin to create a natural relationship with them. The best way to impress is to be an excellent assistant; it will be noticed and in years to come you can probably approach them when your portfolio is ready to show. They do want to see new talent but there is a natural order for this, based on your respect for the photographer and the art director.

First shoot

It's exciting to go on your first shoot or first job with a photographer. It can happen that you will be overwhelmed at some point with a number of things happening that you don't completely understand. You may think you know what's happening but it is important to be open and not assume too much. When something goes wrong it's usually from a mistaken assumption.

On the day

- Be early.
- Be presentable if you are going to be in a studio or controlled environment but don't get too carried away as you may have to get a bit dirty to help set up.
- Offer to make drinks.
- Listen to everything; ask questions! You are expected to learn how the photographer works, to become used to their working methods so that you are more useful to them. They have asked you to come along to help them and they want you to get better so you are more useful and they have less to worry about.

- Try to meet everyone and find out who is who; communication is very important on a shoot – everyone is working as a team. Make a note of everyone's name and how they take their coffee or tea; sounds simple but later in the day, when you have forgotten, it's distracting to be asked twice.
- Always keep one eye on the photographer and one eye on what you are doing, an eye on the other assistant, and one on the client – how many eyes is that? Get used to it. It can be stressful watching a lot of things at once but you need a floating appreciation of everything that is going on e.g. counting frames shot in your head and checking backups, what the photographer is doing, and then what everyone else is doing, time for a cup of coffee? Run a third backup? Lateral and forward thinking are important. Learn to anticipate what is about to happen. As your experience grows you will have a good idea of what is about to happen next. When it does, be near the next event so you can do it quickly. Consider every option. If you are a little confused about what to do and there is another assistant, talk to them regularly.
- Expect to be overworked for the whole day: the majority of jobs do not have the budget for two assistants so you may have a lot on your plate.

  Treat it as a positive experience – you will learn faster if you are working flat out a lot.
- When it comes to assessing the shoot, looking at the screen etc., try to avoid opening your gob to the client. What you are thinking is probably correct but any thoughts should be communicated privately to the photographer or the main assistant first; if they think it's appropriate they will appreciate it, and your tact. It's a good habit to make assessments all the time but keep them to yourself unless asked.
- Double check important tasks that you are doing.
- If you are not sure about a piece of equipment, ask how it works, don't try to wing it, all of the equipment is expensive and breakable.
- Try to relax! If you are tense and worried you are probably not taking things in clearly. You won't learn it all in a day, be clear on the jobs you are asked to do and do them well. That is the easiest way to impress and be asked to work again.
- Make notes for yourself and especially for the shoot. If you are in charge of the digital file management it is your job to keep detailed notes. With complicated set ups it is always a good idea to make a plan of the lighting. With any set up it is a good idea to make notes if you are new to this. You will forget most of it, for example that last minute light that made all the difference or was changed after the last test.
- Develop the ability to make decisions and assessments quickly in your head. Constantly assess and prioritise the jobs that need to be done. Check before doing anything to confirm what is required and then do it immediately without fuss or asking the photographer too many distracting questions – they have enough to deal with, especially at the start of the shoot.
- Try and be aware that the photographer is very busy and mentally occupied. When you are asking about the shoot, deal with the specifics that need to be addressed – What camera, where? What lights where? Later in the day is a good time to ask more detailed questions. If you don't understand, ask.

  The ideal situation is for the assistant to have assessed a problem and suggest the solution in a way that requires the photographer to agree or disagree. In other words pointing out a problem without providing a potential solution pulls the photographer out of their concentration and in fact if you observe the situation and suggest the solution in the same breath then it's a minimal disruption

  E.g. "There is light causing flare on the lens" vs "I have a flag ready for that flare, is it ok to place it in front of the camera?". It's a tiny difference but much more constructive and helpful and crucially it helps the flow of the work.
- Don't expect any photographic jobs to relate to a 9-5 regime, the average job takes place over one day, leading to an early start and possibly a late evening finish to wrap-up. Overtime is not usually paid as the photographer is being paid a fee to do the work that is not related to how long it takes, however if it's possible some photographers do pay a little extra if it all runs on and the budget is not too tight – just don't ask for it as refusal often offends!

And never ask what time the job will finish. To begin with everyone would rather it was over by 5pm but of course the reality is that it will take as long as it takes. The photographer will never commit to a finish time. If you have plans for that evening keep them to yourself. And don't spend the day texting and making calls. Your phone should only be looked at 2/3 times a day at respectful moments. It should never be seen on set and the ringer should be on silent. If you really do have to make or receive a call you must always ask. In an ideal situation the photographer should be surprised you own a phone at all ;-)) Put yourself in the photographers shoes, imagine you are paying someone to pay attention and they keep looking at their phone out of habit and not paying attention. This will be noticed. Some photographers may get annoyed by it, as it can be considered rude, but not necessarily say anything. This can cast a shadow over any good work you have done, with thoughts of "oh but they are always of the bloody phone". Do yourself a favour if you are in the habit of checking your phone all the time. Leave it in your bag, out of sight out of mind.

It's a Business

Back to money and the business of being an assistant. It is very difficult to make a living in England as an assisting photographer. Averaging more than 3 days work a week over a whole year is tricky as you are either available for work or not. No shoot will be arranged around your availability. Subtract one month for the Christmas period, any weeks holiday you might take, and a few more for the quiet times to get the picture. With these cold facts and a calculator to hand it becomes apparent that your income will be low. You will need to make every effort to maximise your income and work towards the goal of being a photographer. What will pay the bills as a photographer over the years will be consistent work from a wide range of clients. The golden rule in business is not to put all your eggs in one basket and rely on a few clients that give you a lot of work. This never lasts and when there is a change and an art director moves on you will be winded by the sudden drop off in work. The same can be said of assisting. Ideally you will need to have a wide base of photographers using you.

When I first made the rounds of photographers in London, as a freelance assisting photographer, because of my previous experience as a full time assistant and the years under my belt I managed to get offered work by almost every photographer I saw. I soon tried to temper the flow by not calling any new photographers. The work naturally levelled itself to the point where I was working for two or three advertising photographers whose work I liked and were infrequently busy, a few 'jobbing' photographers who shot for design groups and some stock, and one or two editorial photographers. This led to a level of work that kept me busy without the photographers phoning me constantly and always finding that I was booked. This did happen and naturally they found someone else who they could use more regularly. It is better for everyone involved to build longer working relationships so that their equipment and working practices become familiar.

Finding out how a photographer likes to work can be one of the most interesting parts of Freelance assisting. This is where, with a little bit of experience, you can be selective in what you learn. You will, over time, start to do the same type of job with different photographers and find that everyone has their own approach to how they do even the simplest of jobs. Study the outcomes and use what works for you. It will all contribute to the quality of your photography. If you can work fast and confidently on any job you will free your headspace and opportunity to improve a shot. Knowledge is never a bad thing; how you use it is up to you.

Most photographers can be rigid in their attention to detail, which probably stems as much from the trickiness of photography as a science as it does from their own personal outlook. You will work with other photographers who are quite creative and relaxed in their methods. Whatever works for them is the right way. Just because you have seen another photographer doing the job in a simpler way does not mean it is a better way.... all to be learnt from your growing experience.

Try to get to the point where you organise the shoot, studio hire, equipment rental, set everything up – lights, camera – and shoot the first exposures for the photographer so they can fine tune it. When you can do this and nothing surprises you, start looking for your own commissions.

Finally

If it all sounds a bit heavy, good! It's a very tough career, not at all for the faint hearted. You must have the resolution to overcome many knock backs and constant rejection. Wait until you start showing your book around. The lack of a fanfare when you open it up is a bit of a shock the first few times. It also takes a while to get used to the fact that you are leaving the office with 'The Best Book In The World' and no actual work.

It takes steely determination to work on your own with very little or no encouragement; as the assistant you are the photographer's future competition and consequently there is really no reason for them to teach you anything beyond what they want you to do for them.

Photography as a whole is a highly competitive field. There are far too many photographers and assistants for the work available. What can be disheartening at every stage is the fact that it is not all about the quality of your work – I learnt very early on that often it is the best business people who survive and prosper in the long run. The sooner you grasp this and perhaps brush up on your marketing skills the better.

In summation I'd like to say that being a photographic assistant can be a tremendously enjoyable job. You will have some great experiences in the diversity of the work and the fact that no two days are the same. To get fulfilment from it and become a photographer, the sooner you are focused on what kind of photographer you want to be and what area you want to work in the better. There is only a finite time that you will be able to survive in England assisting before you will run low on funds and struggle. If you think you might enjoy working as a career assistant, look abroad. In America, for example, because of its rich film industry it is respected as a career and paid as such.

In years gone by there were fewer photographers and assistants and more work about, but the industry has changed considerably. There is also less work because of the advent of new media and the spreading of budgets across a wider range of outlets that are not so reliant on the stills image. Because of the faster broadband and fibre connections available it has become possible to have rich content online so there is now a lot of moving image work. Beware of trying to be a jack of all trades as film is a similar but distinctly different discipline however it is good to learn some basic skills in this area so that you have an understanding of how film shoots work because a lot of photographers are working in both areas now.

Finally I would also like to say that we all think we will be shooting within one or two years of leaving college and will not be assisting very long. I see a lot of assistants burn out after a few years because it's an endurance career not a sprint. No one gets to have a career straight out of college as a photographer despite what you may read online or in magazines. Even with the best opportunities it takes years just to stabilise any new business let alone the multi disciplined demands of being a self-employed and creative business sole trader on top of being a photographer who can deliver under pressure. Try to be realistic about the next few years. The sooner you have a tight grasp on the realties the sooner you will be shooting. The speed of your progress depends on the quality of the assisting you get and how busy you are.

The final golden rule?
Keep working on your portfolio. It is never finished, it never will be, and it is the only thing that will generate work for you that leads to a career as a photographer.

Good Luck.

Standards and Codes for Assisting Photographers

Gwen Thomas

Introduction

The AOP is actively championing a change in profile for 'freelance assistants', particularly those who have a wealth of experience and bring more to a shoot than just a helping hand. Most are already shooting for themselves, actively building up their portfolios and marketing themselves. It is much more a profession in its own right working 'with' the photographer, as oppose to 'for' them, using their expertise to work with only the direction required for the specifics of the shoot.

The first step was to change the name to 'Assisting Photographers' and freelancers are encouraged to print their business cards to reflect this change. To present a more professional look, The AOP has produced invoice pads specifically designed to show all the necessary information, including the Schedule D No. required for the Inland Revenue.

The bottom of the invoice refers to the following guidelines, which provide a code of practice between the photographer and the assisting photographer. These guidelines should be sent, before the shoot, to the photographer in order for them to become part of the contract between the two parties.

The following should be regarded as a guideline only, as photographers and assisting photographers (referred to here as 'assistants') may have their own terms of business. Any terms should be agreed between both parties before confirming bookings.

Bookings

Bookings are usually verbal and both photographer and assistant should understand if the work is provisional or confirmed. On confirmation the following should be agreed:

- Dates, start times, and daily hours
- Venue and travel arrangements
- Special requirements (clothing, equipment knowledge, etc.)
- Fee
- Expenses and overtime (where appropriate)
- Weather contingency for location work
- Possible overlaps with assistant's other confirmed jobs
- Invoicing details (invoice client or photographer?)
- Contact names and numbers

If an assistant has a provisional booking with another photographer, that photographer must be given the option to confirm before another booking is accepted.

Cancellation and Postponement

Cancellation by an assistant is not acceptable without unavoidable reason, eg. illness, and the substitution of another assistant must not be made without the photographer's prior knowledge and consent. The photographer has the right to approve any replacement before commencement of the shoot.

Where a booking is confirmed which may overlap a previously confirmed job, the photographer must be informed immediately and given the option to book another assistant.

Cancellation fees for freelance assistants are only payable for confirmed bookings, although once the booking is confirmed; an assistant should not be cancelled unless the job itself is cancelled. Freelance assistants should be regarded as chargeable items, and therefore covered by expenses when the photographer is charging the client a cancellation fee. In the case of a postponement, where a new date is given and confirmed, fees may become payable to cover costs and inconvenience, by mutual agreement between the photographer and assistant.

Fees

These are charged at a daily rate. A normal day is any 9-hour period worked between 7am and 9pm, and rates are dependant on knowledge, experience, and the type of work the photographer is doing, eg. advertising or editorial. Overtime may be charged for weekends, public holidays and in addition to the standard 9 hours, at a rate previously agreed with the photographer.

Payment

Payment should be made at the end of the shoot unless otherwise agreed at the time of booking. If immediate payment is not agreed, then credit terms of 30 days should be the maximum given. Assistants should give an invoice clearly stating the following:

- Assistant's name, address, and Tax Schedule D Number
- Shoot/booking dates
- Assistant's invoice number
- Photographer's name and order number
- Client/Agency/Product
- Fee
- Expenses itemised
- Total owed
- Payment terms
- VAT number (if registered)

All expenses incurred on behalf of the photographer or client should be agreed in advance and are payable immediately the shoot is completed. Fees and mileage for the use of an assistant's car should be agreed at the time of confirmation.

Location Work

The photographer is responsible for the cost of accommodation and meals whilst on location, but personal expenses (eg. telephone calls) are the responsibility of the assistant. Medical and travel insurance should be discussed with the photographer before the shoot begins.

Weather-permitting bookings should be agreed with the assistant at the time of confirmation, but postponement due to bad weather will result in the assistant, as a photographer's expense, being paid 50% of the fee. The photographer or the client may have weather insurance to cover these events.

Assisting Photographers and Public & Employer's Liability

Whenever an assistant tests to update their portfolio, there may be other people involved acting under their 'care, custody and control', such as models, stylists, set-builders or even a friend who is assisting. Should any of them suffer injury and the assistant is negligent, they may be liable. Any assistant involved in such activities should have Employers' Liability protection.

Similarly, if an assistant's proven negligence damages someone's property whilst testing or shooting for themselves, Public Liability insurance will provide for any payments awarded against them and legal costs incurred.

CHAPTER 9: ADVERTISING

Advertising Photography

Richard Maxted

Gladiators ready!

The lot of the advertising photographer is very much a double-edged sword. On one side of the blade you have all the pressure and stress that surrounds a big budget job. The need to perform in front of the client and agency staff, to make sure everything is bang on, to be almost super humanly confident. To deliver the job on budget and on time, whatever the personal cost to yourself, repeat after me 'anything for the job, anything for the job'. Early starts, late finishes, tight deadlines, no excuses, the buck stops with you and if you mess it up forget being able to re-shoot it, your career will be in the pan quicker than you can say 'But it wasn't my fault', because unfortunately it will be.

The other side of that sword is heavenly. Working with great art directors, brilliant re-touchers, talented model makers, stylists, models, make-up artists, surrounding yourself with genius', they make you look good, they really do make you shine. Catering for lunch, assistants to make you coffee, cab to the agency for a quick meeting, 'Would I like a latte, go on then...' oh, and the money, ohhhh the money.

Of course this is a polarised view of the job, it's nothing like as bad or as good as I've painted it, well it is a bit but there's a reason for it. The pressure, stress, and rewards are all down to the fact that these photos are going to be advertising 'a' product for a given period of time, in a given media and if you're lucky in any number of given countries. To get your images in these places costs the client a huge pile of cash, so the photos have got to be good, they've got to be on the money, they just have to be, end of, no excuses. The client needs you to do your job so they can sell their product, if they can't sell their product then they will be out of a job, they will starve and they will die (professionally), that's where all the pressure comes from. Advertising is powerful, it works, it's important to the client, that's why the rewards are good, but equally that's why stress levels can be so high.

It also goes without saying that we can all do our job in our own comfort zone, in our own environment, in a place or situation where we are relaxed and comfortable. However, imagine having to do what you do when you're not in your comfort zone, you might not even be in your 'normal' time zone. Add to the mix 3 clients from 2 continents, 3 account people, 1 art director, 1 creative director, possibly the copywriter and the art buyer as well, plus your crew which could consist of another 3 or 4 people. On top of that add the task of sorting lunch for them all, getting the cars booked at the end of the day, entertaining them during the shoot, well you can't ignore them can you, that would just be rude. Then you can perhaps start to see the pressure, and by the way, we haven't even mentioned the matter of that whilst you're managing all this you have to try and achieve a photographic hole in one.

Agents and/or carefully employed shoot hosts can of course deflect the pressure when it comes to keeping people off the photographers back, but at the end of the day the buck stops with you, the photographer. It's your shoot, it's your name above the door, it will be your fault that there was no vegetarian option for the client during lunch, even if it wasn't actually your fault.

The Process

So how does the process work? The photographer normally gets involved in the process once the client has approved an idea. The notion that photographers are asked to contribute to the idea process before the client has approved anything is a pretty romantic one and one that happens incredibly rarely. The art director will have drawn up a layout (or scamp/visual) and this will have been 'sold' to the client (normally by the account team) the idea will have been subsequently approved. The agency will then look to commission someone to shoot the layout and this is where the art buyer or producer comes in. These people are tasked with knowing the industry, who's hot, who's new, who's a safe pair of hands etc... The appropriate photographers are chosen to submit estimates and then it's in the lap of the gods really.

The decision on who gets the job varies from job to job. Sometimes there will be a photographer who's style is so right for the job its got them written all over it. Often the photographers in the mix will be asked to call the art director to discuss the layout, this will give the art director a pretty good idea of the photographers take on their idea and a good inside track on whether this is the right person for the job. It's really important to get those phone calls right, for obvious reasons. Other times it might come down to who was the cheapest. It genuinely does vary as to why one photographer does and another photographer doesn't get the job. The big thing is don't take it personally if you don't get it, if you don't get it you don't get it, that's life. The important thing is to be in the mix, if you're not asked to quote on a job that has you written all over it then you have to question your marketing.

How to get in the mix?
It doesn't matter how good a photographer you are, if no one knows you exist you won't get any work, simple. So it comes down to good marketing or advertising, this time you are the product. A good agent will sort all of this out for you, a bad one will bury you into a photographic tundra, so make sure if you do have someone selling 'you' that they are the right sort of person to sell you. A bad agent is much worse than no agent at all.

If you don't have an agent you will have to do your marketing yourself, the best form of marketing is simply going to see people and getting you and your work in front of them. Don't forget that you're not just selling your work you're selling you as a person. Advertising shoots can sometimes be intense long and drawn out affairs, they can at times involve travel, at the very least you will be spending a few hours with the art director, no one will commission someone they don't like. So it's important when you meet these people that you leave a good impression, smiling helps.

With or without an agent you will need a portfolio of images (known as a book) and a website. The old practice of calling in 30 books for a job seems to have gone now, agencies refer to websites and short lists are drawn up from these. So you've got a good website and your book has been called in for a job. The format and presentation of your book is up to you. Landscape, portrait, sleeves, no sleeves, prints mounted, iPad, etc… the options are endless, just make sure it looks smart, professional and sells what you do. Make sure you have some cards to leave behind and the rest as I've already said is really in the lap of the gods.

Who's involved in the process?
Client
The person who pays for everything.

Creatives
Art Director (AD) –Employed by the advertising agency to come up with the idea. The AD's job is to deal with everything visual. Normally they will work with a copy writer (CW) whose role it is to be more focused on the copy and text side of the idea. The AD is normally the person who will attend the shoot on behalf of the agency; it's their idea after all. The AD & CW are also the driving force behind deciding who gets chosen to shoot the job, they choose who gets to visualise their idea. Both the AD & CW 'are' the campaign / shoot.

- Creative Director – In charge of the overall feel and direction of a specific clients campaign. Generally oversees and signs off (approves) the AD's work.
- Executive Creative Director – Basically, runs the whole creative output of the advertising agency.

Account Handling Dept.
Not to be confused with the people who sign the cheques, that's 'Accounts Payable'. This side of the agency deals with liaising between the creatives and the client. Any contact with the client will go through an account person. Likewise when the client has a query, issue or question they will go through the account dept. If the client is attending the shoot, an account person has to be there, this is to protect the photographer and the art director from any client requests they might not have been agreed to. These people have a very tough job and are often the ones caught in the middle. Levels of seniority range from executive, to manager, to director.

Art Buyers & Producers
Historically the point of contact for the photographer at the agency would have been the art buyer. Many still exist but the scope has been widened by the introduction of producers. Both art buyers and producers will call in photographers' books, deal with the estimates and will be the person that the photographer needs to keep in the loop during the job. The purchase order (PO) will come from these guys, without this you don't get paid. When you've finished the job and are sending it to the agency these are the people you send the files to.

Who's the most important?
Easy, accounts payable. They are the ones that actually pay you.

Seriously, all of them, good luck.

Negotiating Licences And Usage

Gwen Thomas

When the photographer is originally approached with a possible commission, great care needs to be taken in assessing the exact needs of the client, because the costing is dependant on this information. Many clients still want to obtain copyright from the photographer for a variety of reasons, the main ones being a lack of 'copyright' understanding and the fear of having to spend more money for further use.

Licensing

Exclusivity

Standard trade practice, with reference to the original commission, will give the client exclusivity for the period of time, in the specific territories agreed, included in the shoot fee. Clients and advertising agencies are concerned that the images they commission, and for which they pay the origination expenses, should not fall into the hands of competitors or become associated with other products after the initial licence period has finished. To prevent this, it has been suggested that the photographer should not licence the images, for example through a library, without client and agency permission, for four years after the end of the licence (unless otherwise agreed). This should be negotiated with the individual agency/client before the shoot takes place, as should other related issues such as confidentiality. The sensitivity of the subject matter should always be taken into consideration, for example, an image that could be used to good effect by a competitor of the original client. Where material is not sensitive, it is unlikely that an agency or their client would withhold this permission. On expiry of the initial exclusivity period, the commissioner should be offered first option to extend the exclusivity clause at a negotiated rate.

It is expected that once any confidentiality period is over that the photographer and agency can use the image for their own PR purposes. This use should include entry into competitions by the photographer and the agency with credits to the photographer, client and agency.

The initial Licence

The original negotiated commission fee would normally include the following:

1 Year UK or any single country – any two media (3rd media may be included depending on its proportion of the media spend)

2 Years UK or any single country – any one media

The licence begins on 1st insertion and 1st insertion can be expected within 6 months of the delivery of finished job to the agency/client.

It is suggested that work should be licensed for a minimum period of 6 months at a negotiated day rate. Less than 6 months in an advertising context is not realistic.

In the UK, the photographer's fee normally includes the first use of the images, but the duration, media and territory are frequently negotiated within this fee. Factors such as the experience of the photographer and the desirability of the commission may affect the negotiated day rate.

Above and below the line

Instead of asking for specific media, many clients will ask for Above the Line or Below the Line media to be licensed. These two categories are becoming common parlance, but there is no definitive description as to which media should belong in each and this can cause confusion as to what the photographer needs to licence. In the 1st instance, photographers are advised to ask the client what media they actually need to ensure they can price the licence fairly.

The following list is not exhaustive, but gives an idea as to which media belongs in each category, and has been developed through experience of negotiating licences by Photographic agents:

Above the Line

Ambient

Internet

Point of Sale

Posters

Press

TV (including interactive)

Below the Line

Brochures

Direct Mail

Intranet

Marketing Aids

PR

Video

Mobiles

CD Ad

Negotiating extra usage

The AOP, together with the London Photographic Agents, have produced a calculator to help with this process. The figures that it produces are a guideline, and give a starting point for negotiations. The calculator can be accessed from the AOP's website http://www.the-aop.org/information/usage-calculator

BUR (Base Usage Rate)

To prevent misunderstandings when negotiating extra usage fees, over and above the use included in the negotiated commission fee, it has been suggested that a Base Usage Rate (BUR) be established. This figure also enables the client to budget accordingly,

The BUR is the figure on which additional use to the areas stated on the photographer's original estimate, accepted by the client, is calculated. It is the figure to which the percentages in the Usage calculator are applied and is a completely separate figure to the negotiated day rate or shoot fee.

It is suggested that the BUR should never be less than the negotiated day rate, and should be pitched according to the expertise of the photographer and the amount of input and involvement required on the shoot from the photographer.

When a photographer is doing a 'budget' job for the client at less than their normal day rate, then the BUR would be set at the figure they would normally charge as a day rate for that type of commission.

When several images from a single day's shoot i.e. the same subject or variations from a single shoot, are used by the commissioner, then each individual image could be subject to it's own BUR.

Additional media and licence period extensions

The calculator is a guideline for use where the photographer has issued, or is issuing, a licence and were produced as a result of discussions between art buyers, photographers and photographers' agents. These are not recommendations, but are provided as guidelines for negotiation based on current trade practice.

The Media listings are not exhaustive and requests for media not shown, can be negotiated by using a similar media with the same style of distribution or viewing. Merchandising should be negotiated separately and the licence cost could be based on a % of each sale (royalty).

Internet

Whilst the Internet is worldwide by its very nature, not all websites will be of interest to the wider community. Most companies, regardless of their size, will have a web presence and so licencing Internet use generically is no longer feasible. It is advised that the kind of business; viewing market; and the relevance in the worldwide market place of each client be taken into consideration before pricing a license. Many smaller/provincial companies presence is 90% web based and photographers may wish to include web use for this type of client within the original day fee. The guidelines include a BUR % by country as well as worldwide to reflect this.

Individual Countries

Countries have been graded by their GDP and then banded from A+ to D with a different percentage allocated to each band. For example the United States is an A+ country, this band has 150% for extra use attached to it – so additional use in the US would cost 150% of the BUR. The list of countries, the band and percentage allocated to them is called Country Grading by GDP.

Geographic terms and acronyms

This listing shows which countries are included in the geographic areas shown on the Additional Territories Usage Chart and in the various acronyms being used by agencies and clients to bundle areas together.

Don't assign copyright

In principle, we are opposed to the assignment of copyright. However, we recognise that agencies sometimes need to negotiate a fee covering any future use of the photographs without continuous reference to the photographer.

In such cases, the Licence to Use will specify "All Media" under Media Use, the Territory will be "Worldwide" and the Time Period will be "Unlimited".

The licence will be exclusive to the Agency/Client and will cover all uses of the photography in relation to the product named on the licence. The photographer retains the right to use the photographs for promoting his/her own work.

The All Uses licence is subject to the general Terms and Conditions and therefore does not permit use in relation to another product or sub-licensing, for example to a photo library.

CHAPTER 9

CHAPTER 10: EDITORIAL

ANDREW WIARD

Introduction

Editorial photography is notoriously badly paid. And always was. Newspapers are the worst – their shift rates have hardly increased in twenty five years. But they do at least pay. Now photographers are facing freetards offering zero pay contracts (we'll give you a credit!), online pound shops selling pictures for a dollar, and competition from "citizen journalists" who do get paid – for their day jobs. So photographers are turning to other ways of making editorial skills pay. Corporate photography. Wedding photography. Videography. And, crowd funding. But this chapter is not about alternative sources of work or income. It is for those who, against all the odds, are still determined to somehow make a professional living as editorial photographers charging professional fees for professional work.

Saying No

The hardest task photographers face is not taking photographs, but selling them. And learning the art of survival in what is without doubt a buyers' market. Why a buyers' market? If intellectual property is so valuable (and it is), why aren't we the creators in control? Supply and demand. Because photography, like acting, is one of the glamorous professions, and there will always, always, be a much greater supply of photographers than there is demand for their work. Editorial photography, particularly photojournalism, is at the most glamorous and overcrowded end of a very glamorous profession. That's why it is so badly paid, and why clients can get away with extortionate contracts – give us your intellectual property rights too, or you will never, ever, work for us again. There is only one way to reply to this if you want to be one of the survivors. It does not require going to Harvard Business School. It does not require any great negotiating skills. You only have to learn one word, and then repeat it again and again, whenever and wherever required. Just say NO. Saying NO is the key to survival in editorial photography. It's no guarantee you will survive, but saying yes to bad deals guarantees that you won't. It's the simplest thing to say: however if you're a young hopeful who has just taken a portfolio round fifty potential clients, before getting a single offer of a job, it's also the toughest. It's a case of going on strike. All by yourself. Many will find that too tough to take.

But those who say YES should remember. If you agree to sell yourself cheap, it will be very difficult to ever raise your price. If you agree to give away your rights, you will never ever sell those photographs again (but your client will). If your competitors charge way below the rate, you can match them, only to find they then charge even less. As it has been said many times, if your USP is that you're cheap, do not be surprised to find that it is not unique. However low you sink into the gutter, you will always find another photographer beneath you. Don't go there.

Working out your Day Rate

Saying no requires a clear understanding of where to draw the line. In editorial, as in any other area of photography, you have to start by working out what you need to make in a day in order to cover your costs, and still make a living. That should be your day rate. I say should, because in editorial this is really a notional figure. You will hardly ever get it, but you still need it as a target, before deciding how far you can risk going below it, without going out of business.

It goes like this. No-one actually takes pictures five days a week. Not unless you're working shifts, sending over the files, and forgetting the rest. You will need at least two days for preparation, post production, and doing everything else when running your own show, including chasing up debts and keeping on top of the figures. No-one works fifty two weeks a year. So let's say you have available three days, forty eight weeks a year, or one hundred and forty four days. Lets say you are aiming for an income of £30,000. On top of this you need to add your overheads, and the purchase, maintenance & regular replacement of all your equipment (your job expenses should be added on top of the day rate). This figure will be lower for editorial than, say, advertising, but will still be substantial. And it will vary from one individual to another. In my case as a rule of thumb, I find I generally have to spend a pound to make a pound, usually more. But let's say you have to aim for total fees of £60,000. With 144 days, that makes nearly £420 per day.

As I've already said, most of the time you just won't get it. Unless you're a big name photographer, or do the kind of studio/location work that's close to advertising – which means higher overheads anyway. You might get it in corporate work, which is why so many use that to subsidise editorial. But not in editorial itself.

Every pound you fall below this target rate comes off your income, not your overheads. And you are very unlikely to get 144 days anyway. Even if you are never ill, there simply aren't enough jobs to go round. Which all points in one direction – you can only make up the shortfall by selling additional rights. Whether by selling extra rights to the original client, or (with the client's permission of course, if straightaway) by syndication, or selling directly to other publications, or re-selling as stock. That means holding on to your rights in the first place. If you agree to work too far below your target rate, AND give away your rights, you are heading for an early grave.

I myself have never been paid £420 per day for an editorial job. Straight editorial one time use, that is, excluding expenses. But I can and do make £420 per day. I can get it by charging less for immediate use, and extra for further rights the client may require. Or charging extra for simultaneous print and web publication. Or by charging "day rate against space", whereby the day rate is no more than a guarantee against publication – so if the space rates exceed the day rate, those rates get paid instead. This enshrines the principle that should be implicit in every commission – you are licensing your intellectual property, not selling your time. I can get it if the job is editorial in style and approach, but really intended for corporate/annual report/PR use. And I can get it by doing a couple of jobs in a day, with a stock sale or two on top. This last will raise eyebrows from those who rightly believe that ANY job should be charged as a day, and so will the minimum I'm prepared to work for. Okay, hands up – it's £250 for a day. Or £150 for a job – and that by the way is what some nationals still pay for a whole day! But for every photographer who thinks this disgracefully low, there will be another who thinks holding out for these fees would drive them out of business.

One should never say never. Yes, I occasionally work for even less. But I stick to my minimum rates as a general rule even if it means losing clients. They are clients worth losing.

Different editorial markets

I have so far been describing editorial as one specific market, whereas in fact there is no such thing. Instead, a bewildering variety of different ways of making a living. Different media, such as magazines, television, newspapers, books or the web. Widely different subject matter – wildlife, news, celebs, sport. Different approaches from reportage to PR. And everything from fully equipped studios to hand held Leicas. To deal with them properly each would need a chapter, and I'd need a book. But I'd like to make a few brief observations.

I won't spend much time on the extremes. Paparazzi photographers can command the highest prices and are in a world of their own. Regional papers pay as low as £18 per photo (yes, really!!) and are a complete waste of time. Nationals pay badly. Time was years at low shift rates used to lead to a well-paid staff job, but those years are gone. The years of staff jobs I mean – the shift rates are as bad as ever! In the 1980s the Express Newspaper group used to employ over 100 staff photographers across all its titles. Now there are only five, and it's much the same everywhere else. Instead of a decent day rate you get the prestige of working for a national. But that doesn't pay the mortgage.

Magazines are a much bigger market and generally pay better, although colour supplements are beginning to take the "we're offering you exposure" attitude. Rates vary widely, and at the high end, lit portraits, or location shoots with assistants and all the rest, are closer to those in corporate or advertising. PR work is the most rapidly expanding area for editorial photographers. Clients often want the editorial approach. Photographers need the money as other markets shrink. It can be much better money, and the range is even wider than it is in magazines. Its very important, and difficult, to assess the usage before deciding a fee. A photo in one or two trade mags and the in-house magazine is one thing. Immediate distribution in all directions, and use in the annual report, is quite another. Often the client doesn't really know what they want to do in the future. Anyway, for extensive rights a good rule of thumb is to charge at least double, and try limiting the licence to a year. If the pictures are that good they are still using them in a year's time, you can then issue a further licence.

Watch out for the "we're only a charity" approach. It's a bit like the "but we're educational" you often get from book publishers. There are charities on really tight budgets, but some can be big business, with staff salaries to match. Likewise some commercial clients have very low turnover and budgets. The charity / commercial distinction is no longer a helpful guide to pricing – judge your fee according to a client's income, and of course the intended usage.

Here let me point you to two very useful guides to rates and rights.

First, the AOP's Usage Calculator: http://bit.ly/17taGHx.

And, the National Union of Journalist's Freelance Fees Guide (Photography Section): http://bit.ly/1dOGC2p.

Expenses

All expenses specific to a commission should be added on top of the day rate. Including travel (mileage, whatever), but most importantly digital production charges. Some clients, who have a little digital compact, and know they can re-use the digital memory card again & again, believe digital files "don't cost anything". Any photographer who has just bought a £5,000 digital camera, a new computer with all the software, and spent hours correcting & captioning digital files, knows that they do. And that in a year or two's time cameras, computer and software will all have to be replaced or updated, often before they have been paid for, or paid for themselves. Digital expenses may have to be very carefully explained to clients, and also the advantages to them. Professionally processed digital files save them a lot of time and money. They must pay those digital production charges. Exactly what they are is up to you, but here's what I do. I charge for digital contact sheets (web galleries). For each high resolution file corrected and captioned, or when producing a large number of files, an hourly fee for. Check professional lab prices for "Photoshop time"! And I charge for digital delivery (email, web, or old-fashioned CD's). What I will not do is just hand over dozens of uncorrected files straight out of the camera free of charge. Why is this practice so wrong? 1) Your reputation is at stake. You risk being judged by the results of uncaptioned, shoddily corrected, and badly edited pictures. 2) Your files are beginning their digital travels in various directions without even your copyright notice, let alone contact details. 3) You are charging little or nothing to cover your digital costs.

For more information on Digital see Chapter 14.

All In Fees

Increasingly clients ask for an all in fee instead of itemised billing. Beware. This can be just another way of saying, we don't pay digital production charges. Or, anything extra for unlimited rights. Or, mileage. However it can provide clarity and simplicity for both parties. You are on safe ground provided you keep in mind a rough total for the appropriate itemised bill. And, specify the rights granted.

Holding on to your rights

The rights are crucial. Everyone wants yours. They want to buy them cheap, and then sell and re-sell them again without paying another penny. "Intellectual property is the oil of the twenty first century". These are the words of Mark Getty, founder of the largest stock photographic conglomerate in the world today, Getty Images. And yes, he is related – he is the grandson of John Paul. The man who discovered that the fast route to wealth and power lay just as much in getting a stranglehold on distribution, as in producing the oil itself. So it is no surprise to find that Getty now controls the distribution of more photographs than anyone else on the planet. When the first edition of this book was printed, Getty Images didn't even exist. The empire that straddles the globe today was only founded in 1995. It depends entirely on the intellectual property, the copyright, in what photographers create. So – hang on to it! Do not agree to "assign" your rights. Strike that term out of any contract you are offered. In copyright law, assignment means surrendering your copyright. All rights granted should take the form of "licences", which is to say you as copyright owner are granting specific limited rights while holding on to your right to issue them.

Protecting your pictures

To hold onto your rights, your pictures need protecting from copyright thieves. I'd like to point you in four directions, each worth a chapter to themselves. First, metadata. It is absolutely essential to put your copyright and contact details in the IPTC section of your photographic metadata. IPTC? The International Press and Telecommunications Council (www.iptc.org). The Photometadata site, http://photometadata.org, is a mine of information about how to go about this. Secondly, everything you need to know about "orphans" – photographs whose parents cannot be found, as yours might well become without the necessary metadata. Best to start here: www.stop43.org.uk. Then, PLUS, the Picture Licensing Universal System, http://www.useplus.com. A developing project for connecting photographers to their pictures and their licenses granted to their pictures using a registry, https://plusregistry.org, searchable both through metadata and image recognition. Finally, the registry of the US Copyright Office, http://www.copyright.gov. Put a lot of your time aside to find out how this all works. Time well spent if anyone makes the mistake of publishing without permission, in the US, one of your photographs registered there. Registration provides for "statutory damages". I won't go further into those here, but suffice it to say they mean you'll have no trouble finding a lawyer to represent you, and infringers should have the sense to settle before the court case.

Professional Fees – Space Rates

Many photographers find working for stock a better way to survive. Not just re-selling commissioned work, but shooting for stock in the first place. Forget low commission rates, shoot pictures that sell, and get the full space rates every time. Or distribute them through an agency or library that will take commission, but will (or should) greatly increase sales. Until recently the major decisions to be taken were whether to sell direct or through an agency, and if so which and on what terms. But now you also have to decide whether to sell RM (Rights Managed) photographs, or RF (Royalty Free). Rights Managed is the traditional method. The copyright holder issues a licence (and gets paid a "royalty") for each and every use publication of a photograph. This is the way I sell my pictures. Royalty Free is – well, it's not free, but if you think its sounds cheap you're dead right, that's exactly what it is. There's no point trying to be impartial about this, photographers either embrace it as the future, or they hate it, and I hate it. The idea is that clients pay a flat fee for extensive use of one or more photographs. The essential point is that the connection between a specific use and an agreed payment is broken. And so is the connection between size on a page and a space rate. Clients can use pictures repeatedly for a wide range of uses for no additional fee. Running a picture full page, or on the cover costs no more than running it one inch square.

There's no point denying that by selling RF in volume, some photographers can and do make large sums of money. But a lot don't. And the effect on the market as a whole, and those still trying to get the proper rate for individual sales, has been catastrophic. Some magazines now fill their pages with RF, and only grudgingly pay for RM when they really have no choice, and then they resent the "high price". The people laying out the pages have been "educated" into thinking that pictures don't really cost anything!

Worse still, a much higher cut of the repro fees goes to the distributor, not the photographer. Some RF sellers pay a lump sum for the photographs, and no further royalties. Others pay ridiculously low percentages, a fraction of the traditional fifty per cent industry standard.

All this is dressed up as modern and customer friendly, while the RM diehards are condemned as luddites. Well, as a luddite who uses all the latest digital kit for everything except making the coffee, I confess to only one antediluvian characteristic – when a picture of mine gets used, I want to get paid. RF is a way of selling photographs like a packet of cornflakes. It cheapens the price, and everything we do. It won't go away, its here to stay, but you don't have to follow suit. If you do, remember it's a one-way ticket. If you ever change your mind, you will find it almost impossible to sell as Rights Managed those of your pictures which are already circulating as RF.

The market is also being wrecked by online sales of photographs that are still rights managed, but simply sold cheap. Low prices, and low mark ups for larger sizes. Some libraries will even sell pictures at a flat fee, relying on bulk sales. Wal-Mart is coming to a high street near you. But if you are a sole trader, you cannot stack them high and sell them cheap. You just won't have enough pictures, and nor will the few remaining smaller agencies. The key to survival here, if survive you can, is specialisation in niche markets. Don't fight a price war you can only lose.

Whatever you do, read any agency/library contract very carefully. Before you step into this minefield, let me point out two or three of the more obvious dangers.

An agency may reasonably demand a degree of exclusivity, whether handling your stock, commissioned work, or both. But if it doesn't work out, you must be able to go elsewhere after a reasonable period of time. What's reasonable? Good question, but don't sign your life away for the next five years. If you do, and your small, friendly agency goes under, you might find yourself sold to one of the big boys like Corbis. You have to be able to walk away.

The best way round this, if you have to concede exclusivity at all, is to grant image exclusivity, not photographer exclusivity. That way you can carry on selling other pictures elsewhere straightaway.

Also, watch out for low commission rates. The industry standard for stock is fifty per cent. The big players are trying to reduce your cut to thirty five or less. Don't listen to all their talk about their horrific digital costs. You have your own, too. All this comes down to power, pure and simple. Let me say it one more time. Don't sell yourself cheap.

For more information on Stock Libraries see Chapter 13

Getting Organised

Freelance photographers fight their own battles – most of the time. They have to. But you are not alone. The only sure way to turn a buyers' market into a sellers' market is to get organised. There are a number of professional organisations for photographers including, obviously, the AOP (witness this book!). I value highly two I belong to, the British Press Photographers' Association (BPPA) and the National Union of Journalists (NUJ). And there are others. If you run your own stock library, there's the British Association of Picture Libraries and Agencies (BAPLA). All are sources of advice and expertise, but beyond that are pretty good at herding cats. And though they don't win every battle, collective strength can produce results.

The AOP took on Getty. After buying up stock agencies all over the globe, Getty decided to impose a new contract on all their contributors. It was a take it or leave it deal, and individuals would have had to sign on the line, or walk. Alone. Maybe walking is not such a bad idea – many have – but most cannot survive the disruption to sales. Photographers whose agency, now Getty, was their sole source of income were in a particularly invidious position. As Getty and Corbis take over the world where else can they turn? The AOP re-negotiated numerous clauses of a non-negotiable deal, and while the result was far from perfect, the company is now in no doubt there are two sides to a deal.

As a trade union the National Union of Journalists is in a position to publish a fees guide (see above). As well as negotiating agreements it fights legal cases and deals with copyright problems, recovering large sums for its members. And provides legal and financial support to photographers prepared to take the publishers on. Here's one they won – defeating a copyright grab by the Scotsman newspaper. Briefly, the Scotsman presented their freelancers with a contract grabbing rights not only future work, but claiming to apply retrospectively on pictures already supplied. They refused to sign. They organised a boycott of the paper. They withdrew permission to publish their photographs on file. When the Scotsman ignored that and continued to publish, the NUJ's lawyers extracted an out of court settlement. The full story is fascinating, no space for it here, but read on: http://bit.ly/18sgL9g.

In addition to working through traditional subscription organisations, with offices and full time staff, photographers now organise and help each other by email and through social media. For editorial photographers in the UK, the brand leader is – Editorial Photographers UK (www.epuk.org). The first stop for the best insider advice and info about the business of editorial photography. Also, though not just for editorial photographers, worth looking at the self-support and campaigning organisation Pro-Imaging (http://www.pro-imaging.org/).

Threats & opportunities

Digital technology has crucially altered the balance of power. The supermarket Goliaths are driving the corner shops out of business. Buyers can now deal direct with big one-stop-shops while sitting in front of their computer screens. They no longer have to rely on a researcher on the other end of the phone, and then wait for the transparencies. All major publishing organisations now have an eye on the future potential of digitised commissioned material, increasing their pressure on individuals to sign away their rights.

But as a lone David you are not powerless. In fact digital technology gives you more power than you could ever have had before. The cost to you may appear crippling, but it is microscopic compared to that of running giant, or even medium and small, agencies. The threat, in other words, is also an opportunity. The market is now polarising between the giants – and you. For a tiny fraction of their investment, you can now for the first time ever fight them on a level playing field. Deal direct and take 100% of your sales. Rent cheap, searchable web space delivering high resolution files straight onto your clients' desktops. You can even run your own. Your pictures can be as instantly accessible as those of Getty and Corbis.

Clients will still need a very good reason to abandon the websites they look at first every day, to then go trawling through thousands of others in order to, maybe, find yours. The keys to survival are, as I've said before, specialisation. And marketing. You must be able to supply something the big players simply can't. And your clients must know that you've got it, who you are, and where to find you. Niche marketing, I'm afraid, is beyond the scope of this chapter. But if you hold onto your rights, and say NO to bad deals, you're still in with a chance – over to you.

CHAPTER 11: ARCHITECTURAL

PAUL MCMULLIN

A personal view

I have a saying. I'll shoot anything so long as it doesn't involve – animals, weddings, portraits or children. That is not to decry those photographers who specialise in these genres as you need to be pretty talented and a good business person to survive in these stretched times. What I am saying is that I like to concentrate on the two main cores of my business, namely architecture and corporate work. For this exercise we shall concentrate on my love for architecture and the built Environment and how to go about shooting this particular aspect of our profession.

So. What makes a good architectural photograph, is it – Light? Composition? Subject? Viewpoint? attention to detail? Probably all of these to be honest. Equipment? Hmmmm maybe less so! We can explore all of these factors later in this piece.

Ok so I'm fresh out of college. I think 'I want to be an architectural photographer' How does one start? Well initially it all begins with the subject, the building. One can study lots of books showing fantastic award winning architecture which are great, often shot in perfect light and with the perfect viewpoint and you can strive to emulate this. It's all subjective of course, a perfect viewpoint for the architect may not be so for the lighting designer or the construction company or the landscaper or the handrail company or the company who installed the paving or indeed the company who fitted out the toilets- the list goes on. These all fall under the auspices of being an architectural photographer and your approach has to vary accordingly depending on who the end client is and who has commissioned you.

For every assignment you receive from a client, there has to be a clear idea of what is required. How many images are expected, delivery method, end usage, clear and concise instructions of which details are important, which elevations and perhaps even instructions about what should be excluded in the shots (whether by viewpoint or judicial cropping). As you work more and more with a particular client you will get to know what they like in terms of composition, angles etc. and more often the brief will be in the form of a phone call just giving you the address, a contact name, phone number and when the finished job is required by. Basically when this happens you have what I would call a 'continuing relationship ' BUT remember you may say your client is 'BEST Architects in the World PLC' but in the real world it is actually J Bloggs in the Marketing Dept. and when he or she moves on, goes off sick, dies, maternity leave or whatever you have potentially lost a client as the incoming marketing manager or different member of the team may also have a favoured photographer. So get to know as many people as you can in your clients office so they know who you are and they know you are a photographer who can do the job and turn in the results.

Licence to use – see Chapter 9

Honestly? I do not have the time to send out a Licence to use for every job that I do! If it is a new client then they receive my terms and conditions (as per AOP guidelines) and then we will discuss the License and what rights they have for usage. I then send them a 'License to use' that covers all the points we discussed and which covers both them and me for all subsequent commissions. Within the Meta Data of every file supplied is all my contact information, copyright, client and agreed usage. Together with the date the image was shot.

Clients

Can't live with them, can't live without them! Unless you are in the fortunate position of being able to self-fund your architectural photography and not need an income – we really do need clients.

These are the people who actually pay you to go out and photograph their creations, their products and their work. I work for a number of large architectural concerns and they trust me to photograph their building at the correct time of day, using the correct equipment and then to provide a suitable digital file ready for publication or for web using my knowledge and expertise. I supply to the client a selection of images as low res jpegs after an initial edit, which have had minimal post production work carried out. From there the client makes a selection of anything (depending on the job) between 10 and 20 images. I then work on the optimisation of each file and provide a full resolution Tiff file in the Adobe 1998 RGB colour space together with a jpeg (SRGB) at a smaller size for web use, all provided on DVD. All images including all the RAW files are backed up to three external hard drives.

Clients, like all of us, are under financial pressures these days. I have often lost out on a commission because the budget had been cut and they had to use the chap in the office or the newly qualified photographer who just happened to contact them at an opportune moment. It happens; I no longer get upset over it. One thing I never do is get angry and let rip, well I did once a long time ago and never worked with that client again. If I'd kept quiet I would have got the job back because the lesser paid/inexperienced photographer cocked it up. Lesson learnt 'never burn your bridges'. Now I am always supportive and helpful as clients mostly never remember favours done (unless gently prompted), though will always remember the guy who either was totally unhelpful or who was publicly critical!

Planning a shoot

Ok we have the brief, we know it's a new build on the other side of the country and it's a shoot for an architect. What next? Phone calls. Find out which way the building is facing (important in deciding whether it is a morning or afternoon shoot). Whether landscaping has been done, rubbish removed, office furniture all in etc. If you cannot speak to someone at the building then your client has to be asked these questions and be given to understand that, potentially, you might need to make a second chargeable visit to the project in the event of them saying it is ready for photography and when you get there it still has two large skips next to the entrance or the paving hasn't been laid. There is nothing that concentrates a clients' mind more than the possibility of further fees if he hasn't checked something and has given the green light for photography to commence.

I find that my working week is a constant juggle, apart from the necessary paperwork, post production of previous work and doing self-promotion (not enough) I need to make decisions about which commissions to organise to shoot first. www (where, when, weather) all play a factor with weather being the decider. There are many on-line forecast sites, apps for your mobile or ipad which I'm not going to list as new versions and types are constantly being introduced. One app I find indispensable and I will mention is TPE (The Photographers Ephemeris) this helps you plan a shoot in natural light and gives time and direction of sunrise and sunset and so much more.

So if it's a distance away it's a pretty important decision to make whether to go for it or shoot a closer job. Whichever way they all need to be done and it becomes a question of which client needs their job quicker. Something that does play a factor once again is the relationship you have with each client. Personally I would prefer to complete a job for a regular client and who pays on time for maybe a lesser fee quickly then for a company who pays more messes you about but then needs constant reminding about payment. Cash flow is crucial.

Winter months are great for dusk shots. Why? Because you can photograph the building at 4pm with all the lights on and people working and then go home for your tea, the downside is that it's cold, there are no leaves on the trees and during the day the sun never gets very high in the sky and therefore planning is even more important especially when your shooting day may only be 5 hours of usable sunlight on a very good day. Summer months are great, early morning light – lovely. Late afternoon and evening light, fab as well. Which is best? Depends on which way your structure is facing of course. Comes back to planning in advance.

The downside to summer shooting- Dusk shots! Worst case scenario (21st June) the sun sets at 21.45 and probably a dusk shot will be between 20 and 30 minutes after that so that can be a pretty late evening and needs to be considered when costing the job. Plus of course most offices will be closed and therefore arrangements need to be made for lights either to be left on or access to the building to have them switched on.

Equipment

A client not so long ago said that in future they wanted me to shoot medium format digital otherwise they would have to commission photography elsewhere. They weren't a regular client and it turned out that one of the partners had been reading up on professional photography on the net and his conclusion was that to be a professional you needed to use medium format digital cameras or backs because the quality was so much better. I hold up my hand here and state I use Digital SLR because it suits my style of shooting. I'm able to afford the best lenses including perspective control types and can afford to update the camera body on roughly a three year basis.

The conversation with the aforementioned client went something like this:

> *'We want you to shoot medium format digital'*
>
> *'Can you tell me why?*
>
> *'better quality and it's more professional'*

'I agree to the first and question the second'

'So in future you will supply what we want?'

'Err—No'

'Why not?'

'Well firstly I'm afraid that I am not going to buy into a system that will cost me a great deal of money and secondly I would add that you will never use the ultimate quality it gives especially since 99.9% of the work you use is less than A4 in size and mainly for web use so you are throwing away a great deal of the information contained in the file. However if you would like to pay me a lot more or perhaps pay for the hire then, yes I will shoot medium format.'

They obviously declined. The conversation was carried out over a coffee in a jovial manner but it was an important point to be made.

Now of course if I were to win the lottery or someone bought one for me that would be a different matter. However we all know that a type of camera doesn't make you a better photographer whether architectural or otherwise – the equipment you use has to suit your style of shooting and working methods and I would never dream of criticising any photographer who works with a lesser camera then I or conversely a photographer who has made the decision to invest in a medium format system and all that entails. Its personal choice and it has to be a business decision, costed and properly thought out.

I confess that sometimes I crave for the clunk click of the Hasselblad and the scrabble to change a film after the 12 exposures as the light is just beginning to disappear or for the hood over my head when shooting on a field camera (especially in winter 'cause the dark cloth acts like a scarf) but DSLR does everything it needs for my business of architectural photography and as mentioned previously, it is affordable, adaptable and I am able to upgrade on a regular basis. An important point though is to look at the quality of the lenses in use. A professional lens though not cheap will last you many years and will still be worth decent money even after five years of solid use so a case can be made for owning all your lenses whereas a camera body depreciates in value quite quickly over this time as new technology comes into play so perhaps a leasing option is a sensible decision in this regard?

All clients have a right to expect a certain quality i.e. to a professional standard but they cannot dictate what equipment you use. It's not their business. My current list of lenses for DSLR architectural photography is 14-24mm, 24mm Perspective Control, 24-70mm, 70-200mm though I am seriously considering investing in some prime lenses which can take full advantage of the latest 'uber' pixel DSLR cameras.

Lighting: I use a number of portable flashguns all with stands and controlled using radio transceivers so much easier then the blue plastic coated flash bulbs (P100's) of yester year when it was a right of passage when a bulb went off in your hand causing blistered fingers and lots of curses.

My first boss used to say:

'Look Up, look at the details'

There is detail we so often miss above our heads and that was an important lesson. On arrival at a commission take the time to look around, get a feel for the building. Decide on the order of shooting the images. Do not, for example, shoot interiors first if you have beautiful light on the exterior expecting it to still be the same an hour later. Take the opportunities as they come and break the commission down into parts. Make a list and tick them off as you go.

AND don't forget your neutral Grad filters and a bubble level!!

CHAPTER 12: CORPORATE & DESIGN

Corporate Photography

Stephen Barnet

Introduction

Corporate photography sits conveniently between the world of advertising and editorial photography, sharing some of the attributes of both disciplines but being a separate area of photography within it's own right. It is used to support and illustrate the public image of a business or organisation. This can be a product or service, or it can be used to illustrate a story in a positive manner. In general terms it comes under the banner of 'Corporate Communications'.

In practice this means shooting for printed publications like corporate brochures and annual reports, establishing and maintaining corporate identity through different media and supporting new territories like the Internet. Commissions will typically come through either a design company or directly from the client company (client direct).

Corporate photography is often seen as the poor relation to its more glamorous advertising cousin. While it is true that budgets are unlikely to be as generous as in a full -blown advertising campaign, shooting for the corporate market can be both rewarding and profitable.

Much of what is written in Chapter 5 about advertising photography is true for making a living in the corporate market. In this chapter we shall expand on some of the points that are skimmed over in Chapter 5 but are more relevant if you are dealing with clients directly or through design groups.

Fees

Practical experience will dictate that there is a market rate for corporate photography, as with any area of business, but it is impossible to discuss actual rates on these pages. What you can charge depends on your experience and what others around you charge. As a rule of thumb, (which like any digit can easily be broken!) rates are approximately 2/3rds of what you would expect to be paid in a straightforward advertising commission. They are also at least 100% greater than you would expect for an editorial commission.

Working Directly with Clients

In some respects working directly with your client is the optimum way of doing business. You will be hired personally for your services and this means you are able to discuss matters without going through third parties. This frees up the creative and decision making process because there is a short chain of command. You are being hired directly for your skills so the responsibility to achieve results is firmly on your shoulders. It should also generally mean that you are paid on better terms. Sticking with AOP Paperwork, you will ask for payment within 30 days, and in practice may well be paid within that period! Practical experience suggests that this never happens when working through a Design Group, were payment terms are usually 60 days or more.

Working directly means it's all the more important to define terms & conditions and make use of your AOP forms! You are responsible for the smooth running of your business and the correct use of paperwork will help to put any problems that may occur into a legal framework.

You may well find that issues such as Licence to Use and Base Usage Rate fall on deaf ears. Best practice says that you will agree a licence period with the client and agree usage for the images. There is very often a wide gap between the expectations of a photographer working within the boundaries of best practice and the reality of building a working relationship with a potential client.

Corporate clients often don't understand copyright issues and expect to have unlimited use of material. They may have been briefed inaccurately by legal departments, or they may want something for nothing. It's up to the photographer to establish the basis for the working relationship at the outset and negotiate a fair deal which can then be enforced.

It is necessary for the photographer to think in terms of the length of a licence, e.g. 12, 24 or 36 months and the use of the photography, e.g. annual report, corporate brochure, trade press, internet etc. Always try to establish that images are for the sole use of the commissioning company, and not to be used by third parties. In the case of large multinational businesses, try to ensure that control of images is kept by the commissioning office. This will usually be their head office, through the communications department supporting the main board of directors. Practical experience suggests that geographical territories are less important than in advertising. For example, the worldwide distribution of an annual report is tiny compared to a worldwide poster campaign.

Having established the needs of the client, the estimate is the easiest way to introduce the concept of additional fees for further usage. If, for example, you are asked to shoot for an annual report you may offer a 2 year licence with additional fees for internet, trade press, corporate brochure etc. at smaller percentages of the day rate. This is a more concise version of the BUR and puts the photographer into a negotiating position. The client can no longer assume that they have carte blanche to use all material.

There has been a rise in recent years of the copyright assignment; a situation that seems particularly bad in the editorial market and is working it's way gradually into corporate business. These 'agreements' are often sprung on the photographer at the very last moment, before a job is about to commence. They tend to be issued by corporate legal departments who don't want to understand the issues surrounding copyright. Blanket assignments make life easier (for the unscrupulous client) without considering individual circumstances. Sadly, there is no magic bullet to overcome these restrictive contracts although at the time of writing the European Union is looking at changing the law on restrictive contracts

If you are unable to negotiate around such a contract, try to settle on an all uses licence as per the advertising guidelines (see Chapter 5 Advertising Photography).

Model Release Forms

When working on jobs that don't use professional models, e.g. when shooting on a client's premises, it's still important that any person photographed signs a Model Release. It's unlikely that your client will be concerned, but it's important that there is no liability on the photographer's shoulders. You may wish to license non-exclusive material in the future to other clients or a library and for this purpose a model release is essential. (See part 1 Chapter2, Contracts, for more information, also Annexe for examples of forms).

Expenses

Unlike in advertising, it is most unusual for corporate or design clients to pay expenses in advance of a shoot. Obviously this depends on budget and the outlay that is required. This will always be a point of negotiation.

Charging mark-ups on expenses is largely a matter of common sense. In general terms, charge everything to the job and mark-up materials and mileage as previously discussed. It is not reasonable to mark-up hotels, airfares, or subsistence. Anything that is purchased with cash or has to be paid directly upon finishing the job should be marked up this includes labour such as an assistant or make-up artist. This is because the photographer will be out of pocket from the end of the shoot, but it may be many weeks before the final invoice is settled. The photographer will effectively be lending the client money and for this service you can expect to charge a mark-up. This does not, however, advocate underpaying assistants or others on the shoot!

Overseas Commissions & The ATA Carnet

On overseas corporate shoots you can expect the client to make travel and accommodation arrangements for you. They should provide tickets and pay for airfares in advance; if the photographer has to make their own arrangements then this would certainly be a case for recovering expenses before the shoot commences. You can reasonably expect that the client will provide a company minder from the local office to deal with problems of transportation, language and logistics.

This leaves the photographer to deal with the headache that is the ATA Carnet. This is an expensive and bureaucratic passport for equipment that is nevertheless essential for the smooth negotiation of customs & excise. Officials can turn a trip into a nightmare of impounded gear, or even refuse entry to the country.

The Carnet can be arranged through your local chamber of commerce and although it is complex to fill in, it's well worth the effort. Its cost, running into several hundred pounds, should be borne by the client. Equipment is then 'booked' in and out of countries with a series of counterfoils that are torn off at each new border post.

Not all countries work under the Carnet system. Broadly speaking, developed countries accept them, third world countries don't. Seek advice from the chamber of commerce about your itinerary.

Where no Carnet system operates, make sure that the client has an agent who is used to dealing with customs in the territory. They may be asked to leave a refundable bond with customs officials and this is most important, as otherwise gear is likely to be impounded. Local officials weald great power and cannot be underestimated. It's best to carry duplicate lists of equipment, including serial numbers, that can be stamped by customs on exit from the UK. Make Airline check-in staff aware that you need to see customs before departure and arrangements will be made for separate loading of your baggage.

For further information on working abroad see Chapter 15.

The only realistic alternative is to travel light as a tourist, aware of the problems that may beset you!

Design Photography

Michael Harding

Working with Design Companies

When compared to the advertising agencies that quite often own them, the rates that design companies typically pay are considerably lower – expect to find them in the region of some 50% lower. The fact that there is less money on offer has several important effects in both the nature of the work that you can expect from them, and the scale of the projects they have to commission photography for.

Although the traditional definitions are blurring more and more daily, much of the print work that design companies do is for application in business-to-business communications such as annual reports and corporate brochures. Whilst these are vital documents, their potential return to the client company can be harder to realise, as these documents are often brand building within an industry or professional context. As a result, the measurable returns for a client company can be lower, as the positive effects that these publications will have for a company are quite long term but they are not usually structured to generate a direct sales response.

Annual reports

In the case of company annual reports, UK law requires that all limited companies must report their financial performance to potential investors each year. This ought to create a huge natural market for images to communicate messages about their successes; in practice though, here in the UK most company stock issues are traded by financial analysts, and so the actual target group that a client might want to address is actually quite a small and intimate audience. This means, in effect, that print runs are fairly short. (If compared to the USA where this marketplace is more retail based, with consumers paying an important role in such investments, the budgets and ambitions can be fairly modest here. Consequently, annual report runs in the USA are much longer, with far greater potential returns to the client company; as a result, rates and production budgets for such work are higher in the USA than here.)

Product catalogues

Even when a project under discussion is for a consumer or retail application, such as a product catalogue, the scale of the application tends to be smaller, say a few thousand copies printed; whereas a classic above the line advertising campaign application might see your work used on billboards globally. Companies have therefore made a link between how widely they are expecting to use your images and how much profit might be returned to them from such extensive usage, and the rates that they expect to pay reflect this.

Packaging

Packaging design is another significant area that graphic design firms produce work for and for which they might commission photographers to create images for. Most consumer brands now realise how important it is to produce visually appealing packaging for their products, and much effort and expense is devoted to producing packaging that will entice a consumer to choose one brand over another. In this instance, the print runs can be vast; in theory, this ought to mean that you could expect the rates to track this increase in frequency of application. In practice, however, the reality is that the day rates to be found in working in this area are similar to those that design companies pay for the print work previously described.

A possible reason for this is that if you were asked to photograph an entire range of packaging for say, a range of convenience foods for a major supermarket chain, you might reduce your advertising rate in respect of the sheer number of continuous days work that this range might take.

How does a Design company work?

The market forces at work in this sector means that even though you might be working for a design company directly, they in turn are usually working to an agreed total price to produce the complete range for their client, in this example the supermarket chain. Your work therefore becomes part of the overhead costs that the design company must factor into their calculations when pricing the job. This differs from advertising in that advertising agencies are often buying your services themselves and then reselling those services to their client with an agency handling mark-up added. You can therefore expect design companies to exert pressure to try to win what additional profit they might at the expense of your day rate.

Furthermore, these fixed price agreements mean that their client company often sees your work as part of the same equation that they might use to purchase any other commodity. This can mean that practitioners in this area can, to some extent, find terms and conditions of work dictated by the client company.

This may sound a slightly downbeat background for making a living, and so it must always be remembered that there is much exciting, stimulating and (even!) profitable work to be found from design groups. For example, one of the pluses to be found when working for design consultancies is the sheer directness of the whole experience. Teams running projects in design tend to be smaller, and designers tend to be expected to run more detailed aspects of the job themselves.

It is, however, a rare design company that maintains a dedicated art buyer, which means that you will get used to contacting individual designers themselves to present your work. This lack of an art buying system means that it can sometimes be difficult to get into design companies, as seeing you and your work personally means that the designer in question is unable to get on with whatever project they are working on at the time. Once again, though, this directness of experience means that the response you get is unfiltered, and this can help you to more accurately define which of your photographs are working hardest for a creative.

You will also find that as there is no art buyer, when your portfolio does get called in for a project, the person at the other end of the line might be the group's receptionist, who is working their way through a long list of fellow photographers, which has been given to them by a busy designer and who expects them to call in portfolios in between answering the telephone. This places additional pressure on you to ascertain exactly what sort of project it is that they are considering your work for, as an incomplete brief has more often than not been given by the designer to the person expected to actually make the phone calls.

Working with a Design Company

Once you get do get a commission, you'll find that the person who is responsible for the day to day running of the project is most likely to be the account manager. They are the person most likely to report project progress to their client, monitor budgets and timetables and oversee practical aspects of the job. Once again, as there is unlikely to be any art buyer on staff, you ought to expect to discuss and agree financial as well as copyright and usage issues with the account manager. As mentioned throughout this book, it is vitally important to maintain a clear and agreed paperwork chain at all times in commercial photography, and it is doubly important in an environment like design, where everyone must multi task, and thus details important to photographers – like rights usage – might slip through the cracks. For this reason the AOP examples that you'll

Getting paid

Equally important to photographers working commercially is getting paid on time. Compared to some famously slow paying ad agencies, design companies are relatively prompt to pay. Always clearly state your expected payment terms – 30 Days Net being standard practice – and reserve the usage rights until your Invoice has been paid in full. Stating that you are reserving your rights might prove to be of some use to you later should the company prove, for whatever reason, to be unable to honour your Invoice. This should be included in your terms and conditions and, to form part of the contract, given to the client prior to the shoot. (see Part 1 Chapter 2 Contracts)

Sending a Statement of Account to the Accounts Department as close to the due date as possible will give you some chance of getting paid promptly, as very few companies today will pay invoices without some nagging. In practice, the difference between getting on the list for eventual payment is often as simple as laying down some sort of marker that gets someone in Accounts to pull your paperwork out of a large pile of those to be paid eventually, and put into that smaller pile for immediate payment.

As the 30 Days Net payment period is now consider period "best practice" by the larger corporate and governmental agency clients that will likely be your ultimate clients, you ought to reasonably expect that this policy should trickle down to the design company that you're in turn working for. Remember: when attempting to collect your debts that it's nothing personal, but be polite, firm and dutiful when you do need to speak to someone in the Accounts Department.

CHAPTER 12

CHAPTER 13: STOCK

Introduction

Ian McKinnell

Image libraries are a multibillion dollar industry providing images for publishing, the web, advertising, and television: any media that uses visual imagery.

Stock can be a valuable source of income for a photographer, complimenting their commissioned work, providing a creative outlet for experimentation & keeping them busy. Some photographers earn their entire income from stock & unlike most commissioned work, royalties from libraries are not a 'one off': images can sell repeatedly for years. There is a vast market out there & the right image in the right place can make a considerable amount of money.

The stock industry has undergone huge changes over the years. The move from print to electronic media has expanded the market exponentially & the internet has changed the way the business operates forever.

Photographer Peter Dazeley has a great deal of experience of the Stock Industry & the following is an edited version of an article he wrote for Photo Professional Magazine.

Stock photography and how to succeed in it

Peter Dazeley

A friend described stock photography as similar to putting a bet on a horse, with some images you win, with some images you lose.

Life is getting tougher for stock photographers; the global recession has had a negative impact on revenues across the board for marketing and advertising services; but a problem should always be seen as an opportunity.

Stock can be a fun & a unique opportunity that few outsiders know about, let alone understand. A supermarket can only sell a packet of sausages once. With stock you can sell the same image over & over again.

Today's top stock photographers rarely do commissioned work, instead they spend hours researching for stock shoots – brainstorming ideas, finding locations, street casting real models, producing mood boards, pre-visualizing and planning shoots that are more like military operations than photo shoots.

When the shoot is completed it does not stop there; it has to be edited, retouched, model release forms attached and most importantly, accurate and concise keywords have to be added. It's also vital to research what images the libraries already have – it's pointless duplicating them.

The stock business differs from most other businesses, as the agency that sells your stock pictures and sets the price is unconcerned about the cost of the production to the photographer. Most of the time agencies don't have a clue about the time and cost that goes into producing an image. A photograph with 50 models on a beautiful beach in South Africa will sell for the same price as a still life of a doughnut on a white background.

The photographer receives a percentage of the fee the customer pays; somewhere between 10-40% is today's going rate (50% used to be the norm). The agency's prices are based on their operating and marketing costs, which have nothing to do with the photographer's costs or the value given to the client. It is a crazy system of pricing. Even so the estimated revenue generated by stock photography in 2010 was $1.45 billion worldwide.

How things have changed

The business has changed out of all recognition in recent years. In the 90's most stock libraries were producing and distributing massive printed catalogues of their pictures and sending duplicate transparencies (occasionally originals!) by post or courier to their customers. In 1990 if you wanted an image of an Easter egg you would reach for the catalogues & maybe find a choice of a dozen after a few minutes searching. If one of those images was yours then it could earn a substantial income from stock because there was more demand than supply. Nowadays the stock business is totally digital; an internet search of just one picture library will bring up thousands of Easter egg images: if one of those is yours your income will be much diluted.

A buyer finds a picture in a stock library by using relevant keywords that best depict his requirement. Keywords describe the subject matter and concepts of an image; without these keywords other photographers' images will appear ahead of yours in a potential buyer's search results, making your picture virtually invisible.

The furthest a lot of art directors and designers go on a shoot nowadays is a quick trip to gettyimages.com. A publisher who needs a sunset picture for an article can choose from thousands of images on numerous stock sites; so why pay a photographer to shoot one?

In the old days, stock photography was considered uncool, with many photographers simply submitting outtakes from their commissioned shoots as a way of recycling their images. Now more and more photographers are earning money from selling their stock images, some shooting stock full time, but fewer and fewer are earning enough to support themselves solely through stock photography.

A buddy's annual family holiday each year was paid for by the income generated from a single picture of a hamburger. Now photographers' income from Stock is more likely to be made up from lots and lots of small sales, with occasional big ones. Quantity is the name of today's game, which is rapidly leading to an oversupply of imagery. All over the world endless photographers have spent the last 10 years shooting too many images of the same subjects.

In this tough economic climate, the internet has become a gigantic, incredibly fast growing market. This is because of the huge number of images needed to fuel the explosion of technology and devices such as websites, blogs and news sites. Most magazines and newspapers will eventually be online, simply because of the costs of paper, printing and most of all distribution. The demand for online pictures will inevitably increase.

Different Flavours

The industry is focused more than ever before on price, with four main licensing models for images: Rights Managed (an image is licensed only for a specific use with the fees depending on use. RM should be the highest quality, highest earning images) Royalty Free (a more flexible license: one payment irrespective of use. A photographer has to give away more rights & is generally paid less) Microstock (lower quality thresholds, more rights given away for even less money than RF. Mainly for amateurs) and Freestock (where amateurs just give their rights away for nothing).

The recent emergence of Microstock has taken the established stock image market by storm. In the past a large file size (50Mb+) was essential for print & posters. Web pages use much smaller images: some picture libraries will even accept images from an iPhone!

Most Microstock contributors are not professionals but amateur photographers, production houses and designers who have a big advantage over photographers in understanding which images are needed. In the future, many of the web and graphic designers will also use their own digital cameras to create their own images, manipulating them in Photoshop, rather than buying pictures.

Many people who participate in Microstock are doing it as a hobby and the buzz (maybe) of seeing their work used by a newspaper, a large corporate company or on the cover of a hip magazine. This rise of the amateur, who often has very high end digital equipment and does not need to cover his costs can be very difficult for a professional to compete against and many previously lucrative areas of stock, such as travel photography, are no longer economically realistic when you need to earn that investment in time & money back.

There has been an enormous amount of PR in the photographic press about the amazing financial success of photographers who have entered the Microstock market. The truth and reality is that very few contributors to Microstock make substantial amounts of money. I asked Jim Pickerell, the photographer, analyst and stock guru for his thoughts on the average price generated from a single Microstock image in 12 months.

> *'I estimate the total gross revenue generated from the sale of Microstock images in 2010 was between $400 and $500 million, lets say $450million. There may be 25 million unique images being licensed as Microstock, because most images are represented on multiple sites, this would mean the average annual income per image would be about $18. Assuming the photographer gets 20%, he would earn about $3.60 per image on file.*
>
> *The gross 2010 revenue from the licensing of creative rights-managed images in the Getty Images collection is unlikely to reach $174 million probably falling short by quite a bit. (These calculations do not consider editorial images.) On average, 35% or $60.90 million will be paid out in royalty to photographers. Getty has about 2 million rights managed images, which would mean photographers are averaging $30 per image on file. But this is Getty, the world's number one licenser of images.'*

One way to succeed in this environment is to shoot a huge number of images, especially as the useful life of an image is getting shorter, as more and more images are uploaded, pushing the old ones further down the customer's search order.

Successful stock shooters spread their work between different brands, but this probably does mean a smaller percentage of your sales than if you put all your work exclusively with one library. Shooting Microstock is more about quantity than quality, they would be aiming to shoot 200 images in a day of 7-8 hours. If you want to make money in this Microstock market, it is clearly a numbers game.

There will always be a few very successful photographers, but in reality, a couple of top photographers have openly said that Microstock has not become the business opportunity that they hoped it would be, and are changing direction.

Networking

One of the most amazing things to come out of Microstock is how the community of Microstock photographers want to share their techniques, lighting, camera tests, tips, and success stories. This seems quite odd to old stock photographers, who guarded the secrets of their success very closely in such a competitive world.

Photographers' networking has become a big part of stock, with Facebook, YouTube, blogs and Twitter. Research photographers; in particular Jonathan Ross of Anderson Ross (http://www.andersenross.com) give a great insight into stock photography, as well as showing images which sell really well.

Yuri Arcurs (http://www.arcurs.com) the worlds highest earning Microstock photographer who has a production company with more than 50 full and part time staff including 4 – 5 other photographers. His team is producing about 11,000 new images per year). Tom Grill, Jim Erickson, John Lund, Tony Sweet who all have blogs and forums, which offer demonstrations as well as tips and support. You can also find Yuri Arcurs, Tony Sweet and John Lund on YouTube. Knowing what is going on in the stock world can be very helpful. Jim Pickerell's Selling Stock online newsletters (http://www.selling-stock.com): a quick Google search will find many others.

Some people may think that it is impossible to earn a living from stock but... a photographer who did not want to be named has a top selling rights managed image which has earned Getty over $175,000. His top 5 RM images have each earned over $100,000. So there is still big money to be made in the Rights Managed stock business; you just need to get going and shoot well-crafted images with very clear concepts, which solve picture buyers' needs. Even portrait and wedding photographers, who shoot modern editorial pictures, should think of asking good-looking couples or interesting characters, if it would be possible to use their pictures for stock and get them to sign model release forms. Remember, your family and friends can radically reduce your model and location costs.

Crossroads

We have arrived at a crossroads for stock photographers. Clients are driving down costs, as libraries fight for market share to combat the advancing choice and saturation of imagery. The world of stock photography has always been speculative; photographers spend time and money to produce pictures that they believe in, in the hope that clients will buy them over and over again. However, sometimes nobody buys them. Producing stock is becoming a bigger and bigger gamble; but it has not stopped photographers rushing to join in. Jim Pickerell researched photographers with the Shutterstock agency in January 2010. They had 208,000 contributors and by October 2010 it had risen to 254,000.

A positive result of the transfer to internet usage of images is the mammoth global market that has opened up. With the digital age and the internet, buyers of stock imagery have an amazing number of pictures at varying price points to choose from. A multitude of sites like DreamsTime and Getty-owned Stock.XCHNG now offer free stock pictures. How all these photographers make a decent return on their investment I just don't understand! There are also billions of images available on Google, Yahoo etc. Google alone has more than 500 billion images on its database.

Commissioned Library Shoots

One modern trend is for large companies and conglomerates to build up their own library of pictures. This clearly makes a lot of sense and eradicates the possibility of using the same stock image as one of their competitors; this sort of PR blunder has happened to many high profile companies in the past. Commissions of this sort can be a very profitable opportunity for photographers as the client will probably want an unlimited, indefinite licence, although it means the photographer will only get the fee once. In reality, it is unlikely that an image will be used by your client globally, indefinitely and in all media. There will always be photographers who intentionally or unknowingly ignore licensing and simply give away unlimited use of their pictures without charging a premium. They tend to be young photographers who don't know any better, or established photographers who have found that either it is the only way to compete, or that they couldn't be bothered with the extra work involved in understanding how image licensing works. This is a mistake, licensing your work professionally should be seen as a big income stream for a photographer's business.

Stock on Request

Another fascinating business area is stock on request. One stop companies like www.onrequestimages.com provide global photography and video solutions. Their clients include American Express, Aviva, T mobile, Coca-Cola, Bank of America etc. Clients are able to send their creative brief, the agency will offer them a selection of suitable photographers and take on the whole responsibility of producing the shoot, including international location scouting, casting, production crew, permits, styling, hair and makeup, editing, and retouching. They represent 450 photographers in 60 countries and they are always looking to recruit more specialist photographers.

Copyright Abuse

Even if you are successful in selling your pictures, it does not mean you will always be paid. A 2009 Deutsche Telekom survey revealed that nearly half (44%) of marketing, public relations and publishing professionals think that a royalty-free image is an image that can be used without payment. Worse still, 37% of respondents admitted having used images illegally by swiping them off the internet.

My pictures are licenced all over the world and bearing in mind that I only ever see a small number of my pictures being used, I am continually discovering images being used without license.

Infringers rely on the fact that, due to the costs involved, small unauthorised uses are hardly worth pursuing by the photographer or the agency. The general view of society today is that if an image is on the web it can be used without paying or worrying about copyright. A 'catch me and I might pay' scenario. The only light at the end of the tunnel is companies like PicScout www.picscout.com who track images to detect and identify its Library customers' unlicensed images. Amy Love, VP for marketing and business development of Picscout states that 85% of the RM uses tracked down for their clients are identified as unauthorised or being beyond their original agreed licence duration. As with the music industry copyright theft is growing at a pace. In Britain it is reckoned that 1 billion songs are illegally downloaded each year and the US Chamber of Commerce estimates that copyright theft costs its nation's economy roughly $58 billion each year.

With these figures maybe there is no way that photographers will be compensated for their efforts in the future: a very serious problem for the next generation of creators. The odds on making a return on your investment are continually being eaten away.

Research

If your agency doesn't offer you an art director or an editor you need to do your own research. Check out the contents of different libraries before you shoot any subject. Find out what they have, whether you can shoot a concept better or differently, check whether there is already an oversupply of what you are considering to shoot. Looking for a gap in the market is one of the keys to successful stock photography. One of the great creative research tools, even if you don't want to put your images into Microstock, is to go into their site, browse their images to find out what producers are shooting and check how many views and downloads each image has made which is displayed on sites like iStock (www.istockphoto.com)

Keep away from niche and speciality collections, because they will probably only have niche demands. My best advice is to fill the gaps in libraries, do not give them more of the same. The key to success is not to give clients what they want now, but what they will want next.

It is important to shoot great, fresh pictures. Try not to include props that date quickly. Old pictures of mobile phones, computers, clothing, look very dated. Having said that, clients will always want the latest technology like Skype and iPads. The simple answer is if you produce modern, carefully researched, beautiful, aspirational, unique images that tell a story and answer customer needs, you will find agencies who will sell them well for you all over the world.

Footage

The future of the web will, I believe, morph still pictures into moving imagery so that shooting footage for picture libraries may well be the future, especially with modern DSLR cameras with video facility, making them very easy to create.

Profitability

For your profitability, you must factor in your expenses. Do not kid yourself. New equipment, car, computer upgrades, even your retirement plan. Successful stock photography is about making sure it is financially viable for you. If you spend 100 hours producing 50 images, keep records of costs and sales, so you can calculate your return on your investment. Using this information, you can work out which images sell and which images did not produce a return, which will give you great guidance for future shoots.

War

There is a war going on, you have to create images that can win the battle of the thumbnails on customers' computer screens. It is not just about great images; the lottery of stock photography today is about having the right image, at the right price, at the right time. Simply put, a great picture is an image lots of customers want to license for money.

Advice from the front line

Finally, I asked my friend Tom Hind, Getty's European Head of Content, for his thoughts on a couple of questions I posed to him for photographers wishing to contribute to stock libraries:

PD: What qualities are you looking for in contributing photographers to Getty Images?

TH: "Above all we are looking for originality, good production values where appropriate, and photographers who are interested in building a body of work."

PD: How should they prepare to contribute to a stock library, and what sort of research would you recommend for somebody starting out in stock photography?

TH 'Stock photography is a unique business and there is no set formula for what will work commercially. For those looking to get into the industry, I would advise reading our creative research briefs to find something that works for you and that you can rework or apply your own twist to. Alongside this, don't lose sight of what interests you in terms of subject matter or approach – the work that you are passionate about always has an edge.'"

PD: What do Photographers do wrong or badly when trying contribute to a stock library?

TH "In general very little! Sometimes photographers use an existing stock image as inspiration, or to help plan a shoot. The fact the image is online seems to commercially validate it, but you can see how this might be a risky approach.'

PD: With the constantly evolving state of stock photography, is there anything else that you think that photographers should be aware of?

"If you are on top of imagery trends and creative research and you are producing innovative work that you are proud of, then it should work for you in fields beyond stock photography. Many of the contributors we work with are approached for commissions because their stock work has something that clients want. That is not to say everything you shoot has to be portfolio worthy or 'edgy', but it is worth mixing it up.'"

CHAPTER 14: DIGITAL TECHNOLOGY & MOVING IMAGE

Digital Technology

Nick Dunmur

Introduction

In the last ten years since this chapter was first written, the landscape of professional photography has changed, perhaps by as much as the shift in perception of image-making which occurred when photography was first revealed to the world. That change continues apace currently, and it is probably true that in another five years, this chapter will need updating again. So, with that caveat considered, what follows is a snapshot of where, broadly speaking, the digital sector of the industry stands now, what is considered to be best practice and how all of that fits together in a digital copyright age.

The Impact of Digital Technology

In the ten years that have elapsed since this chapter was first written, photographers have been exposed to a paradigm shift in business practice as well as having to come to terms with a sea-change in the way that the value of the services photographers provide are perceived by others (clients, especially). The 'new technologies' mentioned in the previous version of this chapter have had an additional ten years in which to develop and mature and one might be forgiven for thinking that that time would have brought some semblance of stability – not so – there is no real indication that the markets that support and enable the trade of digital content have settled into a form that will continue unchanged for any length of time. In fact, the only certainty is that there is no certainty. Content is information and is everything – it forms the basis for entertainment and education and makes digital media very attractive to the consumer. Whatever form it takes; photography, film/video, literature or music or indeed any combination of these, this material is subject to exactly the same protection through the UK intellectual property laws as any other form of creative work. The undeniably huge opportunities that the digital platform offers the creator in terms of new ways of disseminating and communicating with an audience come with a caveat – that of the ease of duplicity and theft which can occur with any digital asset. A complaint often levelled at creators is that they are overly restrictive with what can be 'done' with their work; the internet has provided a platform which reinforces the myth that digital work is somehow free (free to create AND free to use!) and the educational and library communities have been demanding greater freedom to use digital (or digitised) material in greater ways. Indeed there is a substantial group of people and businesses who would like to see copyright as we know it, abandoned altogether. The working life of the professional photographer has become more complex with the management and licensing of the work commanding a greater amount of both time and resources.

Uses of Digital Technology

No one disputes that digital imaging is here to stay. A digital camera has become an indispensible tool much like any other with the exception that new developments are announced in an ever-quickening cycle; whereas a single set of Hasselblad film equipment would see a photographer through their working life, it is not uncommon for digital cameras to be upgraded almost as often as the computers that help control them, as an indispensible part of that workflow.

Online file delivery has largely replaced the 'analogue' methods of delivery (like the courier or the post) and DVDs are barely large enough in size to contain the burgeoning amount of digital data generated by larger and larger sensors. The increase in the speed and availability of fibre-optic broadband has allowed the smallest business to use this technology to their advantage in terms of distribution and exchange. Christmas 2013 saw a larger percentage of consumer spending on gifts carried out online, not in-store. This was the first time this had happened and was facilitated in no small measure by the ease of access to the internet; speeds of 20mbps and upwards are now not uncommon. A professional photographer can be based anywhere (more or less) and be connected to a global market for an ever-decreasing cost.

Digital work has enabled the compilation or mixing of different artforms to become easier. A new language has started to evolve around this, with phrases like 'mash-up' becoming commonplace and while appropriation art as a genre has existed for quite some time, there are generations of new artists and makers who see this as a perfectly usual means of creating. This brings with it new problems in terms of understanding what is acceptable and allowable, morally and legally, and recognising that the law in the form of the Copyright, Designs & Patents Act (1988), [CDPA 1988] has gaps in it that do not cover much of the digital activity that is so easily facilitated.

Digital collage is easy but any maker of such work should remember that any digital-based collage will, inevitably, require the reproduction of any works used, and as such is subject to the same copyright protection.

Computer-generated imaging (CGI) can produce work autonomously, subject to the parameters laid down by an operator, and the copyright-owner of such imagery should be considered the person responsible for setting up and instigating such parameters and not necessarily the person who may have supplied photographic components for that CGI work. Those photographic components may well have had to be licensed in order to combine them into a CGI artifact, but is a good example of the sometimes complex relationships that are becoming more commonplace.

Metadata

With any digital 'product' (a photograph, illustration, piece of writing or music track), comes the opportunity to add information about that item. This is called metadata (which simply means, 'data about data') and is one of the most important and indispensible elements of utilising and implementing a digital workflow. The correct use of metadata in photography allows the creator to input a large amount of information into the file itself. Such metadata can be broken down into three main types; descriptive (author, image caption, keywords…), structural (how the pages of a chapter of a book are put together, or how an image in a series might be laid out in order) and administrative (date of capture, file type…). In the case of photography, the EXIF data (Exchangeable Image File data) provided by the camera is also stored in the image file (information such as focal length, image dimensions, ISO and exposure…) EXIF data is a part of metadata.

The IPTC header system (IPTC is short for International Press & Telecommunications Council), originally created by the newspaper industry and incorporated in Adobe Photoshop (under File>File Info from the top menu bar) as well as into many other photography software used for capturing, editing and manipulating digital imagery, allows for such information (metadata) as creator, creation date, copyright owner, contact information and so on to be input and saved in the image file which is not only vital for establishing provenance but also preventing the creation of more orphan works*. Deliberately removing this metadata is a criminal offence, but proving that its removal has been deliberate, is more difficult.

Correct use of metadata templates allows a photographer to automatically embed a huge amount of useful information right from the moment that those files are captured and downloaded to a computer system and worked on. As stated, this information acts as a label, identifying the photographer (and indeed any other contributors or different copyright holders), aids in the prevention of the creation of orphan works and helps ensure that the work is correctly attributed to the photographer and therefore, more importantly, that any fees due for usage can be paid.

As a bare minimum, a photographer should structure their workflow to input metadata in the fields that describe 'author/creator', 'copyright status' and a contact email or telephone number. Make sure that any emails/telephone number that are used are ones which have longevity – it is pointless embedding metadata that becomes out of date. Set up a specific email address that is only used for metadata as this can aid in identifying the source of any contact that has come about through the use of an image file's metadata. All the main software used for capturing, processing, cataloguing and manipulating imagery have the ability to set up metadata templates which can be populated with the relevant information and embedded automatically. Adding metadata should not be an onerous task.

As a general rule of thumb, where a digital process has an analogue equivalent, there is no real reason to alter the manner in which that process is perceived and understood from the point of view of copyright and licensing.

A reminder – The Rules that Govern Usage

It is worth reiterating the rules that govern the production of creative work.

The main economic right that photographers control through their copyright, is the reproduction right; that is, the right to prevent or permit copying.

The majority of laws across the world now recognise that the reproduction right includes:

- making a digital version of an analogue original (format-shifting);
- making a digital copy of a digital image;
- transmitting or disseminating the digital image (a copy of) across an intranet or over the internet.

It does not matter whether the resulting digital copies are transient or temporary, for example, where a user views an image from a website on a screen for a minute or two, the law still treats this as reproduction.

As more and more material that used to exist in analogue form, now exists digitally, (particularly the written word, but latterly as much music and imagery), there are tensions between the creator and the audience, or to use more oft-used terms, the content-maker and the consumer. These tensions centre around the primary concerns of the creator of being able to protect their work adequately and only allow such access as has been paid for, and the consumer who needs reassurance that they have indeed paid and will not be locked out of their right to access such material in the future. The assumption in the previous paragraph is that the creator IS the copyright owner and, although obvious, it is worth pointing out that the two are not necessarily one and the same. Copyright owners are concerned that once their works are available in digital form, they will be copied again and again without further recompense (financial or otherwise). Digital Rights Management (DRM) systems allow for control of this (think of Apple's iTunes store as one of the best examples of this working, albeit arguably, too restrictively) but there is a balance to be had between over-zealous restriction on what the consumer can do with their licenced material and allowing what must be considered to be reasonable use of that content (for example, allowing a song to exist on two or three personal music devices, or as part of a back-up).

Digital Rights Management

Digital rights in practice

Making a digital version of an analogue photograph – This includes storing a photograph in digital form as an archive copy, for example, by copying or scanning a print or negative/transparency and storing it on some form of computer media (hard drive, DVD, flash memory...)

Making a digital copy of a photograph already in digital form – This includes downloading an image from a website and storing it as described above, or downloading it and making a print. It also includes copying an image held on a DVD/CD to a new DVD/CD and includes viewing a digital image on-screen which has previously been stored.

Transmitting or disseminating the digital image across an intranet or over the internet – This includes attaching the digital image to an email or publishing the image on a website/blog and making it available to view.

Digital manipulation – Anyone wishing to manipulate an image (analogue or digital) will either need to scan or digitise it or store and view it on-screen. Either way, the photographer can rely on the reproduction right and also their moral rights, for protection, particularly the integrity right.

Clearing digital rights

The person responsible for clearing the rights to use an image is the person who makes the copy or who authorises/initiates the copy. If your images have been copied and distributed without your permission, these are the people to pursue – in addition, it may be able to pursue those responsible for assisting in the transmission of such (an) image(s).

Licensing digital use

Licensing digital usage is no different to licensing other forms of media, however, clients are often unclear about the extent of the Licence to Use and the type of media involved. The answer is to be very clear about what can and cannot be done with the images and to try to licence to as narrow a set of uses as possible. This has the two-fold effect of allowing the client to return at a later date to negotiate further licensing if appropriate and desirable and allows the photographer to keep costs to the client as low as possible. It is advisable to always couch narrow licensing in the context of lower costs, which highlights the benefit to the client. By following a publisher's example of 'licensing narrowly', a photographer can grant only those rights and limit use to specifically what is required now, and not predicated on speculation of what 'might' be needed in the future. The photographer should not agree rights that allow 'all electronic rights' as this will only harm the photographer's future earning potential. This is business, after all. What is desirable and what is achievable, however, will often, if not always, be in two different places and it is equally important to recognise the importance of some flexibility and of long-term business relationships. Each situation will have its own mitigating circumstances.

Once the photographer is aware of the uses required and what rights apply and has negotiated and agreed a fee, an appropriate Licence to Use can be completed and issued (see Appendix). Listed below are some of the key points to be addressed when licensing digital imagery:

- Publisher's/producer's name
- Any other parties involved (many projects have more than one person involved in the decision-making process)
- Title or working title of the project or work
- Short description of the project or work
- Title of the image (if different)
- Confirmation of copyright byline to be used if appropriate
- Type of use – this always includes storing the work in digital form and then whatever other type of use is required. Such as;
  (1) It may be appropriate to consider whether any rental or lending rights are granted and
  (2) Whether any right to allow inclusion into a cable or online service of some sort is permissible. Also,
  (3) Whether there is a right to public display of the work granted, and
  (4) Whether printing out or the making of hard copies is permissible,
  (5) Whether any form of manipulation is allowable
  (6) Whether any use of the work is allowed in any packaging or advertising
- Format/platform – hard drive, DVD/CD/other removable media
- Quantity – not applicable in all circumstances, but helpful where DVD/CDs are being reproduced
- Image quality
- Territory/language – very difficult to restrict this to anything less than worldwide but can be applicable in some circumstances
- Completion or publication date
- Term of the Licence (years/months/in perpetuity)
- Procedure for approval of further rights if required
- Inclusion of any DRM or copy-protection mechanisms (PLUS identifier, digital watermarking, and so on)
- Express terms relating to any transference of copies of photographs in digital form (this relates to Section 56 of the CDPA 1988)
- The quality of reproduction
- Any assertion of moral rights
- Number/quantity of complementary copies of the final product for the photographer

Uses of Digital Technologies

Moral rights apply in the digital world just as they do in analogue media. The main difficulty, as with traditional media, is in enforcing and policing these rights and it is recommended that any contractual conditions dealing with moral rights issues are included in the terms of any licence issued. Moral rights have a great significance in the digital area, because of the ease with which photographs and other digital copyright works can be copied and transmitted.

With the possibility of an infinite number of exact copies of a photograph a reality, a photographer would no doubt prefer to be continuously associated with their work wherever it appears. In addition, the provenance of a photograph is something that should be of general interest to a consumer/audience, particularly if there are to be adaptations or manipulations. The photograph should carry its pedigree so that those with an interest can see who has created what, when and why.

The correct use of metadata will assist in the prevention of the creation of orphan works and in maintaining a link between photographer and image, but it is not a failsafe. The removal of metadata can occur through file processing (uploading to social media sites, for example) and while deliberately removing this metadata is a criminal offence, proving that its removal has been deliberate, is more difficult. Any photographer who uses social media and is concerned about the removal of their metadata from any pictures uploaded and the creation of orphan works should refer to a survey of online and social media sites conducted by David Riecks at Controlled Vocabulary (http://www.controlledvocabulary.com/socialmedia/index.html)

Work continues on the development of unique identifying systems for authors and their work. The purpose of such a system is to provide a means for a unique identifier to be firstly permanently attributed to an author and then for that identifier to be embedded into the work in some way, either through the metadata (as the PLUS system operates: https://www.plusregistry.org works) or into the very image pixels themselves as a digital watermark (as the Digimarc system operates: http://www.digimarc.com). Both methods are continuously being developed and of the two, the PLUS system is arguably the more widely used at the moment and is free to register with. Neither method is foolproof or a failsafe method, but it is recommended that the photographer makes use of one or the other as a minimum and continues to monitor the development of such systems to allow them to make use of the latest developments.

The right to object to, and prevent, derogatory treatment which is damaging to the honour or and/or reputation of the creator is intended to preserve the integrity of the photographer and their work. Moral rights are personal to a creator (a part of their personality, if you like) and as such cannot be assigned to anyone else.

However, the other issue at stake, particularly in a digital world, is the one of authenticity and provenance. There is a desire to know whether a work is authentic or 'truthful' or whether it has been manipulated and if so, to what extent. This is important, not just in an historic or aesthetic sense but in terms of newsworthiness and current affairs. The workflows adopted by many currently are such that a photographer sending images back to a picture desk or an agency may not be aware of exactly what has been done to a particular picture before it is published.

Adaptations, Appropriation, Derivative Works and copyright in a digital photograph
For more information, please refer to chapter 1 Copyright.

The UK has no adaption right for artistic works or photographs and artists and photographers must control adaptations or manipulations of their work through the reproduction right.

Appropriating the work of another artist or photographer without permission and using parts of it, or manipulating and adding to it to create a 'new' work is not good practice, nor is it likely to be legal (see the many copyright cases involving the appropriation artist, Richard Prince).

No separate copyright exists in the digital version of an analogue photograph – the digital version is merely a copy of the original. Photographers entering into contracts which state that such a separate right exists (sometimes under the guise of a Derivative Work, for example) should exercise caution and check with their professional trade organisations for the latest advice.

Two important and separate issues exist which need to be considered when investing in a digital workflow;

Firstly – and contrary to what people might think, more easily resolved – is the issue of which type of digital platform to invest in. What resolution and type of sensor is required...what capabilities (video?)...what kind of work does the photographer get involved in – all these considerations are highly important but should be relatively easy to resolve.

Secondly – and more problematic – is the consideration of how to manage, cost and charge for the digital pathway that inevitably involves more time (& therefore, cost) on the part of the photographer. Digital workflows have been around for long enough for the reality of these to be well-known among photographers and image-makers, although many clients still seem to believe that 'digital' is a synonym for 'cheap', and in the worst cases, 'free'!

Many photographers still work with film and indeed in some areas of the industry, it has enjoyed somewhat of a renaissance, but it is a set of tools like any other and has its own criteria for costing (and therefore charging). The donkey-work of a film-based workflow is handled by the lab (the clip-tests, chemistry balancing, processing and finishing) but the digital workflow usually transfers all that equivalent process to the photographer and many people become unstuck by not allowing for the time this part of the job takes.

What exactly IS post-production?
In many people's minds, this phrase covers a huge amount of activity; everything from processing the digital raw files to retouching and compositing. However, it is useful to think of it more specifically and say it is the handling, indexing and preparation of camera files to suit the final requirements of the brief. It does not necessarily include retouching, therefore – although clearly, that can be a lucrative additional service.

For all the time spent shooting, a good rule of thumb is to allow an additional 25-40% of time for post-production. The percentage will vary depending on how automated the workflow is for a given job, how much individual attention is required to the pictures and how fast the computer equipment driving the whole scenario, is. That means, one day shooting needs between 2 and 3 ½ hours to review, edit, process and output.

Delivery of the finished files can be done in a number of ways, but if uploading large quantities of data, ensure that the broadband connection available will allow it and will not add additional charges for extra bandwidth consumption. Many photographers use small bus-powered external hard drives to drop files on to and give that to the client. Arguably the slowest and most cumbersome delivery method is the creation and delivery of DVDs. Whichever route is taken, there are time (& cost) implications for each.

The concept of a 'digital surcharge' was mooted in this chapter and it still remains a valid notion albeit one that does now not warrant a separate line item entry on an invoice. It is important to remember that the provision of digital files provides the client with a range of benefits and cost-saving, regardless of the fact that clients may well have come to expect this, it is still an advantage for them. Investment in digital platforms is expensive and the requirements to continually upgrade are huge compared with a film-based workflow. This investment needs to be paid for so it is recommended that any calculation of a 'day rate' includes a provision for re-investment in digital camera gear AND computing power to drive it all.

This Code of Practice is based on commonly accepted 'best practice' among AOP professional photographers and also in part on the Pic4Press guidelines, produced by the Pass4Press consortium, of which AOP member, Bob Marchant, is a member and contributor.

Colour calibration

Monitor, workspace and system must be calibrated, profiled and set up correctly. Note that there is a difference between calibration and profiling;

Calibration being the act of returning a piece of equipment to a known, pre-determined state and profiling being the act of creating a set of parameters that define exactly a piece of equipment's response a particular set of circumstances. Calibration should precede profiling.

Colour working space

Finished work can be submitted as RGB, CMYK or greyscale files – the format used for supply and the working space should be agreed with the commissioning client.

- ***RGB***

  Originating and archiving files in an accepted RGB colourspace with an embedded ICC profile means the fuller gamut (range of image colour information) remains available for any subsequent conversion to CMYK or re-editing. Whilst it is generally accepted by many that Adobe (1998) RGB has become the industry-standard RGB colour working space, it should be noted that many other colour working spaces are available (such as Don RGB, Best RGB, eciRGB v2, Bruce RGB and many more) and that depending on the gamut of the image in question, a different working space may produce better results. A better alternative to Adobe (1998) RGB would be eciRGB v2, produced by the European Color Initiative, and geared to the print and publishing industry.

  Of course, if producing work destined solely for the internet or for screen display, it would be appropriate to work in sRGB (sRGB IEC61966-2.1 is the same colour space, just with its full name attached).

  Care should be exercised when using much larger colour spaces such as ProPhoto RGB as the gamut is too large to be displayed on current monitors and unless the operator has experience in editing by numbers, its use should arguably be restricted to archiving a master file that may be used as future developments in technology allow greater gamuts to be displayed.

- ***CMYK***

  Because CMYK files are, by their nature, targeted files, they are produced to match specific output conditions. It is recommended that the photographer only supply CMYK files when they have (a) been supplied with the relevant output/destination profile and (b) are experienced in converting from RGB to CMYK colour spaces (Note: It is NOT as simple as using Mode>CMYK from the Photoshop menu bar). Alternatively, the client may supply sufficient information to allow the photographer to make a targeted conversion using information relating to dot gain, ink set-up, GCR/UCR and USM.

  In the absence of any specified CMYK profile and a continued insistence to supply CMYK files, it is recommended that the photographer supply files in either ISO Coated v2 (ECI) or ISO Coated v2 300% (ECI), which are good choices (correct at time of going to press) where the intended printing condition is not known.

Sharpening

In either case, output sharpening should only be applied where the files have been prepared to the finished size. If in doubt, under-sharpen and state clearly in a Read Me file accompanying the files that this is the case. Sharpening can be thought of as a three-stage process: capture sharpening; creative sharpening and output sharpening and whilst it is not the remit of this chapter to lay out all of the technical possibilities for a digital workflow, care should be taken at all stages. If the photographer is in doubt, further advice should be sought before proceeding.

Hard copy

For the peace of mind of both parties, it is recommended that some form of hard copy be submitted along with the files – this can take the form of an 'aim print', which is not the same as a proof. The 'aim print' can be produced on a decent ink-jet printer using an appropriate paper/ink/profile combination and provides a visual guide to the image. A proof, by contrast, must be produced to far more exacting standards and is made to the same output/destination conditions that the printing press uses. Contract proofs can be made using ink-jet technology but the operators require FOGRA certification before such a print can be considered a proof.

Submission media

Three main platforms for file delivery exist: removable media such as flash drives (USB sticks and pen-drives), DVDs/CD-ROMs (NOT re-writable); external bus-powered (simply for convenience) hard drives and online file transfer. Of these, the unalterable nature of a DVD/CD-ROM provides evidence of the original state of the photographer's work and as such, has an advantage over the other methods, which sacrifice that element of irrefutability for convenience.

If using a pen-drive/USB stick or a bus-powered/mains powered external hard drive, it is important that the client or receiving party can attach and read the files on the drive. Where the computer platforms are known (Mac or Windows), this can be handled easily, but in the absence of such information, it is possible to format the drive to the FAT32 file system. This can be done on a Mac using Disk Utility and setting up a new partition (or partitions, depending on the size of the drive as FAT32 will not allow a partition greater than 2TB), and on a Windows PC in the Disk Management utility (Start>Control Panel>System and Security>Create & format hard drive partitions). The two drawbacks using the FAT32 format is the 2TB individual partition size and the fact that a single file cannot exceed 4GB.

An alternative is to use the NTFS format (New Technology File System) which will allow Macs running Snow Leopard and newer, to read the files (but not write to them whilst still on that drive).

Many photographers use external hard drives as a fast method of transferring large amounts of data to their client and also because the cost of large capacity drives has fallen so much, they are pretty much a consumable item.

Online file transfers can be very effective as long as the broadband connection used is a decent quality and upload speed. Remember that most ISPs sell their wares on the basis of fast DOWNLOAD speeds and the UPload speed is likely to be anywhere between a twentieth to a tenth of the DOWNload speed. The exception is a symmetric DSL line (SDSL instead of ADSL) where the upload and download speeds are identical, but these types of line installation are not offered by every provider and are less common and usually more expensive. It could be a good option if a photographer needed to regularly upload large amounts of data. Online file transfer can be very simple – if a photographer has their own website, simply uploading a folder of files via ftp to the website and sending the client the link can do the job – or additional functionality can be added in by hosting the files on a gallery site that allows the client to browse, rate, comment and download different sizes of the same file. Sites like Photoshelter and Photodeck as well as SmugMug offer this kind of service, which comes at a cost. In between sit various web-based file transfer platforms (WeTransfer, Hightail –was YouSendIt – and MailBigFile being three) which allow the upload of a certain volume of data and an email to be sent to one or more recipients notifying them of the arrival of such.

There are as many file transfer platforms as days in the month and it is beyond the scope of this chapter to address all of the options available, plus no doubt, these platforms will continue to evolve as connectivity and speeds improve.

File submission and compression

Some forms of online file transfer apply compression – the photographer should be aware of this and where possible allow as little compression or select lossless compression methods in preference. Similarly, when burning files to DVD/CD-ROM or saving to an external hard drive, minimum compression should be used wherever possible (for jpegs, level 9 compression or greater and for tiffs, either no compression or lossless LZW or ZIP compression). Of course, there may be circumstances where greater compression is unavoidable.

File size
As a guide to file size to be supplied:

- (i) for average print purposes, an RGB tiff file at 300ppi where the printing press screen is 150lpi, would translate to about 25MB for a full A4 page.
- (ii) for higher quality brochure work, at 400ppi, the same A4 page would be abut 44-45MB.
- (iii) far less commonly, for output to a 5x4 transparency or inter-neg, the file would be about 40-80MB
- (iv) for large packaging work, file sizes required to be in excess of those above are occasional but rare.
- (v) work intended for posters or hoardings varies depending on the type of screen density being applied but can often only be in the range of 80-120MB, although some producers of media of this type require higher resolutions such as 450ppi with the artwork being at 25% of its final size.

As a rough guide, use the following, but CHECK with your client for exact file size requirements:

- 96 sheet: 3048x762mm at 300ppi (25% of final size)
- 48 sheet: 1524x762mm at 300ppi (as above)
- 32 sheet: 1016x762mm at 300ppi (as above)
- 16 sheet: 508x762mm at 300ppi (as above)
- 4 sheet: 254x381mm at 300ppi (as above)

Note that these dimensions are 25% of the final size and are intended as a guide – it is always important to verify exact file specifications with the client.

Copyright
Where copyright security is a concern, it is recommended that some sort of digital watermark be embedded into the file or that an agreement is secured as to the exact usage of the imagery before the files are submitted.

Information
It is recommended that a 'Read Me' text file is included with the image files which clearly establishes ownership of the material, contact and transaction details, license terms, any relevant information relating to layout of the files on the media (disk or drive), technical information such as the amount and type of USM applied (if any), and so on. This file should be in a widely-accessible format such as a PDF.

Shooting Moving Image

Nick Wilcox-Brown & Nick Dunmur

Introduction

Stills and Video have been running in parallel for years; same principles, similar hardware but very different industries.

Although the process really started far earlier, the arrival of Canon's EOS 5D MkII in 2009 will be the date that most will remember for the convergence of stills and moving image.

Moving image is not only the practice of lighting and capturing an image but of telling stories, bringing scenes and subjects to life, and in many cases, capturing quality sound.

For most photographers at AOP level, moving image is now or will soon become an everyday reality. Some clients will expect you to capture "just a little bit of video for the web", others will expect full blown commercials or documentaries.

What is the best way forward?

Moving image, Film, Motion, Video – many words are used to describe the practice of capturing moving images of a subject. Technically the whole process is very similar to working with stills, but in practice, requires a substantial leap into storytelling, the ability to think ahead to the edit and levels of collaboration that may be beyond the experience of many stills photographers.

The approach you take will in most cases be directed by:

The Client

Clients not only dictate the industry; commercial, TV, corporate, they also dictate the level of production, the usage and the budget. Like photography, different industries have different production standards and different rates. If you're working for a television production for instance, you will be expected to hand over all material shot and have no further control. Usage will be all rights, including copyright. No negotiation.

Commercial or Advertising work is much more akin to photography; everything is by negotiation, rates and production values will normally be higher, as will the level of equipment required.

Generally rates for shooting moving image are in line with stills but the breakdown is very different. The headline day rates are low, but moving image projects are often multi-day, much longer than equivalent stills projects. If your thing is editorial or documentary, projects of 30 days are not unusual.

Equipment costs are on top of day rate and it is customary to charge your own equipment at hire rates. Quotes are often produced as menus, with different levels of cameras or equipment depending on the client budget. Adding in, for instance, tracks and dollies or a Steadicam adds substantially to the 'production value' and is reflected in the look of the finished product as well as in the additional time and costs incurred.

As per stills, all other costs, including the edit are charged on top.

Bear in mind that as with advertising work, recces, pre-production meetings, script amends and overseeing special effects may be part of the deal and are all chargeable.

Story

The most significant part of any production is getting the story right: the 1st step is normally a treatment or overview, followed by a script or a shot list in either order, depending on the production. The script may be a full-length manuscript which will usually be refined through a few or many drafts, sometimes right up until it is being shot. Alternatively it may be a simple storyboard with basic text which will do double duty as a shot list.

Normally the treatment and or script will be put together by a 3rd party but it may fall to you, the photographer, to establish the client's requirements and put this together yourself or to get a writer or producer involved to deal with it for you.

A key lesson for stills photographers here: working with "talent' or more often, non-talent, who may be narrating the story, being interviewed or just a participant. Put a stills camera in front of someone and they may freeze or giggle. Rare is the time when the problem can't be surmounted within a few minutes and the required images captured.

Put a movie camera in front of someone and ask them to perform, or worse to talk to camera and make sense, and things can be tougher. Many people freeze, constantly 'Err,'Um' or repeat themselves. Steps are usually needed to ensure accurate rendition of text, particularly as audiences traditionally have very short attention spans.

To prevent boredom, a key editing techniques is to constantly change the shot: head shot, 5 seconds; view from side, 3 seconds; cut away to background, 3 seconds. This means that when the shot is being captured, the subject needs to answer the same questions or to describe the event twice. Occasionally 2 cameras may be used in which case it is essential to match white balance, exposure, 'looks' presets and timecode.

The lessons here are to script everything possible and leave enough time for, and make sure you have multiple takes to draw upon in edit.

Continuity and repetition
Continuity is often overlooked when shooting, but can jump out and bite in edit. If you are matching up questions, the answers must also match for each shot as the slightest repetition or discrepancy will be obvious.

Similarly if you have two shots of the same person, they should be wearing the same clothes in each, holding the product in the same hand and lighting should match – no good to go back and re-capture half the shot later in the day, with different lighting and shadows. The human brain is very sensitive to slight changes, and while many cannot describe precisely what is wrong with a scene, they will know that it doesn't look 'right'.

Production
Much of this will be familiar to still photographers: call sheet, preproduction, contingency, logistics, planning and insurance.

Team
The team is very important to large and small productions alike. In addition to the usual client / model / make-up / assistant, there is audio and movement to be considered.

Audio constitutes 50% of a film and the ear is very discerning. It is not simply a case of putting a mic on the camera and getting levels right. Bad audio will be picked up far quicker than bad pictures, so it is worth taking the trouble to get it right. Get some training and practice hard, but if you doubt your abilities or those of your team, get a sound guy. Their day rates are affordable and it offloads a whole lot of responsibility onto someone else's shoulders. Similarly, camera movement, very much a specialised skill; Cranes, Pole cams and Steadicams bring high production values, but they are not a tool that you can pick up and run with. Operators will usually have their own kit and all you need to provide is the camera and direction. This is also a particular case where audio recording will need to be done externally, as camera audio is likely to be unusable – cue the sound man!

For larger productions other members of the team will be needed. If you have regulars you can draw upon, then this will provide the optimum solution, however if you are called upon to work within or to direct a larger production with a ready assembled crew, it is well worth remembering that in the film world there is a strict and historical hierarchy that is useful to be aware of: Director, 1st AD, 2nd AD, Director of Photography (a much abused and very hard earned title – use it at your peril), head of lighting, Key grip, Best boy, 1st and 2nd camera AC and so on.

Most will not work to this level, but if you do, take the trouble to look up and get familiar with the roles. It will be appreciated.

Lastly, don't forget to feed people properly, crews march on their stomachs and hospitality is expected and essential.

Skills and Equipment

At the beginning we talked of the similarities between still and moving image work; there are also some significant differences with the way that equipment is used in terms of shutter speeds, pulling focus, and other basic techniques. Multi-tasking leads to mistakes: If you are embarking on a significant project, make sure you get some proper training, or better still, have someone with you who really does know what they're doing.

The range of equipment, and the speed of change within the movie industry is such that is not appropriate to make kit recommendations here. Much of the equipment will be hired for specific projects and there are many specialist hire companies that can provide as little or as much of the equipment as you will need for your production. Look beyond your current photo dealer, they are trying to learn too and there are so many established providers employing skilled staff who know the answers already. It is worth building relationships with one or several of these companies. Many have specific areas of speciality and in most cases they will be able to suggest, recommend and hire equipment to you for particular types of work.

DSLRs are familiar tools for stills photographers and they are capable of shooting good quality motion footage, but look beyond, there is plenty of other equipment available for hire that may be more suited to your project.

If you have doubts about your ability to use specific kit, take the trouble to hire in a tech assistant, or somebody who really knows their way round the gear. At this point in time, one of the favoured cameras is the RED One. Very good for high-quality production, multiple frame rates and other such functionality, the camera is known throughout the TV and film industry for being a particularly difficult product to use. This is exactly the reason why specialist tech operators are so useful. Remember that some people will have spent many years learning how to use specific products and that hard earned experience can only help to improve the quality of your production.

Moving image is all about nicely composed frames and capturing motion within the frame, don't overlook the possibilities of adding in further motion: pans and zooms are familiar techniques, try using track and dollies, cranes and other accessories to add new dimensions to the production. Ultra small cameras offer new perspectives and if the budget is available, aerial sequences will add new dimensions.

Edit and Post-production

So you can use Final Cut, Avid Media Composer or and other editing software. But can you edit?

Editing is a craft that has traditionally taken many years to learn. Not just a matter of using software effectively, it is all about having an eye for the story, knowing exactly how to cut to create tension, to enhance emotion. If your project is a personal one, and you are starting out, then learning to use one of the editing packages is a great idea. For a client project or one where significant budgets are involved, don't scrimp; a decent editor will be worth their weight in gold.

Don't just grab the first editor that comes along, ask around, get recommendations, work with different editors, find one that you are comfortable with. When you have done so, sit with them and watch the way your sequences are cut and assembled. Not only another set of eyes, the whole process is fascinating and the knowledge you gain will provide useful insight for your next project.

A good editor will make or break your project, but don't assume that an editor will also be good at colour correcting or grading your footage; some are very skilled, others think they are, and many will recommend a colourist and perhaps an audio production or effects specialist as well. The film industry has plenty of room for specialists and happily, people are still prepared to pay for them.

One last thing – don't forget the 180 degree rule, both of them.

CHAPTER 15: WORKING OVERSEAS

Working Outside the UK

Norman Childs

One thing that we must all avoid is comparing the European Union with say the African and Asian continents or any other continent for that matter. European countries have gone a long way down the road of standardisation. Therefore, we must remember that a continent such as Africa is made up of wildly different countries, from many aspects; such as laws and legal issues, financial or fiscal arrangements, customs both conventional and tribal, as well as the obvious language issues and significant differences in weather patterns.

If anyone is contemplating photography whether commissioned or not in such countries, they could do no better than read very informative and comprehensive guides such as the 'Lonely Planet' guides or the 'Rough Guides To' books of the countries where they wish to work. 'When to go' is a very important aspect. Sometimes in the rainy seasons, the roads are impassable, making assignments very difficult to finish on time. Photography in temperatures in the forties can be curtailed simply due to exhaustion. In such cases make sure you have plenty of bottles of water with you.

In any event, always allow more time than the client suggests. Inevitably you will over run the schedule.

Over the last twenty years, the world of commerce and industry has been both challenging and exciting. Much of Britain's heavy industry moved to cheaper labour markets in South East Asia and beyond. In addition the digital age came upon us very quickly and adapting to the constantly changing world around us, became a necessity and part of survival.

I have been very fortunate in that in my photographic career right from the beginning thirty five years ago, I was able to travel around Europe and the other parts of the world at other people's expense. Namely; I had a job of running a Photographic Unit for an engineering company. I was fortunate in that I learnt much about marketing and financial objectives and how to apply photography to illustrate these principles.

Then after having run my own business for ten years, I hit my first recession in the early nineties, when many of my clients moved their manufacturing facilities overseas to cheaper labour markets. It was then that I realised that I had to follow them. At a time when British companies were still experimenting with setting up overseas, the fact that a UK photographer made contact with them to help illustrate the benefits of making such a decision to investors, became a huge bonus to all my clients.

In three years I had filled my passport to far flung places around the world. Many of them quite dangerous to operate in then, and some even more so now. I am now on my fifth passport in twenty years. So the first thing to be aware of, is to keep your passport up to date and make sure you have enough pages to accommodate endless visas as well as the customary stamps in and out of each country. At the time of writing, bear in mind that certain Arab countries will not allow you entry if you have an Israeli stamp in it. Equally, the US will not accept you if your passport has a Cuban stamp in it. Of course the thing to do quite legally is to obtain a separate passport for such countries.

So how do you get work overseas? I believe you need to address several of the following aspects to convince clients that you know that you are capable of taking on such assignments overseas, with minimal supervision.

1. Firstly, try to think of niche markets. Those markets where photography can really make a difference to a company's profile, and thus to its public, both in the western world and the countries in which it operates. Think carefully how photography can solve a client's visual communications and improve their relationships with investors, employees, customers and not least, the local communities in which they operate.
2. This means you have to have some knowledge of marketing principles and how to apply them through your photography. The understanding of marketing and financial profiles of your clients is as important as being able to add that creative flare to your images.
3. This often creates a 'chicken and egg' situation where you need to gain knowledge of operating in different parts of the world, whilst at the same time gaining experience to help you cope with the awkward situations and local procedures, that you will inevitably come across. This will vary from such knowledge of how to greet people correctly; how to cope with the many scrums you will meet as your cases come off the carousel on arrival in a strange airport, to how to get your equipment through customs with the minimum of fuss and delay.

Some attention to detail here will help immensely such as having the right currency in your pocket to offer tips. In Africa, you will be inundated with porters with trolleys wanting to carry your bags and expect an exorbitant amount of money for such a short lift of kit. Make sure that you either have the currency of the country you are visiting, or if it is a 'third world' developing country in Africa or other continent, then usually the dollar is still 'king' albeit having taken a battering of late. Next favoured is the Euro, with Sterling coming a lowly third these days. Five dollars will suit most bag carriers! If you have over 100kgs of kit then expect two or three 'trolley experts' at five dollars each. Therefore make sure you have sufficient cash with you on arrival.

Also don't forget that when you get to the hotel there will be 'bell hops' so another five dollars each for the upward journey and the same again for the trip down in the lift the morning after! Suddenly, you have spent 25 dollars in tips and haven't gone very far at all!

In the cities in South East Asia it is less of a problem and in China the main thing is to be polite to indifference. At any airport where you end up, make sure you keep a level head and don't get worked up with the slowness of procedures. It will only make things worse if you do!

4. The world has shrunk in terms of communications, which makes it an amazing market place for the enterprising, entrepreneurial photographer. The UK is no longer a large enough market place to sustain the truly creative photographers, seeking to constantly 'push the envelope' of ability and experience.
5. Whilst it still maybe desirable to maintain an operating base in the UK or your home country, it should be considered as an essential part of marketing, to make oneself known to buyers of photography from all over the world. These can be drawn from the familiar areas of the advertising and PR world, but increasingly there is a move by many final clients to commission photography directly with an enterprising photographer. As I have made this my world, 99% of my experience has been generated by direct commissions.
6. Whilst the conventional methods of presenting work to clients may still be considered normal; increasingly the use of electronic means of communications of presenting work is now becoming more and more acceptable. Indeed, with potential clients in other parts of the world, it maybe the fastest, most appropriate way of putting forward your expertise.

   Apart from having an attractive website; consider the use of specifically designed presentations to suit each prospective commissioner of photography. Use the clients' house colours and logos or typeface if possible to top and tail your presentation. There are many programmes available to do this simply and easily by the photographer. Not only does this impress and flatter, but shows that you have researched the clients' activities and their potential requirements, together with styles that they understand.
7. Many individuals responsible for the marketing aspects of their own companies are extremely busy people. They are often looking beyond the portfolio as to whether a photographer can produce excellent images. They frequently look for someone who can perform in a business like manner and take control of organising complete assignments. This will encompass arranging all the appropriate flight details and if necessary arranging your own passport and visa issues. It is therefore essential that you also get from the client, the name of a contact person in each country with whom you can build up a relationship for all the additional aspects, such as cars and drivers and hotels, to be brought together for a successful trip.

   Tackling large assignments under such conditions, requires the photographer to be 'clued up' as to operating in different countries and with different nationalities.
8. Make sure that your passport is in order and that you have the correct visas. Sometimes taking photographs on a professional basis means that a business entry visa is required. Often a visitor or tourist visa is not sufficient. Check with your client.

   Sometimes you must have a letter of invitation (LOI) with you on arrival at immigration. This must be produced by your client and also be in your possession before you leave your home country. It enables you to get a visa on arrival in the country where your assignment is taking place. Be aware that the visa could cost as much as 250 dollars per person, payable in cash when you arrive at the immigration kiosk in your assignment country.

   Equally, many airlines will not allow you on the flight to start your journey without these documents.

9. Be aware of the legal formalities of arriving with a large itinerary of photographic equipment in any country. Check whether an ATA Carnet is required for entry into that country. The London Chamber of Commerce and Industry is a very good organisation for such information. If not a carnet, ensure you have a Duplicate List (available from HMRC) of equipment. A copy of this must be in your possession on arrival in most countries. Ensure that your client has a copy of this too before you arrive in their country and in particular the person meeting you. This involves the client meeting you airside as the equipment comes off the carousel. You will also need either of these two documents to get your equipment back through customs on return to your home country! Most clients will already know the procedures for getting through their own customs, even if this just means a twenty dollar note.

   Do not, under any circumstances expect to 'wing it' through customs of any country with very expensive looking equipment. Even if there are no specific formalities, be sure there could be informal ones which unless you are prepared for, will result in delays. Although the EU allows for easy passage of such photographic items, further afield it can be a very different story in say Africa, Middle East and Asia.

10. When operating overseas, be aware that you could end up far from any major city or town. In many parts of the world, countries are very desolate apart from the cities. Temperatures, (both very high and low), humidity and dust can play havoc with digital and electronic equipment. Therefore make sure your equipment is in good working order. Consider taking back up equipment to cover for any major break down. Few cities in Africa and Asia have hire facilities to supplement you own gear. So consider taking some additional means of downloading camera cards, should your computer go down. Be prepared to back up not only onto your computer, but also to external hard drives. I back up twice at the end of each day. Then keep the hard drives and computer in separate bags. Take a second camera with you and if possible double up on a main lens. Similarly with any lighting equipment. Try to take some extra units to cope with any failures. Any attempt at trying to secure replacements whilst on location, will inevitably be costly and time consuming.

When travelling to remote or difficult areas, always ensure that you have adequate travel insurance. In the case of assignments that have an element of risk, ensure that this covers personal injury and even the facility to be medi-vacced out of the country and back to the UK or your home country, if necessary.

Also make sure you have adequate medication, particularly all necessary vaccinations for the countries you are visiting, together with malarial prophylaxis if appropriate. You local GP or travel clinic will be able to advise. Believe me, these things are necessary. In the normal course of photography twelve months ago, I picked up the notifiable disease Shigella, when drinking tea with the nomads in Mauretania. Acidophilus is very helpful with keeping the stomach in check!!

Finally. Most of the world speaks English in one way or another. Some people are amazing with their knowledge of our tongue. Others less so. However, from my own experience, their ability to speak English has always far out weighed my attempts to speak their language. So try not to get irritated when what they say is not necessarily what they mean. Much can get lost in translation, so be patient and kind. It will serve you well when things go 'belly up' on your assignment! As a passing shot. Learn to speak Mandarin!

Being a Location Photographer

Philip Lee Harvey

To my mind, being a location photographer is the best job in the world. It's taken me to incredible places, brought me in contact with amazing people and has given me perspectives and experiences I'd never have otherwise have had. But however enjoyable this job can be, it's definitely not a holiday.

Shooting a Masaai warrior at sunrise with Kilimanjaro as a backdrop might seem like a career defining moment – but shots like that won't arrive on a plate. Imagine, for instance, that your guide accidentally takes you to the wrong spot, that Kilimanjaro is shrouded in clouds or that the Maasai warrior you had arranged to meet up with the previous day shows up sporting a pair of jeans and a T-shirt.

Some of these obstacles you'll be able to overcome, others you won't. Being a location photographer is all about anticipating problems and making the most of what luck comes your way. It's about thinking on your feet, trusting your instincts – **and above all, always having a plan B.**

Do your research

The success or failure of your location shoot can be determined before you've even left your own front door. **You can never research your location too thoroughly** – from something as obvious as checking the weather usual for the time of year you're working, to getting technical and anticipating the angles of light. Use Google images to see what might be achievable – but always take these pictures with a pinch of salt. Trees get chopped down, people get older and buildings get demolished. I once spent a whole day in Scotland looking for a beach that had been washed away years ago

Thorough research will help you manage your client's expectations, and let them know what you can realistically accomplish. It's important to stay in touch with your client throughout the shoot to let them know what they can expect from your work – it will make your job much easier if you encourage them to keep an open mind too!

Pack Wisely

Tempting as it may be to pack everything but the kitchen sink, being a location photographer is all about being nimble and getting mobile at short notice – **so pack light and pack sensibly**. Wheels on your suitcase might seem like a great idea in the departure lounge, but they won't be so welcome when you're slogging your way up a mountain in the driving rain.

At the same time, **two is the magic number** – it's a good idea to carry a spare for everything you need, so the job won't be jeopardised if a crucial item gets lost, stolen or broken. I carry two bags, each containing a set of equipment that I can work with, and I always back up my work in at least two different places – in the past I've been known to FedEx extra hard drives home if I'm nervous about getting them through customs. If you're flying to your location, always carry enough equipment to get the job done in your hand luggage – you'll be able to work without a fresh pair of pants for a few days, but not without your camera.

Keep a low profile

More often than not, it'll make your job easier if you stay as inconspicuous as possible on location. Excited as you may be to work on a shoot, try to be discreet in telling people what you're doing – I always prefer to dress and behave just like an ordinary tourist.

Find a good guide

However much research you do in advance, local knowledge can make or break the shoot, **so take time to find a good guide**. I tend to email four or five companies from the UK in advance – the speed with which they respond is often a good indicator of how efficient they might be, and personal recommendations also count for a lot.

Don't always opt for the young guy who shouts loudest, talks smartest and wears flash Ray Bans – in my experience, older guides tend to be wiser, better connected and be more familiar with the landscape. While it's important to find a hard working guide who understands that being a few minutes late can scupper the job, it's worth taking the time to relax with your guide, and make them feel they're part of your project. Just to be on the safe side, I always pay guides at the end of a shoot – I once paid a guy on our last night in Mexico, and had to find my own way to the airport the following day while he nursed a hangover.

Working with people

When you're out on a shoot, **never assume that people don't want to help you** – I've found that 99% of the time, people love getting involved and will gladly stand in as your model or temporary fixer. Sometimes however, you have to appreciate that time is money, and it's fair to pay people if they go a long way out of their way to help you – particularly in third world countries. When you do pay someone, do it proportionally to local wages – but do bear in mind it's fair to add a bit of foreigner tax on top!

If you're making a gift to more than one person (such as a village), consider doing it in front of the whole group and make it clear that this is a gift to everyone – don't reply on just one person to hand it out. Try to avoid paying bribes to officials wherever possible – these can quickly get out of hand when everyone wants a piece of the pie.

Above all...

Never...

- Make clever remarks in front of people in uniform!
- Take anyone's opinion as gospel – accept that tourist boards and guides will often have a hidden agenda in where they take you, and someone who says their wife would be your perfect model could possibly be biased...
- Assume anything, except that something will inevitably go wrong. The secret is visualising potential problems in advance, and being able to adapt to them.

Always

- Be stern but courteous – don't be afraid to stop a guide if they're taking you to their uncle's carpet shop!
- Send people your pictures when you say you will – people who don't do this give photographers a bad name.
- Work like everyday is the last day of your shoot. Imagine that tomorrow the heavens will open and you'll drop your camera in a puddle – so make hay (and take pictures) while the sun shines!

CHAPTER 16: SHOOTING ON THE STREETS

GRANT SMITH

Photographers' rights in the UK

In recent times there has been much confusion surrounding photographers' rights in the UK.

What you need to know

At the time of writing there is NO law preventing you from taking photographs of whoever you want and whatever you want so long as you are standing on public land and not on private property. This includes photographing police officers. There are a few exceptions to this rule including sensitive government buildings such as the MI6 building and MoD properties, and those where a photography prohibition order is in place. This will be clear in signage that prohibits photography. Parliament and Trafalgar Square have photography prohibition notices in place – commercial photography is not permitted without prior arrangement.

However, it can sometimes be hard to distinguish between what is public and what is private land, especially now as more and more supposedly 'public spaces' are in fact owned by private companies. However, the majority of pavements and footpaths are public land. There are a couple of indicators to look out for to let you know if you are on public or private land:

Metal studs or tracks running along the pavement – the area of pavement alongside the road will be public property but the other side of the line will belong to the nearest private estate.

Wall mounted plaques – these can be hard to spot but will be mounted on a wall somewhere on the private estate, stating who the land belongs to and some of the restrictions on your behaviour when on the estate. Other plaques may have a graphic of a camera, informing you that you are being filmed and surveilled for the prevention of crime.

Answers to important questions

Can I take photographs of people and places (without their permission) as long as I am standing on public property?

YES! If you are standing on public property you are legally allowed to photograph anyone or anything you like, even if your subject is on private property or is a private building. However, if you continue to photograph the individual or individuals persistently and aggressively, your behaviour may be deemed as harassment, and you may be subject to arrest.

A right to privacy exist in UK law, by virtue of Article 8 of the European Convention on Human Rights, which may result in restrictions on the publication of photographs. However this does not mean that you can take as many photographs as you want, as your behaviour may be deemed as harassment if you persist after the subject has made it clear that they do not want to be photographed. This article appears contrary to Article 10, which is the right to freedom of expression. Exercising common sense in these circumstances, and being courteous and respectful to others when taking photographs is the simplest way of ensuring you get the photograph.

Can I take photographs on public land that I intend to use non-commercially and commercially?

YES! You are within your rights to use images editorially, in a book, on a website or in an exhibition. However if a person is recognisable and you use their picture or that of a privately owned building without their permission to endorse a product such as in an advertising campaign, this could result in legal action. A signed model release will be needed to use the images for endorsement of any service or product.

Can I take photographs of private property that I intend to use for profit-making and commercial gain?

YES! Unless you have gained entry illegally. A land or property owner may impose conditions of entry, which may restrict photography to non-commercial use. In this case you may need permission from the property owner if you intend to use the image commercially. Many institutions such as the National Trust, English Heritage, Disneyland and Graceland that allow ticketed access to the public, make it a condition of entry that photographs may be taken, but may not be used for commercial gain of any kind. No prior permission is required to publish a photograph of any property in the UK for commercial gain, if the photograph was taken from a public place. However most image libraries now request a property release is obtained from the building's owner. This is difficult when the building is a commercial office, as a property release will not be easily secured. This is much easier to obtain on a private residence. Organisations like the National Trust, English Heritage and the Royal Parks will grant permission for commercial photography on their property after the organisation is satisfied that the photographs will not compromise the reputation of the organisation and a fee is paid.

Am I required by law to give my personal details to private security staff?
NO! When stopped by security guards, you are not obliged to provide any personal details. Private security guards do not have any police powers, nor do they have any powers to view or delete images or confiscate equipment. Security guards cannot obstruct individuals from taking photographs.

Am I required by law to give my personal details to the police?
NO! Unless the police have reasonable suspicion that you are involved in terrorist activities, they have no powers to take your details, look at your photos or to confiscate your camera. Since the abolition of section 44 of the Terrorism Act 2000, this is now covered under section 47a (see below). Police have no power to delete digital images or seize film without a court order. However, failing to cooperate with the police when questioned may lead to a charge of obstruction. Cooperation and politeness are the most efficacious ways of dealing with police enquiries.

Common sense and knowledge are your best friends. Avoid taking photographs of children without consent, exercise caution and empathy when photographing victims in traumatic situations and be prepared to be questioned if photographing sensitive buildings such as government premises, banks and embassies. Develop your knowledge of the law and carry a print out of your rights.

Keep a print out of your rights with you at all times
Amateur Photographer magazine has produced a Photographers' Rights Card. Print it out and keep it with you. The organisation 'I'm a Photographer Not a Terrorist' (PHNAT) also has a bust card on its website, as do the NUJ. PHNAT is monitoring any stops on photographers in the vicinity of the Olympic sites.

Police guidance issued to police officers
New guidance was issued in April 2010 stating that police have no powers to view or confiscate photos without reasonable suspicion of terrorist activities. In July 2010, section 44 of the Terrorism Act 2011 was repealed and replaced by section 47a, which states that police officers must have reasonable suspicion that the individual (or group) is involved in terrorist activities. Section 44 gave the police the authority to stop and search anybody without need for suspicion in designated areas. Where the designated areas were was not public information.

Section 47a, Terrorism Act 2000
Used as a part of the counter terror legislation, section 47a allows police to stop and search photographers when a police officer reasonably suspects that photographs or film are being taken as part of a hostile terrorist reconnaissance. Section 43 allows for the arrest of such individuals. Film and memory cards may be seized as part of the search, if the officer reasonably suspects there is evidence that the individual is a terrorist. Images cannot be deleted by a police officer. A court is required to do this. While terrorists may undertake hostile reconnaissance using photographic equipment, police officers should not automatically consider photography or filming as suspicious behaviour.

Furthermore, you do not need a permit to photograph/film anybody, any building or anything in a public place. It is not an offence to photograph or film a public building. It is a common fallacy that the image of a building is copyrighted – no such provision exists in UK law. The Eiffel Tower is often used as an example. The image of Eiffel Tower is not copyrighted, but the lighting arrangements are. Copyrighted. This means that any images of the Eiffel Tower depicting the lighting scheme require permission to be used commercially

Police have no power to stop the filming or photography of incidents involving police personnel.

Recent government guidance issued to security firms
Security guards are privately employed and have no public accountability. In guidelines for security guards released by the Home Office in November 2011, it was recognised that approaches by security guards to members of the public taking photographs was regarded as unwarranted intrusion. These guidelines addressed size and type of camera, stating that a larger professional camera is no more suspicious than a compact camera. Security personnel have no right to prevent an individual from photographing a public or private building, if the photographs are being taken from a public place. If the photographer is on private property, permission **ought** to be sought before taking photographs. If prior permission has not been obtained, security personnel may inform the photographer of the restrictions and politely request that the photographer stops taking photographs. If the photographer refuses to comply with this request, security personnel may request that the photographer leave the premises and could use reasonable force to effect this. Reasonable force is the justified response to the situation. For example a verbal threat will result in result in a verbal response. As the level of threat rises, so does the response. Security personnel may use reasonable force to remove an individual from private property that they are protecting

NB Security personnel cannot delete images nor seize photographic equipment.

APPENDIX & INDEX

AGENT/PHOTOGRAPHER AGREEMENT

Agreement dated .... between .... (hereafter called The Agent) and .... (hereafter called The Photographer).

Territory

The Agent will represent The Photographer in the following geographical areas: ....

Field of Photographer

The Agent will represent The Photographer in the following fields of work: ....

Responsibilities

The Agent will:

a) solicit photographic assignments on behalf of The Photographer;

b) negotiate contracts and fees with the client as agreed with The Photographer;

The Photographer will:

a) provide a portfolio of work to a standard agreed by both parties;

b) update and replace work in the folio as necessary.

Responsibility for collection, storage and mounting of published work/tear sheets for the portfolio, shall be with the Agent/Photographer*.

Accounting

- The Agent/Photographer* is responsible for estimates, VAT invoices, and licences on Agent/Photographer* letterhead.
- VAT invoice to client to be raised by The Agent/Photographer*, promptly on completion and acceptance of the commission.
- Payment to The Photographer, less commission, to be made 5 days after receipt and clearance of the client's cheque/Commission payment to Agent to be made ....*
- Statements of account to be sent on a monthly basis and outstanding debts chased by The Agent/Photographer* on a regular basis.
- The Agent/Photographer* will keep an accurate and up to date book of accounts which can be checked on demand by The Agent/Photographer.
- Copies of orders, estimates, invoices and licenses to be kept by both parties.
- VAT returns, accountant and auditing fees are the responsibility of the Agent/Photographer*.

House Accounts

The following are live client accounts held by The Photographer at the date of this agreement, on which no commission is due to The Agent unless otherwise agreed as, and when, future commissions are negotiated:

....

....

....

....

Commission Structure/Calculation

- Commission is payable to The Agent at ....% of The Photographer's fee (excluding expenses) on jobs solicited and confirmed by The Agent.

continued...

Agent/Photographer Agreement – available free from www.the-aop.org/information/downloads/legal-business-forms

- Commission is payable to The Agent at ....% of The Photographer's fee (excluding expenses) on jobs solicited and confirmed by The Photographer, but not on the above House Accounts.
- The fee shall be deemed to be the balance of the invoice (excluding VAT) after actual expenses are deducted.
- Commission is payable to The Agent at ....% on re-usage fees of work originally solicited and confirmed by The Agent.
- The Photographer reserves the right to refuse work solicited by The Agent.
- Commission shall not be payable if for whatever reason any work is not completed.

Promotional/Portfolio Costs

- Promotional material and advertising costs will be borne by: ....
- Content of promotional and advertising material shall be to a standard agreed by both parties.

Expenses

Travel, telephone, office administration, entertainment, delivery and general business expenses incurred by The Agent will be paid by The Agent.

Insurance

The Agent/Photographer* confirms that, as of the date of this agreement, insurance to cover the portfolio and its contents to the sum of £............. is now in effect and will be maintained throughout the term of this agreement.

Termination

This agreement shall terminate 30 days after receipt of written notice of termination given by either party, subject to the following provisions:

On termination of this agreement by either The Agent or The Photographer:

a) The Agent will receive commission of ....% on work in progress or previously arranged.
b) The Agent will receive commission of ....% for a period of .... months from the date of termination on work received by The Photographer from clients previously solicited on his/her behalf by The Agent.
c) The Agent will for a period of .... months from the date of termination, pass on all enquiries from past or future clients to The Photographer or the new agent.

- Throughout the term of this agreement, the portfolio remains the property of The Photographer and will be returned into his/her possession immediately on termination.
- The relationship between The Photographer and The Agent shall be that of principal and agent, and nothing contained herein shall constitute this arrangement a joint venture or partnership. The Agent shall not acquire any rights in any of The Photographer's work.
- This agreement constitutes the entire understanding between the parties and no modifications shall be of any force and effect unless made in writing and signed by both parties.
- This agreement is governed by the laws of England and Wales, to the non-exclusive jurisdiction of whose courts the parties submit.

Signed

.... On behalf of The Agent

.... On behalf of The Photographer

** delete as appropriate*

THE ASSOCIATION OF PHOTOGRAPHERS 1993

Agent/Photographer Agreement – available free from www.the-aop.org/information/downloads/legal-business-forms

COMMISSION ESTIMATE

The Agency :

Photographer's Name :
Agent/Rep :
Photographer's Ref. No. :
Date :
Art order No :
Product :

The Advertiser :

Job Description :

Media use/period of use/territory : ☐ **Right to a Credit**

Exclusivity period : Term of the licence plus ___________ years (Subject to clause 5 overleaf)

Fees :

Commission fee	______________
Pre/post production fee	______________
Other (specifiy)	______________
Base Usage Rate ______________	
Total fees	______________

Expenses :

Film, Processing & Polaroid	______________
Prints	______________
Location services	______________
Travel	______________
Subsistence	______________
Production co-ordination/Assistants	______________
Stylist	______________
Make-up/Hair	______________
Set build	______________
Props/Wardrobe	______________
Studio hire	______________
Equipment hire	______________
Models/Casting (billed direct?)	______________
Rush charges/Overtime	______________
Special insurance	______________
Messenger/Delivery	______________
Miscellaneous	______________
	______________
	______________
Total Expenses	______________

IMPORTANT NOTE: the terms and conditions printed on pages 198, 199 or 200 should appear on the reverse of this form. Make sure you use the terms relevant to your country of residence ie. England and Wales, Scotland or Eire.

ESTIMATE TOTAL (exc. VAT) ______________

Contingency ___________ % of ESTIMATE TOTAL (exc. VAT) ______________

Advance required before shoot commencement (exc. VAT) ______________

THIS COMMISSION IS SUBJECT TO ALL TERMS AND CONDITIONS ABOVE AND OVERLEAF.
UNDER CLAUSE 4 OVERLEAF, NO USE MY BE MADE OF THE PHOTOGRAPHS UNTIL THE INVOICE IS PAID IN FULL

Estimate template – available free from www.the-aop.org/information/downloads/legal-business-forms

COMMISSION INVOICE

The Agency :

Photographer's Name :
Agent/Rep :
Photographer's Ref. No. :
Date :
Art order No :

The Advertiser :

Product :

Job Description :

Media use/period of use/territory :

(for full details see attached 'Licence to Use' No. __________)

Fees :

Commission fee ____________
Pre/post production fee ____________
Other (specifiy) ____________
Base Usage Rate ____________

Total fees ____________

Expenses :

Film, Processing & Polaroid ____________
Prints ____________
Location services ____________
Travel ____________
Subsistence ____________
Production co-ordination/Assistants ____________
Stylist ____________
Make-up/Hair ____________
Set build ____________
Props/Wardrobe ____________
Studio hire ____________
Equipment hire ____________
Models/Casting (billed direct?) ____________
Rush charges/Overtime ____________
Special insurance ____________
Messenger/Delivery ____________
Miscellaneous ____________

Total Expenses ____________

IMPORTANT NOTE: the terms and conditions printed on pages 198, 199 or 200 should appear on the reverse of this form. Make sure you use the terms relevant to your country of residence ie. England and Wales, Scotland or Eire.

Sub-total ____________
VAT ____________
TOTAL COST ____________
Less Advance Paid ____________
TOTAL AMOUNT DUE ____________

THIS COMMISSION IS SUBJECT TO ALL TERMS AND CONDITIONS ABOVE AND OVERLEAF.
UNDER CLAUSE 4 OVERLEAF, NO USE MY BE MADE OF THE PHOTOGRAPHS UNTIL THE INVOICE IS PAID IN FULL

Invoice template – available free from www.the-aop.org/information/downloads/legal-business-forms

LICENCE TO USE

Granted to (The Agency) :

Photographer's Name :
Agent/Rep :
Photographer's Ref. No. :
Date :
Art order No :

The Advertiser :

Product :

Description of photograph/s covered by the licence:

Terms of the licence :

Media Use

- ☐ Artist reference
- ☐ Brochure
- ☐ Catalogue
- ☐ Inserts
- ☐ Magazine consumer
- ☐ Magazine trade
- ☐ National press
- ☐ Packaging
- ☐ Point of sale
- ☐ Poster (less than 10sq metres)
- ☐ Poster (more than 10sq metres)
- ☐ Television/Cinema
- ☐ Test
- ☐ Other (specify) : ____________

Territory :

- ☐ UK
- ☐ Single EC Country
- ☐ Continental Europe
- ☐ USA
- ☐ English language areas
- ☐ Worldwide
- ☐ Other (secify) : ____________

Time Period

- ☐ One year
- ☐ Two years
- ☐ Other (specify) : ____________

IMPORTANT NOTE: the terms and conditions printed on pages 198, 199 or 200 should appear on the reverse of this form. Make sure you use the terms relevant to your country of residence ie. England and Wales, Scotland or Eire.

Right to a credit ☐

Exclusivity Clause

I confirm that subject to clause 5 overleaf I shall not publish or supply the material to any other person for publication during the term of the licence plus ________ years, without the express permission of the Agency or the Advertiser.

I confirm that the Agency and the Advertiser are hereby licensed to reproduce and publish the Photographs, for the above purposes, territories and time period, on the terms and conditions set out overleaf.

Under clause 4 overleaf, no use my be made of the Photographs until the invoice has been paid in full.

Signed : ______________________________ Date : ______________

APPENDIX

Licence to use template – available free from www.the-aop.org/information/downloads/legal-business-forms

TERMS AND CONDITIONS [England & Wales]

1. DEFINITIONS
For the purpose of this agreement "the Agency" and "the Advertiser" shall where the context so admits include their respective assignees, sub-licensees and successors in title. In cases where the Photographer's client is a direct client (i.e. with no agency or intermediary), all references in this agreement to both "the Agency" and "the Advertiser" shall be interpreted as references to the Photographer's client. "Photographs" means all photographic material furnished by the Photographer, whether transparencies, negatives, prints or any other type of physical or electronic material.

2. COPYRIGHT
The entire copyright in the Photographs is retained by the Photographer at all times throughout the world.

3. OWNERSHIP OF MATERIALS
Title to all Photographs remains the property of the Photographer. When the Licence to Use the material has expired the Photographs must be returned to the Photographer in good condition within 30 days.

4. USE
The Licence to Use comes into effect from the date of payment of the relevant invoice(s). No use may be made of the Photographs before payment in full of the relevant invoice(s) without the Photographer's express permission. Any permission which may be given for prior use will automatically be revoked if full payment is not made by the due date or if the Agency is put into receivership or liquidation. The Licence only applies to the advertiser and product as stated on the front of the form and its benefit shall not be assigned to any third party without the Photographer's permission. Accordingly, even where any form of 'all media' Licence is granted, the photographer's permission must be obtained before any use of the Photographs for other purposes eg use in relation to another product or sublicensing through a photolibrary. Permission to use the Photographs for purposes outside the terms of the Licence will normally be granted upon payment of a further fee, which must be mutually agreed (and paid in full) before such further use. Unless otherwise agreed in writing, all further Licences in respect of the Photographs will be subject to these terms and conditions.

5. EXCLUSIVITY
The Agency and Advertiser will be authorised to publish the Photographs to the exclusion of all other persons including the Photographer. However, the Photographer retains the right in all cases to use the Photographs in any manner at any time and in any part of the world for the purposes of advertising or otherwise promoting his/her work. After the exclusivity period indicated in the Licence to Use the Photographer shall be entitled to use the Photographs for any purposes.

6. CLIENT CONFIDENTIALITY
The photographer will keep confidential and will not disclose to any third parties or make use of material or information communicated to him/her in confidence for the purposes of the photography, save as may be reasonably necessary to enable the Photographer to carry out his/her obligations in relation to the commission.

7. INDEMNITY
The Photographer agrees to indemnify the Agency and the Advertiser against all expenses, damages, claims and legal costs arising out of any failure by the Photographer to obtain any clearances for which he/she was responsible in respect of third party copyright works, trade marks, designs or other intellectual property. The Photographer shall only be responsible for obtaining such clearances if this has been expressly agreed before the shoot. In all other cases the Agency shall be responsible for obtaining such clearances and will indemnify the Photographer against all expenses, damages, claims and legal costs arising out of any failure to obtain such clearances.

8. PAYMENT
Payment by the Agency will be expected for the commissioned work within 30 days of the issue of the relevant invoice. If the invoice is not paid, in full, within 30 days The Photographer reserves the right to charge interest at the rate prescribed by the Late Payment of Commercial Debt (Interest) Act 1998 from the date payment was due until the date payment is made.

9. EXPENSES
Where extra expenses or time are incurred by the Photographer as a result of alterations to the original brief by the Agency or the Advertiser, or otherwise at their request, the Agency shall give approval to and be liable to pay such extra expenses or fees at the Photographer's normal rate to the Photographer in addition to the expenses shown overleaf as having been agreed or estimated.

10. REJECTION
Unless a rejection fee has been agreed in advance, there is no right to reject on the basis of style or composition.

11. CANCELLATION & POSTPONEMENT
A booking is considered firm as from the date of confirmation and accordingly the Photographer will, at his/her discretion, charge a fee for cancellation or postponement.

12. RIGHT TO A CREDIT
If the box on the estimate and the licence marked "Right to a Credit" has been ticked the Photographer's name will be printed on or in reasonable proximity to all published reproductions of the Photograph(s). By ticking the box overleaf the Photographer also asserts his/her statutory right to be identified in the circumstances set out in Sections 77-79 of the Copyright, Designs and Patents Act 1988 or any amendment or re-enactment thereof.

13. ELECTRONIC STORAGE
Save for the purposes of reproduction for the licensed use(s), the Photographs may not be stored in any form of electronic medium without the written permission of the Photographer. Manipulation of the image or use of only a portion of the image may only take place with the permission of the Photographer.

14. APPLICABLE LAW
This agreement shall be governed by the laws of England & Wales

15. VARIATION
These Terms and Conditions shall not be varied except by agreement in writing.

NOTE : For more information on the commissioning of photography refer to Beyond the Lens produced by the AOP.

Terms & Conditions (England & Wales) – available free from www.the-aop.org/information/downloads/legal-business-forms

TERMS AND CONDITIONS [Scotland]

1. DEFINITIONS
For the purpose of this agreement "the Agency" and "the Advertiser" shall where the context so admits include their respective assignees, sub-licensees and successors in title. In cases where the Photographer's client is a direct client (i.e. with no agency or intermediary), all references in this agreement to both "the Agency" and "the Advertiser" shall be interpreted as references to the Photographer's client. "Photographs" means all photographic material furnished by the Photographer, whether transparencies, negatives, prints or any other type of physical or electronic material.
2. COPYRIGHT
The entire copyright in the Photographs is retained by the Photographer at all times throughout the world.
3. OWNERSHIP OF MATERIALS
Title to all Photographs remains the property of the Photographer. When the Licence to Use the material has expired the Photographs must be returned to the Photographer in good condition within 30 days.
4. USE
The Licence to Use comes into effect from the date of payment of the relevant invoice(s). No use may be made of the Photographs before payment in full of the relevant invoice(s) without the Photographer's express permission. Any permission which may be given for prior use will automatically be revoked if full payment is not made by the due date or if the Agency is put into receivership or liquidation. The Licence only applies to the advertiser and product as stated on the front of the form and its benefit shall not be assigned to any third party without the Photographer's permission. Accordingly, even where any form of 'all media' Licence is granted, the photographer's permission must be obtained before any use of the Photographs for other purposes eg use in relation to another product or sublicensing through a photolibrary. Permission to use the Photographs for purposes outside the terms of the Licence will normally be granted upon payment of a further fee, which must be mutually agreed (and paid in full) before such further use. Unless otherwise agreed in writing, all further Licences in respect of the Photographs will be subject to these terms and conditions.
5. EXCLUSIVITY
The Agency and Advertiser will be authorised to publish the Photographs to the exclusion of all other persons including the Photographer. However, the Photographer retains the right in all cases to use the Photographs in any manner at any time and in any part of the world for the purposes of advertising or otherwise promoting his/her work. After the exclusivity period indicated in the Licence to Use the Photographer shall be entitled to use the Photographs for any purposes.
6. CLIENT CONFIDENTIALITY
The photographer will keep confidential and will not disclose to any third parties or make use of material or information communicated to him/her in confidence for the purposes of the photography, save as may be reasonably necessary to enable the Photographer to carry out his/her obligations in relation to the commission.
7. INDEMNITY
The Photographer agrees to indemnify the Agency and the Advertiser against all expenses, damages, claims and legal costs arising out of any failure by the Photographer to obtain any clearances for which he/she was responsible in respect of third party copyright works, trade marks, designs or other intellectual property. The Photographer shall only be responsible for obtaining such clearances if this has been expressly agreed before the shoot. In all other cases the Agency shall be responsible for obtaining such clearances and will indemnify the Photographer against all expenses, damages, claims and legal costs arising out of any failure to obtain such clearances.
8. PAYMENT
Payment by the Agency will be expected for the commissioned work within 30 days of the issue of the relevant invoice. If the invoice is not paid, in full, within 30 days The Photographer reserves the right to charge interest at the rate prescribed by the Late Payment of Commercial Debt (Interest) Act 1998 from the date payment was due until the date payment is made.
9. EXPENSES
Where extra expenses or time are incurred by the Photographer as a result of alterations to the original brief by the Agency or the Advertiser, or otherwise at their request, the Agency shall give approval to and be liable to pay such extra expenses or fees at the Photographer's normal rate to the Photographer in addition to the expenses shown overleaf as having been agreed or estimated.
10. REJECTION
Unless a rejection fee has been agreed in advance, there is no right to reject on the basis of style or composition.
11. CANCELLATION & POSTPONEMENT
A booking is considered firm as from the date of confirmation and accordingly the Photographer will, at his/her discretion, charge a fee for cancellation or postponement.
12. RIGHT TO A CREDIT
If the box on the estimate and the licence marked "Right to a Credit" has been ticked the Photographer's name will be printed on or in reasonable proximity to all published reproductions of the Photograph(s). By ticking the box overleaf the Photographer also asserts his/her statutory right to be identified in the circumstances set out in Sections 77-79 of the Copyright, Designs and Patents Act 1988 or any amendment or re-enactment thereof.
13. ELECTRONIC STORAGE
Save for the purposes of reproduction for the licensed use(s), the Photographs may not be stored in any form of electronic medium without the written permission of the Photographer. Manipulation of the image or use of only a portion of the image may only take place with the permission of the Photographer.
14. APPLICABLE LAW
This agreement shall be governed by the laws of Scotland
15. VARIATION
These Terms and Conditions shall not be varied except by agreement in writing.

NOTE : For more information on the commissioning of photography refer to Beyond the Lens produced by the AOP.

Terms & Conditions (Scotland) – available free from www.the-aop.org/information/downloads/legal-business-forms

TERMS AND CONDITIONS [Eire]

1. DEFINITION

For the purpose of this agreement '"the Client" shall where the context so admits include their respective assignees, sub-licensees and successors in title. In cases where the Photographer's client is a direct client (i.e. with no intermediary), all references in this agreement to "the Client" shall be interpreted as references to the Photographer's client. "Photographs" means all photographic material furnished by the Photographer, whether transparencies, negatives, prints or any other type of physical or electronic material.

2. COPYRIGHT

The entire copyright in the Photographs is retained by the Photographer at all times throughout the world.

3. OWNERSHIP OF MATERIALS

Title to all Photographs remains the property of the Photographer. When the Licence to Use the material has expired the Photographs must be returned to the Photographer in good condition within 30 days.

4. USE

The Licence to Use comes into effect from the date of payment of all sums due by the Client to the Photographer for use of the Licence. No use may be made of the Photographs before payment in full of all sums due without the Photographer's express permission. Any permission which may be given for prior use will automatically be revoked if full payment is not made by the due date or if the Client is put into receivership or liquidation. The Licence only applies to the Client and product as stated on the front of the form and its benefit shall not be assigned to any third party without the Photographer's permission. Accordingly, even where any form of 'all media' Licence is granted, the photographer's permission must be obtained before any use of the Photographs for other purposes eg use in relation to another product or sublicensing through a photolibrary. Permission to use the Photographs for purposes not agreed must be sought and will normally be granted upon payment of a further fee, which must be mutually agreed (and paid in full) before such further use. Unless otherwise agreed in writing, all further Licences in respect of the Photographs will be subject to these terms and conditions.

5. EXCLUSIVITY

The Client will be authorised to publish the Photographs to the exclusion of all other persons including the Photographer. However, the Photographer retains the right in all cases to use the Photographs in any manner at any time and in any part of the world for the purposes of advertising or otherwise promoting his/her work. After the exclusivity period indicated in the Licence to Use the Photographer shall be entitled to use the Photographs for any purposes.

6. CLIENT CONFIDENTIALITY

The photographer will keep confidential and will not disclose to any third parties or make use of material or information communicated to him/her in confidence for the purposes of the photography, save as may be reasonably necessary to enable the Photographer to carry out his/her obligations in relation to the commission.

7. INDEMNITY

The Photographer agrees to indemnify the Client against all expenses, damages, claims and legal costs arising out of any failure by the Photographer to obtain any clearances for which he/she was responsible in respect of third party copyright works, trade marks, designs or other intellectual property. The Photographer shall only be responsible for obtaining such clearances if this has been expressly agreed before the shoot. In all other cases the Client shall be responsible for obtaining such clearances and will indemnify the Photographer against all expenses, damages, claims and legal costs arising out of any failure to obtain such clearances.

8. PAYMENT

Payment by the Client shall be within 30 days of the date of the Photographer's invoice and in default of payment interest shall be charged on all sums due from the 31st day of the date of the Photographer's invoice at the rate of 8% per annum until payment is received in full.

9. EXPENSES

Where extra expenses or time are incurred by the Photographer as a result of alterations to the original brief by the Client, or otherwise at their request, the Client shall give approval to and be liable to pay such extra expenses or fees at the Photographer's normal rate to the Photographer in addition to the expenses shown overleaf as having been agreed or estimated.

10. REJECTION

The Client may not reject a photograph on the basis of style or composition unless he pays a fee acceptable to the Photographer.

11. CANCELLATION & POSTPONEMENT

A booking is considered firm as from the date of confirmation and accordingly the Photographer will, at his/her discretion, charge a fee for cancellation or postponement.

12. RIGHT TO A CREDIT

If the box on the estimate and the licence marked "Right to a Credit" has been ticked the Photographer's name will be printed on or in reasonable proximity to all published reproductions of the Photograph(s)

13. ELECTRONIC STORAGE

Save for the purposes of reproduction for the licensed use(s), the Photographs may not be stored in any form of electronic medium without the written permission of the Photographer. Manipulation of the image or use of only a portion of the image may only take place with the permission of the Photographer.

14. APPLICABLE LAW

This agreement shall be governed and construed in accordance with the laws of Ireland. Both parties submit to the non-exclusive jurisdiction of the courts of Ireland.

15. VARIATION

These Terms and Conditions shall not be varied except by agreement in writing.

NOTE : For more information on the commissioning of photography refer to Beyond the Lens produced by the AOP.

Terms & Conditions (Eire) – available free from www.the-aop.org/information/downloads/legal-business-forms

ASSISTING PHOTOGRAPHER'S INVOICE No. ________

Date :

Ref No. :

Photographer :

Address :

Client/Job Reference :

Fee for Photographic Services :

Job Date/s:

Total Fee ________________

Expenses (specify) :

Total Expenses ________________

Subtotal ________________

VAT ________________

TOTAL AMOUNT DUE ________________

Payable to :

Assisting Photographer :

Address :

Schedule D No. :

VAT Reg. No. :

Payment due on completion of shoot subject to guidelines issued by The Association of Photographers Ltd

APPENDIX

ASSISTING PHOTOGRAPHER TERMS & CONDITIONS

Bookings

Bookings are usually verbal and both photographer and assistant should understand if the work is provisional or confirmed. On confirmation the following should be agreed:

- Dates, start times, and daily hours
- Venue and travel arrangements
- Special requirements (clothing, equipment knowledge, etc.)
- Fee
- Expenses and overtime (where appropriate)
- Weather contingency for location work
- Possible overlaps with assistant's other confirmed jobs
- Invoicing details (invoice client or photographer?)
- Contact names and numbers

If an assistant has a provisional booking with another photographer, that photographer must be given the option to confirm before another booking is accepted.

Cancellation and Postponement

Cancellation by an assistant is not acceptable without unavoidable reason, e.g. illness, and the substitution of another assistant must not be made without the photographer's prior knowledge and consent. The photographer has the right to approve any replacement before commencement of the shoot.

Where a booking is confirmed which may overlap a previously confirmed job, the photographer must be informed immediately and given the option to book another assistant.

Cancellation fees for freelance assistants are only payable for confirmed bookings, although once the booking is confirmed, an assistant should not be cancelled unless the job itself is cancelled. Freelance assistants should be regarded as chargeable items, and therefore covered by expenses when the photographer is charging the client a cancellation fee. In the case of a postponement, where a new date is given and confirmed, fees may become payable to cover costs and inconvenience, by mutual agreement between the photographer and assistant.

Fees and Payment

Fees

These are charged at a daily rate. A normal day is any 9-hour period worked between 7am and 9pm, and rates are dependant on knowledge, experience, and the type of work the photographer is doing, e.g. advertising or editorial. Overtime may be charged for weekends, public holidays and in addition to the standard 9 hours, at a rate previously agreed with the photographer.

Payment

Payment should be made at the end of the shoot unless otherwise agreed at the time of booking. If immediate payment is not agreed, then credit terms of 30 days should be the maximum given. Assistants should give an invoice clearly stating the following:

- Assistant's name, address, and Tax Schedule D Number (where applicable)
- Shoot/booking dates
- Assistant's invoice number
- Photographer's name and order number
- Client/Agency/Product
- Fee
- Expenses itemised
- Total owed
- Payment terms
- VAT number (if registered)

All expenses incurred on behalf of the photographer or client should be agreed in advance and are payable immediately the shoot is completed. Fees and mileage for the use of an assistant's car should be agreed at the time of confirmation.

Location Work

The photographer is responsible for the cost of accommodation and meals whilst on location, but personal expenses (e.g. telephone calls) are the responsibility of the assistant. Medical and travel insurance should be discussed with the photographer before the shoot begins.

Weather-permitting bookings should be agreed with the assistant at the time of confirmation, but postponement due to bad weather will result in the assistant, as a photographer's expense, being paid 50% of the fee. The photographer or the client may have weather insurance to cover these events.

AOP www.the-aop.org

MODEL RELEASE FORM

Photographer: ______________________ Agency/Client: ______________________

Model/s: ______________________ Art Order No.: ______________________

Product: ______________________ Brand Name: ______________________

Date/s: ______________________ Hours Worked: ______________________

For valuable consideration *(insert consideration)* received *I/we hereby grant the *photographer/agency/client, and any licensees or assignees, the absolute right to use the photograph(s) and any other reproductions or adaptions, from the above mentioned photographic shoot, but only for the product or brand name specified above, solely and exclusively for:

Media

- ☐ Advertising - national press
- ☐ Advertising - trade press
- ☐ Editorial - consumer press
- ☐ Editorial - trade press
- ☐ Editorial - national press
- ☐ Catalogue
- ☐ Test/personal/portfolio (not for commercial use)
- ☐ Internet
- ☐ Brochure
- ☐ Point of Sale
- ☐ Inserts
- ☐ Poster ______________________ *(specify)*
- ☐ Packaging
- ☐ Television/Cinema/Video
- ☐ Full library use
- ☐ Other ______________________ *(specify)*

Territory

- ☐ UK
- ☐ Single EC country ____________ *(specify)*
- ☐ Continental Europe
- ☐ USA
- ☐ English language areas (book publishing)
- ☐ Worldwide
- ☐ Other ________________ *(specify)*

Period of Use

- ☐ One year
- ☐ Two years
- ☐ Other ______________________ *(specify)*

For specific restrictions/conditions/agreements see attached. Electronic rights must be negotiated separately.

---

* I / We understand that the image shall be deemed to represent an imaginary person unless agreed otherwise, in writing, by my agent or myself.
* I / We understand that I / we have no interest in the copyright, or any moral rights, in the photograph.

**I am over 18 years of age.

Name of *model/model agency : *(print)* ______________________________

Signature of *model/model agency : ______________________ Date : ____________

***Parent/guardian or model agency must sign for models under 18 years of age. *Delete as appropriate*

In accepting the above release it is the responsibility of the *photographer/agency/client not to use or authorise the use of the material except for the above media, territories and time periods. Further usage must be negotiated and agreed beforehand, in writing, with the *model/model agency.

ISSUED IN 1995 BY THE ASSOCIATION OF PHOTOGRAPHERS LTD, THE ASSOCIATION OF MODEL AGENTS AND THE INSTITUTE OF PRACTITIONERS IN ADVERTISING

Standard Model Release Form – available free from www.the-aop.org/information/downloads/legal-business-forms

INDEX